RUMRUNNER

THE LIFE *and* TIMES *of* JOHNNY SCHNARR

MARION PARKER AND ROBERT TYRRELL

ORCA BOOK PUBLISHERS

First printing, 1988
First paperback printing, 1992

Canadian Cataloguing in Publication Data
Parker, Marion.
  Rumrunner

  ISBN 0-920501-12-5 (bound). – ISBN 0-920501-94-X (pbk.)

  1. Schnarr, Johnny, 1894-   2. Smuggling–Juan de Fuca Strait Region (B.C. and Wash.)–History–20th century.   3. Smuggling–Washington (State)–Puget Sound Region–History–20th century.   4. Prohibition– Juan de Fuca Strait Region (B.C. and Wash.)–History–20th century. 5. Prohibition–Washington (State)–Puget Sound Region–History–20th century.   6. Smugglers–British Columbia–Biography.   7. Smugglers– Washington (State)–Biography.   I. Tyrrell, Bob, 1948-   II. Title
  HV5091.C2P37 1988   364.1'33   C88-912484-7

Publication assistance provided by The Canada Council
Cover design by Susan Fergusson
Cover illustration by Jim Ketilson
Cover photograph by Lawrence McLagan

Printed and bound in Canada

Orca Book Publishers
P.O. Box 5626, Station B
Victoria, BC,   Canada
V8R 6S4

In memory of Alma van der Est
a teacher
a second mother
a friend

TABLE OF CONTENTS

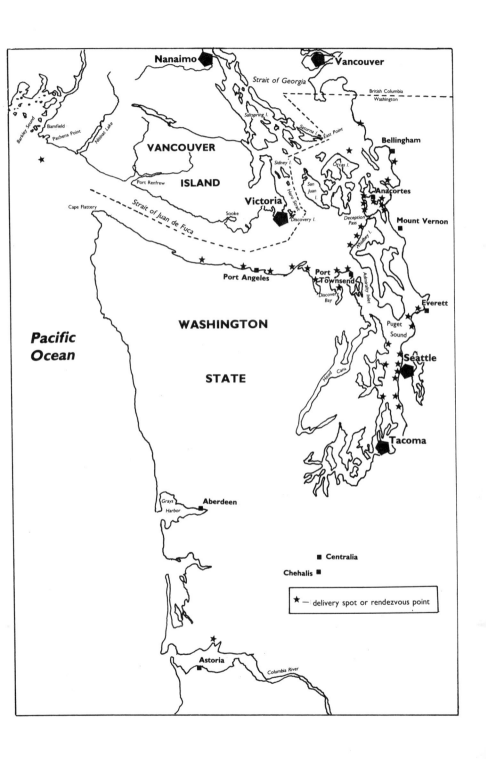

Nanaimo

Vancouver

Strait of Georgia

British Columbia
Washington

Barkley Sound

Bamfield
Pachena Point

Nitinat Lake

Saltspring I.

Satturna I.

East Point

Bellingham

VANCOUVER

Sidney I.

Orcas I.

San
Juan
I.

Anacortes

Port Renfrew

ISLAND

Haro Strait

Victoria

Discovery I.

Deception
Pass

Mount Vernon

Cape Flattery

Strait of Juan de Fuca

Sooke

Whidbey I.

Port Angeles

Port
Townsend

Discovery
Bay

Admiralty Inlet

Everett

Puget
Sound

WASHINGTON

Pacific
Ocean

STATE

Hood Canal

Seattle

Tacoma

Grays
Harbor

Aberdeen

Centralia

Chehalis

★ — delivery spot or rendezvous point

Astoria

Columbia River

INTRODUCTION

RUMRUNNER IS JOHNNY Schnarr's story just as he remembers it.

Much of the credit for the writing of the book, however, must go to Johnny's niece, Marion Parker. Over a period of five years, she patiently gathered her uncle's reminiscences on tape. The process was slow; many evolved gradually as an event was recalled several times. Marion made it a rule never to stop her uncle from repeating a story that he might already have told. She soon found that a little nugget of information was always added with each telling.

As the tapes were carefully transcribed, the manuscript grew. Even after the repetitions were edited out, the finished product totalled seven hundred and fifty pages. The story covered Johnny's life from his birth in 1894 until he retired from commercial fishing at the age of seventy-five.

When the project came to me, the task was a relatively simple one. It was obvious that the story was worth telling. There is no doubt that Johnny Schnarr is a genuine West Coast character — one who has lived his life according to his own standards, and done so successfully for over ninety years. It was equally obvious that the most interesting period of Johnny's life occurred during the era of Prohibition in the United States. His experiences in the rum trade were the kind of adventure that the rest of us only dream of. The midnight rendezvous, the high-speed boat chases, the bullets flying in the night, all of this was real and very exciting!

There is one unfortunate aspect of Johnny Schnarr's story. We have been unable to locate any photographs of the boats that he used so successfully in his escapades. In some respects this is not surprising. At the time he went out of his way to keep a very low profile as far as his clandestine activities were concerned. Nevertheless, Johnny himself had pictures of several of the rumrunners, one in particular of *Revuocnav* that he describes as being an exceptional shot of the boat at high speed. Sadly, all of these pictures were lost when his marriage ended shortly after the era of Prohibition.

Even without the photographs, however, Johnny Schnarr has provided us with an accurate recounting of a life of excitement and adventure during a fascinating period in the history of the West Coast. *Rumrunner* is his story.

Robert Tyrrell
April, 1988

SHIPWRECKED

ONCE WE WERE out of the Columbia River and headed south along the coast again, the weather was fine. There was no wind to speak of, and only a light ground swell. But I continued to do all the steering, unwilling to put my fate into Harry's hands after the fiasco he had made of navigating coming out of Victoria. Harry seemed happy enough with this arrangement. I kept us a good ways offshore just to be on the safe side.

We motored through calm seas and clear weather for two days. The little two-cylinder engine was running fine, pushing us along at a steady six knots. But I was the one who was finally running out of gas. At this point I'd been five days without any real sleep, and it was catching up with me. I was exhausted. I knew that I was in danger of passing out on my feet. Finally, about nine o'clock on the evening of our second day out of Astoria, I reluctantly turned the wheel over to my mate.

"Look, Harry," I said. "I've got to get some sleep. We're ten miles offshore. Keep on this heading due south and we'll stay that way. Keep a close watch on the compass."

In fact, the heading that I had set would take us slightly farther away from the coast, but from what I had seen of Harry's abilities as a navigator, I didn't want to take any chances. I figured that there was no way that he could get us into any trouble in the three or four hours that I planned to sleep. I tended to the engine and then lay down in the bunk.

But I was never really able to sleep on a boat that was running. For the longest while I tossed and turned, but, in spite of how tired I was, I mostly just lay there and dozed a bit.

It must have been a couple of hours later, maybe a bit longer— I was half asleep—when I suddenly felt the boat list heavily to one side and then level out again. I jumped up off the bunk and stood waiting to see what would happen next. Nothing. I figured that we'd been broadsided by a large swell. Maybe the wind had picked up. I lay back down again. Something didn't feel quite right. A moment later a wave crashed right over the top of the boat, cracking the beams in the deck over the bunk. Water flooded in. I jumped up and found myself standing in a foot and a half of cold sea water. The little engine sputtered a few times and died.

My first thoughts were for the boat. "If we can get this water out of here, the engine will be warm enough to dry the plugs and she'll start again." I grabbed the pump and shouted for Harry to come and bail. He showed up soon enough, but was white as a ghost. I handed him a bucket.

"Bail, you bugger," I shouted. "Bail!"

I hadn't been above decks yet, and my thought then was that we were on a reef. I knew that Cape Blanco was not too far south of our position, and that there was a reef there. We would have cleared it by at least ten miles on the heading I had set, but I wasn't thinking of that. I'd deal with Harry later. There were more pressing problems!

"Goodbye, Johnny," Harry whined as he began to toss buckets of water out the hatchway.

"Goodbye, hell," I answered. "Not as long as this thing floats!"

We soon had the water level down enough that the engine was dry. Then, just as I was about to try to restart it, another huge wave crashed over the boat. This time the whole hull was filled and we were right under the water. I held my breath and, half swimming, half climbing, made my way out of the forward cabin and up into the pilothouse. I took a quick look out the companionway. What a surprise that was! In spite of the darkness I was able to make out a sandy beach as the wave receded around us! I couldn't believe my eyes! I went out on deck and stepped off. Harry had steered the *Rose Marie* straight onto the beach. Fortunately for us he had hit one of the few stretches of sandy shoreline along this part of the Oregon coast.

The last big wave had pushed the boat further up the beach; she wouldn't float again on this tide. I stood and watched as the next foaming breaker broke over the top of the six-foot mast on the stern of the little boat. With the hull full of water the waves could no longer move the *Rose Marie*. Instead, they began to pound her to pieces. It was funny, I thought we must be in the midst of a sudden storm, but there was no wild wind blowing, only a breeze. The large waves—every sixth or seventh one to hit the beach was a monster—must have been the result of a big off-shore swell running up onto the shallows.

When the next big wave went out, I climbed back on board to find Harry. I figured that by this time he was probably half-drowned down below. Much to my surprise he was still bailing. He had held his breath as each wave filled the boat and then continued to bail as the water went down. I guess he was in a state of shock. I had quite a time just getting him to stop bailing.

Now that I realized that we were safe, I got pretty angry at Harry. He had obviously not paid any attention to the compass heading that I had told him to steer. In order to get us to the beach in the time that I was trying to sleep, he would have had to head due east instead of south. Anyway, my cussing snapped him out of his state of shock long enough for me to get him up on deck and ashore between waves.

Once on the beach I chewed him out again, running back and forth through my list of expletives a couple of times. When I tired of that, there was very little to do but take stock of our situation. Here we were, shipwrecked on a desolate beach on the coast of Oregon, helplessly watching the little boat and its cargo of illegal liquor being smashed to pieces by the powerful surf. This was not exactly what I had in mind when I decided to go into the rumrunning business!

GROWING UP

OF COURSE, I didn't start out to be a rumrunner.

And rumrunning was not the only thing that I did in my life. In my early years I did a lot of hunting and trapping and logging. I went overseas in World War I and fought at the front in France. After the war I did some more logging and this and that. And then Prohibition came along in the United States. For a young fellow with a sense of adventure, getting involved in the rumrunning seemed like a pretty good way to make a living. And it turned out to be just that for me. I didn't get rich in the rum trade. But I lived well and I had some exciting times and I met a lot of interesting people. And I was good at it!

Between the years 1920 and 1933 I made over four hundred liquor runs, and I never once got caught. There weren't too many who could say that. I delivered liquor to almost forty different spots along the Washington coast of the Strait of Juan de Fuca and down into Puget Sound. I also made trips down the west coast to California and Mexico. I was so successful that the United States Coast Guard offered a $25,000 reward for the capture of my boat! But no one ever collected it.

Looking back over my years in the rum trade, I can see that there were two basic reasons for my success. First of all, I was always very interested in boats and engines and I was good with motors—this is what got me in the rumrunning in the first place. I always had about the fastest boat around. I always wanted to have a boat that would go twice as fast as the Coast Guard cutters. And most of the time I did. That was why I was able to outrun ten of them when they tried to ambush me in Discovery Bay up on the Olympic Peninsula. I spent a lot of time and a lot of money making sure that my boats were fast!

The second reason for my success was more simple—luck. I was a lucky guy! There's no doubt in my mind. God knows, I tempted fate often enough. There were many times in my life—not only during the rumrunning years, but before and after as well—that I knew that the only reason I was not dead was blind luck. I was shot at with everything from handguns to machine guns to four-pound cannon. And I went through some terrible storms at sea that might have easily sunk the boat. But I was always lucky.

After the rumrunning years I had lots of other adventures. I was a logger again, and then a fisherman. I fished out off the west coast of Vancouver Island until I retired shortly before my seventy-fifth birthday. Now I am going on ninety-four and looking forward to telling you about my adventures. And I think I'm still a pretty lucky guy!

I was born on a hundred-and-sixty-acre homestead in the Saltser Valley near Centralia, Washington on November 16, 1894. My parents had met and married in Kansas and come out west in the early part of the decade. I was the youngest of four children. August, the eldest, was about seven years older than me; Gus was next, two and a half years younger than August; then Minnie, who was about two and a half years older than me. We were pretty evenly spaced out.

I have only one strong memory of those days on the homestead. When I was about three and my sister Minnie five, I came pretty close to drowning. We were playing in the front yard one day when Minnie suggested we get a drink of water from the well. The water in the well was only about a foot below the level of the ground, so there were no boards covering it. We raced each other to the back yard. I was always quicker than my sister, so I got there first. I remember reaching down with the dipper to get some water. And that was the last thing that I remember until I woke up about six hours later. Minnie pulled me out of the water and ran to get my father, who was working in the fields. They rolled me over a log for awhile to get some of the water out of me. Then they put me to bed. The funny thing is that I always thought that I had fallen into the well. It was only many years later—when I was about seventy years old, in fact—that Minnie finally admitted that she had pushed me in because I had beaten her to the well. Apparently she watched me struggle until I quit kicking and then got scared and ran for help. She was so frightened that she had never told anyone what had really happened.

When I was six we left the homestead and moved onto a twenty-six-acre piece of property on Coal Creek, about three miles out of Chehalis. We lived in kind of a ramshackle little house for the first few years and kept a team of horses and a wagon, a cow and some chickens. We grew most of our food in a large garden.

By this time my father was not around very much. He worked in the logging camps and only came home from time to time. When he was home, he tended to spend a good deal of his time drinking in one of the many saloons in Chehalis. When he was drunk he often treated August badly and beat him for any little thing.

Once August had taken the old muzzle-loading gun that Father kept hanging fully loaded on the wall and went out to hunt a deer. He had asked if he could go hunting, but Dad had refused. We really needed the meat so August finally decided to go anyway. He didn't see a deer, but he couldn't resist firing the gun, so he shot a small bird. When Father found out the gun had been fired, August got a real licking. After that Dad always took the gun with him when he went to town.

When he was drunk, my father sometimes beat my mother as well. When August was about fourteen and Gus twelve, they finally decided that they had to do something about it. One night they waited along the trail from town and met my father as he came home from the saloon. They jumped him and took the gun away from him. August told him that they had had enough of being beaten and were not going to put up with it anymore, that they did not want him drinking up all the money, and that he should go away and not come back. And that's what happened. After that our father stayed away.

August, being the oldest, took charge of the family from then on. He was a hard taskmaster and I always tried to stay on his good side. Of course, that wasn't always possible, but I didn't fare too badly. Being the youngest, I suppose I probably got away with more. August and Gus had some terrible rows!

My mother was a good woman and a hard worker. She was always busy; she canned a lot of fruit and vegetables to get us through the winter. In looking back on it now, I can see that we had a pretty tough life in those days, but, of course, when you're going through it, it just seems like the way things are. I certainly don't recall feeling hard done by at the time. We really didn't know any different.

I started school when we moved to Chehalis. I went as far as the sixth grade, but I don't think I finished that year. I was never that fond of the schooling, but I enjoyed the games we played outside the schoolhouse. We didn't have room to play baseball, so we played games like Hide-and-Seek and Pom-Pom Pull Away. I was always very small for my age; I hardly grew at all until I was ten or twelve. But I was very quick and I could dodge around the bigger kids and was very difficult to catch.

I was about ten, I think, when we started cutting cordwood. We used to work from daylight until dark. Boy, that was hard work! I can remember that I used to be pretty good at pulling the saw in the morning, but later on in the day I would get so tired that I could only pull it one way, then I'd have to hesitate before giving it a push back the other way. I used to load the wagon and take the wood to town and sell it door to door for three dollars and fifty cents a cord. Nowadays, of course, that doesn't seem like much, but back then a dollar went a long way.

The next year we built a new house on our property. The Brown Logging Company was running a railway up the valley to bring their logs out and they wanted to cross our property. They offered to give us the lumber to build a new house in exchange for the right-of-way across our land. We agreed to that.

We were very proud of the house we built. It was forty feet long and twenty feet wide and had two floors. The outside walls of the house were made of logs. Inside those we built two-by-four walls which we filled with good dry sawdust. That house was well insulated so that it was warm in winter and cool in summer. In the living room we built a large stone fireplace which easily heated the whole place. In the kitchen we had the latest in kitchen stoves; it had a warming oven and a hot-water reservoir alongside the oven. All in all it was a pretty good house, especially considering it was built by four not-very-big kids. I believe that house is still standing today.

We didn't have a lot of entertainment in those days. I remember how excited we got when the circus came to town. When the posters for the Ringling Brothers Circus went up, it was all anybody could talk about until the big day came. By the time the circus actually arrived, we were in a state of high excitement.

On the big day Mother packed up a lot of food and loaded us kids into the wagon, and off we went to town. We arrived around noon, even before the tents were up. Part of the thrill was being able to watch as the whole show was put together. They used horses for raising the big tents. If there was something really huge to move, the elephants were brought in to help. The circus opened about three in the afternoon and went on into the evening. We would all be exhausted by the time we arrived back on the farm late that night. But it gave us something to talk about for weeks and weeks.

Even more exciting than the circus was the Buffalo Bill Wild West Show. There was a real feeling of adventure and danger about that show. The sense of danger was enhanced in their stop in Chehalis because accidents took the lives of three men while they were in town. One man was run over when they were unloading one of the huge wagons that carried their props. Another died in some kind of accident when they were packing up to leave. But the one that I saw died right during one of the performances. It happened during the bronco busting event. There were three or four other men on horseback in the ring to assist the bronc rider if he got into any trouble. One of these riders was distracted by something that was happening at the other end of the ring when suddenly the bronco stopped bucking and ran full-tilt at him. The bronco crashed into the rider's horse, throwing him out of the saddle, and knocking the horse over on top of him, killing him right there in front of the whole crowd. It seems kind of shocking now, but back then they just carried that cowboy out of the ring and went on with the show.

Another part of the Wild West Show featured a group of sharpshooters. These were men and women—I think Annie Oakley was there—who would shoot at all kinds of objects thrown up in the air. Everything that they shot at exploded with a bang. It was funny, but, even to a young kid like me, that act didn't add up. I had handled a few guns by this time—in fact, I was a real good shot for my age—and I sure knew that you didn't shoot at something on the fly with a bunch of people sitting directly in your line of fire! I figured that there were no bullets in those guns and that they had devised some way of making all those things explode.

Anyway, that was all the entertainment we had, and everyone enjoyed it and talked about it for the longest time.

Although we didn't have much in the way of modern conveniences, I guess my early years were pretty much like those of a lot of other country boys. We tried to stay out of trouble as far as we could. We did get arrested once when I was ten or eleven, but not too much came of it.

August, Gus and I went on a camping trip towards the end of summer that year. We set off with enough supplies to last for four days. First we went up Coal Creek to where there was a trail that cut across the hills. We walked that trail until we came out on a road which we followed to the New Waukum River. Then we went up alongside the river for a long ways. When we stopped to make our camp we must have been ten or fifteen miles beyond any of the farms that were in the valley.

We stayed there for several days. There were lots of fish in the river and we had a pretty good time. On the second day August shot a deer. This was before the hunting season opened, so we stripped all the meat off the carcass and smoked it over the fire until it was nice and dry like jerky. We didn't want to carry any extra weight for our walk home.

We came back down the river to the road and then followed the road for about three miles through an area of small farms. When we came to the bridge over the river, we planned to leave the road and follow the trail over the hills, the same way that we had come on the way in. When we got to the bridge, there was a crew of fifty or sixty men doing repair work on it. The crew boss stopped us. He said that he was the game warden for the district and ordered us to open our packs.

"So you've shot a deer out of season, have you?" he asked when he looked in the packs.

"No," August answered. "That's bear meat."

"Oh no it's not!" the man insisted. "You boys are under arrest."

The warden took our names and then told us to wait there by the bridge while he went to his farm to get a wagon to take us to town. As soon as he was out of sight, the men on the work crew started laughing and told us that we should just go off home.

It seemed that they weren't too fond of the game warden, either. This seemed like a pretty good idea to us, so off we went.

The next day the game warden showed up at our place with the sheriff from Chehalis. He wanted the sheriff to arrest us and throw us in jail. When the sheriff asked to see what was left of the smoked meat, we showed it to him.

"What kind of meat is this?" he asked as he examined the hard, dark jerky.

"Bear meat," August answered. The sheriff continued to look the meat over closely.

"Well," he said. "There is no proof that it is anything else. I can't arrest you without any proof."

Since there were no bones or horns, there was no way to prove that it was deer meat. With that the sheriff and the game warden headed back to town. The sheriff was none too pleased about being dragged out for nothing, and the game warden seemed to be in a particularly black mood. But we were very happy.

UP NORTH TO JOHNSTONE STRAIT

IN THE SPRING of 1910, August and Gus were hired to work in a logging camp near Port Harvey on Cracroft Island up off the coast of British Columbia, about one hundred and fifty miles northwest of Vancouver. They worked up there all summer and came back to Chehalis when the camp closed down for the winter.

The following spring I was allowed to go with them when they headed back to camp. In Vancouver on the way up, we paid forty-five dollars for a sixteen-foot, double-ended boat from Turner Boatbuilders in Coal Harbour. We had it shipped on the *Cassiar*, the Union Steamship that took us up to Port Harvey.

We stayed in a little cabin on the bay at Port Harvey, about ten or twelve miles around the island from the camp where August and Gus had worked the year before. After a few days the camp boat came into the bay and my brothers were hired back on. They went to stay at the camp, while I was left by myself in the small cabin. I had no trouble amusing myself, as this was all a brand new adventure for me. I fished in the bay, dug clams, explored in the woods, and generally enjoyed myself.

But my holiday only lasted a couple of weeks. When two of the men at the logging camp quit, August told his boss that he thought I could handle their jobs. So one day, the camp boss showed up in the bay again and asked me if I wanted to try firing the donkey. I said that I'd sure like to give it a go.

It turned out to be a pretty good job. That donkey did not have a heck of a lot of work to do. It only hauled the logs a short distance and booted them into a chute. I don't know why, but the two men who'd quit had a hard time keeping the steam up in the donkey. One of them was bucking the blocks off of the woodlog, and the other was splitting the blocks and feeding the fire. Still, the two of them couldn't get enough steam up in the boiler to keep the donkey running when they had logs to haul. Doing both jobs myself, I had no trouble making that old steam donkey do its work. I guess it was all that cordwood I had cut as a kid that gave me the training that I needed for the job. Anyway, the boss was so pleased with the job I was doing, and the fact that I was saving them one man's wages, that he gave me an extra dollar a day. August and Gus were falling and bucking and making six dollars a day; I was getting five dollars a day. I felt pretty good about that!

I really enjoyed that job. I had no trouble keeping the fire fed and the steam up. And it was fun to watch the donkey drop those big logs in the chute and see them scoot down the mountainside and into the water. The chute was about five hundred feet long and steep. The logs went down like bullets, hitting the water with a loud smack. Most of the cedar logs would split open when they hit, sometimes in half or quarters; other times there would be nothing left but splinters floating around the boom. The fir and hemlock logs would be all right, but would often end up in a terrible tangle. Logs would shoot down under the water for quite a ways and sometimes come up under another log. Then those two would get in the way of another one, and so on, until there would be an awful mess that the boom man would have to pull apart with a winch.

The main excitement that we had that year was when Dan J. arrived in camp after a month-long drunk in Vancouver. The first day or so he seemed to be all right, but then things got pretty strange. I guess old Dan had a bad case of the D.T.'s. He would jump out of bed in the middle of the night and start yelling at the woodstove. It was getting towards fall and we kept a good fire going to dry out our wet clothes.

"Come up, devil, and get me!" Dan would yell. "I'm ready for you."

After a good deal of coaxing, we would get him back to bed. Then he'd likely start talking to animals on the ceiling. He seemed to have a zoo full of different animals that appeared to him in the night. This was fine for him, but it did not make the rest of us too comfortable. It made it difficult to get to sleep.

One night, Dan jumped straight up out of bed and yelled, "I'm going for the chuck."

Dressed only in his long underwear, he ran out of the bunk-house and headed for the beach. He stumbled out into the water as far as he could and threw himself down. Of course, a bunch of us took off after him in the dark. Nobody really wanted to go into the cold water, though, so a couple of guys grabbed the rowboat to paddle out to where the lunatic was. At first, no one could find the oars. One of the other men and I had used the boat the day before to go fishing, and had not put the oars back where they were usually kept. We didn't say anything. I guess we wanted the guy to drown because we were pretty fed up with him keeping us up all night. Anyway, someone found a board and used it to pad-dle out and drag poor Dan out of the water. He had passed out by the time they brought him ashore.

But it wasn't too long before he came to. Funny thing was, he now appeared to be as normal as can be.

"Pretty cold bath, wasn't it?" he asked.

We walked him back to the bunkhouse, changed him out of his wet clothes and put him to bed. This time he dropped straight off to sleep.

But when we woke the next morning, Dan was nowhere to be found. After it was determined that he wasn't in camp, search par-ties were formed and we set out to hunt. Given the performance of the night before, we weren't too sure what we were likely to find.

We searched all day. Finally, about three o'clock in the after-noon, one of the men found him about a mile and a half from camp. He was standing on the edge of a bluff looking down at the ocean a hundred feet below. The fellow who found him said, "Come on with me now, Dan, and we'll go back to camp."

"No," came the reply. "I'm going to drown myself."

"You don't want to do that," the searcher said. "Come on. Let's just go back to camp and have some lunch."

"No, I've had all I can take," Dan said. "But I just can't quite get myself to jump." After a moment or two of silence, he contin-ued, "Look, you come and give me a push, OK?"

"No way! You just step back and come with me."

Suddenly, Dan turned and looked hard at the fellow who had found him.

"If you won't push me," he said, a fierce look in his eye, "then I'll put you over."

And with that he tried to grab the other man. Naturally, the other fellow set off at a good clip through the bush. And that's the way they finally arrived back at camp—Dan hard on the heels of the fellow who had saved his life.

Everyone was back in camp by this time and the general consensus was that we had to do something with this guy before somebody got hurt or ended up dead. We decided that we would tie him up and send him to the hospital over in Alert Bay. Naturally, we didn't expect to have Dan's cooperation in this procedure. Being small and quick, I offered to get behind him and knock him down, provided everyone else would then dive in to help. I was able to get behind Dan unnoticed. I grabbed him around the neck and pulled him over on top of me. The others quickly came to my aid.

We tied Dan onto a set of bedsprings and kept him that way. He ranted and raved for most of the night. By the next morning when the camp boat set out for Alert Bay, he was delirious and only semi-conscious. By the time they reached the hospital, they thought he was dead.

Old Dan never did come back to that camp—which was just about how we wanted it. He did recover after a couple of weeks in hospital, though. But he told the nurses that he would never go back to the camp because "they were nothing but a bunch of devils there. You could see the fire coming out of their mouths when they spoke."

When the logging camp closed down late that fall, August, Gus and I decided to do some exploring around that part of the country to see what the prospects were for trapping. We were looking for something to keep us busy during the winter months when there was no logging. First, we rowed across Johnstone Strait to the mouth of the Adams River on the east side of Vancouver Island. There seemed to be lots of game around that area, so we began to set out a trapline along the river.

We did not have to build a cabin because there were a number of Indian cabins that were abandoned for the winter. The Indians only used them when they were fishing in the summer and early fall. They came to catch and smoke the salmon when the fish were going up the rivers to spawn. In just about every one of the cabins there would be a hundred or more smoked salmon stored up in the rafters. I guess they took what they could back to the reservation and then came back for more when they needed it. The salmon were always in good shape, smoked nice and hard so that they would keep for a long time.

Although I already knew how to set a trap and stretch and skin a pelt, I was learning a lot of other new things at this time. We now had tow boats and did a good deal of travelling up and down the coast around the Adams River, so I learned about the sea and the weather. We soon found out that the sail was not as useful as we had hoped it would be. It seemed that, for the most part, the wind was either calm or blowing in the wrong direction. We rowed and rowed and rowed some more! The wind, coupled with the strong tides that were common in the area, could be a formidable foe. If the wind was too strong and the tide flowing in the wrong direction, there was often nothing to do but head for a quiet spot and wait it out. We didn't always end up where we thought we were going, but then we weren't running on a schedule, either.

We didn't think anything of rowing twenty or thirty miles in a day. In those days, there were some considerable distances between places where you'd find other people. We used to buck some awfully strong winds. It had to be blowing a gale before we couldn't make it to where we were going.

We did use the sail when we had a favourable wind. We took great delight in sitting back and letting the wind do the work for a change. To have our little boat rushing through the water far faster than we could row, waves splashing over the gunwales in our faces, was one of our greatest pleasures.

After we had got ourselves established around the Adams River, we decided that it was time to take a trip down to Chehalis to see how the rest of the family was doing. Gus agreed to stay behind and tend to the trapline and look after our camp and August's two dogs, Bounce and Jack.

August and I left one of the boats with Gus and set off in the other. We rowed over to Port Harvey, where we took passage on the freight boat to Vancouver. From there, we went on down to Chehalis by train.

We stayed with Minnie in the house that we had built in Coal Creek. By this time, our mother had moved to an old folks home. We visited in the area for awhile and told all our friends about our adventures up the coast. Everyone thought the life we were leading was quite exciting. When it came time to head back, Harry Brown, who was just about my age and the youngest of the boys in a family that August knew quite well, asked if he could come with us. We agreed to take him along and set out once again for the trip north.

We got off the freight boat in Port Harvey and rowed back across the Strait of the Adams River and joined up with Gus again. Gus had got pretty well set up and seemed able to manage the lines there by himself. He did not mind working alone. After talking it over, we decided that we would leave him there and that August and Harry and I would head over to Bute Inlet to look around.

We took one of the boats and the two dogs and headed back across the strait. We started setting our traps at the lower end of the Inlet. We even set some up behind the lake in back of Fawn Bluff. Gradually, we worked our way up the inlet, taking up traps that had been out about three weeks and leapfrogging them on ahead of us. When we got to the mouth of the Orford River, about twenty miles up on the east side, we set a line along its banks. We continued in this way until we worked our way to the head of the inlet.

The Southgate River flows into the head of Bute Inlet on the east side, and the Homathko River drains from the north. We decided to explore the Southgate first. Our rowboat would not be much good in the river, so we took a few days and felled a spruce tree and made ourselves a dugout canoe. This was our first canoe. We had seen the Indians build them, so we had a fair idea how to go about it. Later on we built several more, whenever we needed one for something. We got pretty good at making canoes. This was my introduction to boatbuilding. I seemed to have the best eye for the lines the boat should have, and my brothers soon learned to leave that up to me. This was a skill that would come in very handy later on when I began to design and build boats for speed.

When the canoe was finished, August, Harry and I paddled and poled our way about twenty-five miles up the Southgate. We built a small cabin on the east bank, not too far from where the Bishop River joins the Southgate. This would be our headquarters for the winter.

August liked to travel alone, so he headed further up the river and left Harry and I to manage the traplines in the vicinity of the cabin. There was not too much snow that winter, but I do remember that it was cold enough for "mush ice" to be flowing in the river.

Although we thought of ourselves as experienced woodsmen by this time, we were still pretty green in a lot of ways. I remember one day when Harry and I set out with Bruce and Jack to check the lines north of the cabin. We ran the lines up along the east side of the river for about four miles. We crossed over on a long pool where the ice had frozen hard enough to support our weight. Then we hiked down the west bank until we were right across the river from the cabin. Now we were faced with a dilemma. We either had to retrace our steps to cross the river on the frozen pool, or wade the river. Right opposite the cabin the water was covered with mush ice, but a couple of hundred feet downstream, there was a wide riffle where the current was shallow and fast enough to stay ice-free. Being young and naturally averse to anything that seemed like extra work, we decided to cross there.

We hated to wade in and get our shoes and socks wet so close to home, so decided to take them off and cross barefooted. There was no place where the water was above our knees. The river was one hundred and fifty feet wide at this point. Unfortunately, however, the water was too deep for the dogs to wade, and too fast for them to swim. They would be carried down the riffle by the swift current and dragged down under the mush ice that was built up on the pool below. There was nothing to do but carry them across.

We each hoisted a dog. I had Jack in my arms, Harry had Bounce. Our shoes were tied together and hung around our necks. The bottom was covered with round, river-worn rocks from six to twelve inches in diameter. As we waded, the force of the current, combined with the slippery bottom, caused our unprotected feet to be pinched between the rocks with nearly every step. The whole process was so painful that, by the time we were halfway across, we had to stop. There we were, knee-deep in near-freezing water, a dog each in our arms. For someone standing on the bank, it would have been a comical sight.

Fortunately, in some respects, the icy water soon numbed our feet until we could no longer feel the pain of the beating they were taking from the rocky bottom, and we were able to set off again. As soon as we hit the far bank, we dropped the dogs and ran for

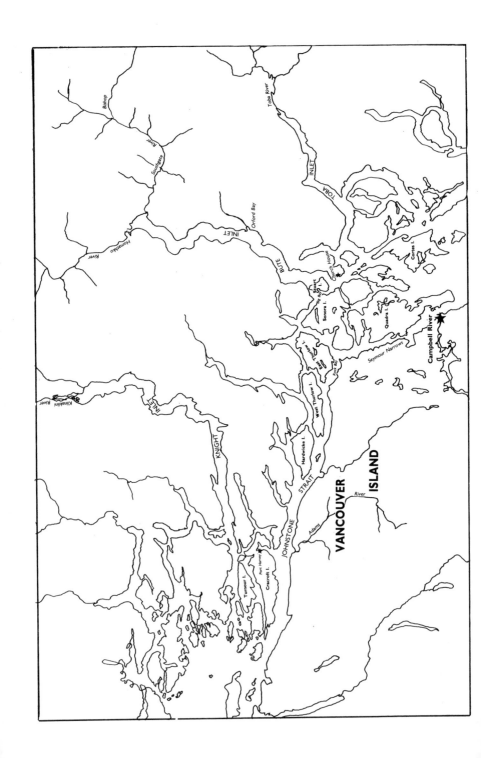

the cabin as fast as our frozen feet would carry us. We soon had a fire roaring. Then the real pain began! As long as I live, I'll never forget the agony as the feeling slowly returned to my feet!

In late winter, August decided that he had seen all he wanted to see on the Southgate River, so we gathered up all our gear and headed downstream. This time, we set up camp in a cabin on an abandoned homestead on the flats at the head of Bute Inlet. A group had tried to start a settlement there quite a number of years before, but had finally been starved out. The place had been abandoned for a long time and was all grown up in bush and trees. August continued to trap the lower reaches of the Southgate, while Harry and I set our lines around the flatlands at the head of the inlet.

It seemed that we spent a good deal of our time crawling on our bellies through the long grass of the flats, trying to get close enough to a Canada goose to shoot it with a rifle. We weren't often successful. As I remember it, we spent an awful lot of our time eating, or thinking about eating, when we were that age.

Once or twice, that got us into trouble. One day, Harry and I found some plants alongside the bank of a stream. They had nice-looking white roots on them, and looked and tasted very good. It was still early in the spring, so they did not yet have any leaves on them. We ate two or three each.

Before too long we both began to feel dizzy and weak. We knew right away that it was the roots. We headed for the cabin, weak-legged and wobbly. By the time we made it back, we were staggering so badly that we could hardly talk. We were very scared, thinking, what the devil can we do if we've been poisoned? Fortunately for us, August was off up the Southgate for a day or two. We each drank a cup of Pacific milk and crawled into our beds. This was about four o'clock in the afternoon. We passed out immediately and didn't wake up until late the next morning.

When we woke up, we were fine. Another lesson learned the hard way! We had eaten the roots of the wild parsnip. The odd thing was that I should have know what it was because it grew around our place back in Washington. But I had always seen it with big green tops and flowers and I never made the connection. We were very lucky that we hadn't eaten more.

It was getting quite late in the spring when we picked up our traps and headed back to see Gus at the Adams River. It was a

long row back down Bute Inlet loaded down with all our gear and
the dogs and the pelts that we had trapped. We got mostly marten
up the Southgate River, with a few mink and otter taken along the
shoreline of the inlet.

When we got to the Arren Rapids on the north side of the
Stuart Island, the tide was just at the end of the ebb. We were
rowing with the tide up the right-hand side of the channel next to
the mainland, and were just rounding the last point, when we met
the incoming flow. There were two or three inches of water flowing back over the current that was still running out. With two of
us rowing, we were not able to butt the tide and it soon carried us
back the way we had come. There was nothing to do but wait, so
we camped in the bay on the east side of the pass for six hours
until the tide changed. And even then, we found out that there
really was no period of slack water that day. We went through the
pass on a fast-flowing ebb tide that was just like riding the river.

It was good to see Gus again. We spent time telling each other
of our separate adventures. Gus had trapped all the way up to the
headwaters of the Adams River. He, too, had caught mostly marten. After we had rested for a few days, we put all our pelts
together and hauled them over to Port Harvey for shipment to
Vancouver to be sold.

It was also about this time that Harry left us. I think that he
went back down to Chehalis for awhile and then came back up to
British Columbia to go logging on Vancouver Island. I met him
many years later when we were both around seventy years old. He
was living in a cabin on the MacMillan Bloedel Logging Company
grounds, six or seven miles south of Port Alberni on the Bamfield
road. He had some cougar dogs and was doing a bit of hunting,
but he was pretty crippled up by then and spent most of his time
around the cabin.

That spring we ran into an Irishman named Paddy McCallum. He
was travelling around the area in a boat of about twenty-four feet
with a small cabin on it. He had his wife and ten-year-old daughter
with him. In the course of telling him about the trapping we had
done up the Adams River, we happened to mention that there
were quite a number of fir trees that had been washed out of the
riverbank and were now in jams and scattered along the river.

Paddy seemed to think that we might be able to get the handlogging rights to the area from the government for nothing. We all agreed that, if we could get the rights, that's what we would do for the summer months.

Paddy headed down the coast to Vancouver to arrange to get the logging rights, while August, Gus and I went to a spot about a mile up the river to establish our camp. We built a fairly large cabin for Paddy and his family to live in. Paddy's wife was going to do the cooking for the lot of us. I believe that the three of us boys managed in a tent for the summer.

After a few days, the McCallums arrived back at the Adams River. The good news was that Paddy had been able to acquire the logging rights that we needed. The bad news was that his young daughter had come down with the measles.

A week or so later Paddy came down with them too. And the epidemic was on! Over the next few weeks, the only one who didn't get the measles was Mrs. McCallum; she'd had them as a child. The poor woman got to nurse the rest of us! Paddy was the oldest of the bunch of us, and the disease hit him really hard. He thought he was going to die for sure. It hung on him for nearly a month. August came down with them next, and he was awfully sick for three weeks. Then he made the mistake of going back to work too soon and ended up in bed for another spell. Gus got them a little bit after August, and he was pretty sick as well. Last of all, it was my turn.

By the time they got to me, I guess those measles were just about worn out, because they didn't bother me nearly as much as the others. I was only in bed for a day or two. The rest of the time, I was up and around. But I did not feel good. Worst of all, I had lost all my ability to taste. No matter what I ate, it tasted dry like hay. After about two weeks of that, I got the idea that a nice tender Willow grouse would taste really good. I went out and shot one and brought it home. Paddy's wife fried it up real nice in butter. What a disappointment it was! I'd wasted my time, for I still couldn't taste a thing!

That bout of measles certainly slowed up our logging operation that summer. Even when we finally did get everyone back to work, none of us felt really lively for quite awhile.

The trees that we were after were good-size firs that had been washed out of the riverbank by the current during the spring flood. They still had the limbs and roots on them in most cases. We were working during the summer months when the water in the river was low and we could get at the trees. We trimmed off all the limbs we could get at with an axe and cut off the roots with a bucking saw. Then, we'd roll the tree with a jack to get at the remaining limbs. Finally, we'd cut the tree into logs from twenty-four to forty feet long. We would then roll the logs down the bank and out onto the bars where they would float free when the high water returned with the fall rains.

In places, the trees were piled up in jams and all tangled together. We had to work a lot harder for those logs and be especially cautious when we cut them. We had to be careful that we did not cut one log and have another one roll on us. The trees that were still hanging partially out in the current were also dangerous. The flow of the current against them put a lot of pressure on the trunk. We had to cut them very carefully; they could easily snap and jump back at you. Some that were just too dangerous, we didn't even try to take.

All summer, we picked out any really long logs to be used as boomsticks. We bored a hole in each end of these with a boom auger and fastened them together with chain. At the mouth, the river was about one hundred and fifty feet wide. The boomsticks were strung on a long slant, about one thousand feet up the river from the lower end of the slough on the north side, to a rock bluff on the south side. The slant was so gradual that, when the timber came down in the fall, we didn't lose a single log under the boomsticks. They just floated down the river and were herded into the slough. Most of the logs floated free with a high water. We had to use a peevee or jacks to roll a few out into the current and on their way.

The slough was a perfect place to boom up the logs. While the river would be boiling with high water, there was hardly any current at all in the slough. After we had a section made up, we brought it out on a high tide. The incoming tide would back up the current in the river and we were able to use long pikepoles to move the section from the slough out into the river. We tied the section up outside the river mouth where it waited to be picked up by a tug that towed it to Vancouver for sale. We managed to get two or three sections out of the Adams River that summer.

After the logging was all wrapped up in the fall, we parted ways with Paddy McCallum and his family. We loaded all of our belongings into our two boats and headed over to Bute Inlet where we planned to trap for the winter. On the way down Cordero Channel, we stopped in at the store in Shoal River, right opposite Phillips Arm. We ordered a lot of new traps, for August had plans to enlarge our operation.

The supplies would be sent back to us on the freight boat that made a trip up the coast every two weeks, and off-loaded at Church House at the mouth of Bute Inlet. We would pick it up there and take it up to the Southgate River.

Church House was an Indian reservation. We knew most of the Indians there and stopped in to get a few supplies from their store from time to time. When we went in to get our freight, the chief invited us to supper. We were happy to accept and went up the hill to his house.

It was interesting to see the homes that the Indians lived in because all we had seen before were the primitive cabins that they had on the fishing grounds. The chief's house was nicely furnished. There was a big dining room table and all the furniture you would see in any house. We were a bit surprised when the time for dinner came and a blanket was spread on the floor in the living room, and all the dishes of food were placed on it. Everyone sat around the edge of the blanket to eat. It seemed a bit unusual, but I can recall that the meal was a very good one.

That fall, we established our camp about twenty miles up the Southgate River where the rapids prevented further canoe travel. We spent the first couple of weeks building a cabin there. It was about ten by twelve feet with an overhang at the end where we could stack firewood. We had always enjoyed having the fireplace at our home in Chehalis, so we decided to put one in our little cabin. We had no cement; we just used stones that we could fit together.

I found a nice big slab of rock that I thought would make a great hearth for the fireplace. It was about four inches thick and four or five feet across. It was much too big to move in one piece, so I decided to split it. I took a stick of dynamite and, using poles to pry up the rock, put it right under the middle where I wanted it to break. Then I started shooting at it with the .22 rifle. It was quite cold by this time and the dynamite was frozen. I shot three or four holes through it, but I couldn't set it off. Then I got out my 25-35 and shot it with that. Boom! She went off all right! The rock went up in the air and split just where I wanted it to. It made a damn good hearth. We certainly enjoyed having that fireplace when the weather got really cold.

And it did get cold that winter. We had one solid month of freezing temperatures, clear sky and a strong north wind. We would get a big fire going in the fireplace at the cabin at Twenty Mile and keep it roaring until about nine o'clock at night. The rocks would be really hot before we went to bed. We would then put a four-gallon can of water in the fireplace and hope that it wouldn't freeze by morning. But during that cold snap, it was always frozen solid when we went to get up. We would have to thaw it out to have water to make our breakfast.

We trapped up the Southgate River all that winter. Fairly early in the spring, we came down the river and spent some time around the head of Bute Inlet. We had a look around up the Homathko River and generally just did some exploring. By this time it was quite late in the spring and the pelts were no longer prime, so there was no sense doing any trapping. We hauled our winter's catch down to the mouth of the inlet and shipped it to Vancouver for sale.

After that, we decided to head further north and explore Knight Inlet. We spent most of that spring rowing and sailing around. It was a good life. We would catch fish when we wanted to, dig clams or shoot a deer if we needed meat. All the time, we would keep our eyes out for any sign of cougar. There was still a bounty on them, so we were always looking to get the dogs on the trail of one. That was a good way of adding a little money for our next winter's provisions. In all the time we were hunting and trapping, we must have killed at least thirty cougar.

FIRST ENCOUNTER WITH KOHSE

LATER THAT SUMMER, I went to work for a logging camp at Menzies Bay, just below Seymour Narrows. Then we spent another winter trapping. This time, we worked the drainage of the Homathko River at the head of Bute Inlet.

In the spring, we made another trip up Knight Inlet. We went up the Klinaklini River until we came to the canyon section. There we found a huge, clear pool that was full of Dolly Varden trout. We camped there for about a week on a lovely sandy spot below a big bluff right beside the river. And what fishing we had! Those trout went from twelve to thirty-four inches long, averaging about twenty-two inches. They were lovely and fat. We made a rack over our campfire and smoked the fish as we caught them. I think we left that spot with about one hundred and sixty smoked fish. That was some of the most enjoyable work I think I ever did.

On our way back down the river, we stopped on a gravel bar to see if we could find any deer tracks. We were two or three hundred yards from the canoe when we saw a man coming towards us from the bottom end of the bar. He was still a fair ways off, but we could soon see that he was dressed only in his long underwear. We figured he must be some kind of nut or something to be walking out in the bush in his Stanfields. He didn't even have shoes on.

We went down to meet him. The first thing he did was ask if we were the Schnarrs. When we said we were, he told us that he was looking for us—that he'd been told we were up the river above where he was—and that he needed our help.

The fellow went on to tell us that his name was Fred Kohse and that he had come up the river to stake some timber claims. But when he had started back down, he'd run into trouble trying to navigate the river and had run his speedboat onto a gravel bar at the upper end of an island, a couple of miles downstream from where we were. He soon found that he could not free his boat himself against the strength of the current that held it on the bar. Knowing we were somewhere upstream, he had left his wife and young son on the island and swum to shore to come looking for us. This, at least, explained why he had abandoned most of his clothing.

We loaded Fred into the canoe with us and headed downstream. His wife was much relieved to see us. I guess she wondered if she would ever see him again.

Kohse's boat was about thirty feet long with a five-foot beam and powered by a forty-horsepower Redwing engine. It was quite a boat and looked to have lots of power. He'd put a hole in the bottom of the hull when he ran onto the gravel bar. Together, the four of us were able to tip the boat back against the current far enough to get at the damage. We put some boards over the hole and covered it all with a piece of canvas that we tacked down all the way around.

We camped on the island that night. Sitting around the fire after a meal of smoked trout, potatoes and beans, we learned a little about Fred Kohse. He was a German who had worked as a head waiter in France and Italy before coming to Canada. He was fluent in German, French and English. He had worked in a great many high-class hotels. Before coming out west, he had worked in a big hotel in Montreal. He told us that he had been head waiter at the Empress Hotel in Victoria for several years. Then he had become interested in boats and the water and he started up the boathouse. First he did it in his spare time. In the summer he would run tours up the Gorge. Gradually his business had expanded to become full-time.

While he was working at the Empress Hotel, Kohse had heard that there was a lot of money to be made staking timber claims. In spite of the fact that he knew absolutely nothing about timber and logging—he had never even been out in the woods—he had set off with his family to see what he could make of it. You had to give the guy credit for having a sense of adventure.

We told stories of our various adventures until late into the night. Kohse told us that, in exchange for helping him get his boat off the bar, we were welcome to catch a ride with him down to Victoria if we were interested. He had a larger boat, a thirty-six-foot sailboat, anchored at the mouth of the river.

The next morning, we pushed the boat back up against the current until we got it into enough water to float it. Then we worked it down the side of the island until we got it into deep water again. Our patch worked quite well; it only leaked a little.

Gus and I took our canoe, while August went on board with the Kohses to navigate them the rest of the way down the river. August wanted to steer the boat himself, but Kohse would have none of that. They soon left us far behind.

But we weren't too long in catching up to them again. Kohse had not followed August's directions closely enough and he had again grounded them on a sandbar. August was furious when we found them waiting for us to tow them free. He gave Kohse an ultimatum.

"Either you let me steer this boat and take it the rest of the way out of the river, or we leave you right here to make it on your own!" August was used to getting his way.

By this time, I think even Kohse had decided that it would be wise to let August handle the boat. August took the steering wheel and we came the rest of the way down the river without further mishap.

After spending so much time in small rowboats and canoes, Kohse's sailboat looked like a luxury yacht to us. It had a beam of about twelve feet and a really big sail. There was also a ten-horsepower auxiliary engine that was used to make landings or if there was no wind at all. It looked quite grand sitting there at anchor at the mouth of the Klinaklini River. We soon decided—or at least August decided—that we would take the trip to Victoria. We tied our rowboat and canoe behind the speedboat and off we sailed down Knight Inlet, a little Armada with the larger boat towing the others behind.

As we came by Cracroft Island, we stopped at Port Harvey to pick up our mail and leave our boats. From there, we were about three days sailing down the Strait of Georgia to Victoria. It was a wonderful trip. We ate smoked trout, which everyone enjoyed, and generally just relaxed. It was a real treat not to have to row to get where we were going!

By the time we arrived in Victoria, we'd got to know Kohse quite well. He seemed like an easygoing guy to get along with. I wasn't really surprised when he asked us if we wanted to go into business with him, operating the Empress Boathouse. With his job at the hotel, it was obvious that he didn't have time to do it all by himself.

Gus was not interested in staying in Victoria at all. He had made up his mind to go back down to our place in Chehalis. Our father had left the property to me when he died. This had long been a bone of contention between August and Gus because August felt that, being the oldest, he should be entitled to it; whereas Gus argued that the old man had the right to leave it to whomever he wanted. I suppose the old man did it for spite because I had not been there when my brothers had driven him off. The thing was, it didn't really make much difference to me. I wasn't planning on going back to it anyway. So when Gus said he was going back, I told him to send the papers over to me, and I signed the property over to him.

August and I decided to give the boathouse business a try. The Empress Boathouse was built on a raft of logs on the upper part of the beach, just west of the CPR wharf in Victoria Harbour. Fred and his family lived in the boathouse. When the tide went out, the raft would be sitting on the mud flat that ran about one hundred feet beyond the boathouse at low tide. A float ran from the raft out far enough so that you could always tie a boat to it, even at the lowest tide. As well as renting launches and running tours up the Gorge, Kohse also ran boats out to the big ships entering the Strait of Juan de Fuca. At that time, ships had to anchor over at William Head and wait until a pilot and a doctor came on board. The doctor would inspect the ship for disease, and, if it passed inspection, the pilot would then take over and steer the ship to wherever it was going, usually Vancouver. We would run the doctor back in to Victoria. Then when the ship was on its way back out to sea, we would run out and pick up the pilot again.

We ran the boathouse operation for a few months, but there was not enough money in it for all of us. On top of that, August soon got so that he wanted to manage everything, and that did not go over too well with Kohse. A lot of tension developed between the two. Finally, August left and went back up to Port Harvey. I decided to stay on at the boathouse.

When it was quiet one day, I started fiddling around with an old motor that was really worn out. A bearing was so worn out that, when it ran, it sounded like a threshing machine. It was a one-cylinder, five-horsepower gasoline engine. I'd never worked on a gas engine before, so I was interested to have a look at it. When I got it apart, I discovered that, not only did it have the bearing worn so thin that metal was riding on metal, but the crankshaft was also worn until it was lopsided. It must have been at least a sixteenth of an inch flat on the sides.

I put in a lot of hours on that engine. I filed the crankshaft until I got it round again and then I poured a new babbitt bearing around it. It was a big job for me at the time. But when I put everything back together, it worked perfectly. I really felt good about that. I had learned a lot and really enjoyed doing it. Kohse was very happy to have his old engine back and used it all the time after that.

We sometimes got caught in some pretty rough weather running those boats out to the big ships in the strait, and I began to learn a lot about operating a powerboat on the ocean. All of this would prove to be very valuable experience for me later on.

When World War I started, Fred Kohse and his family were put in detention up in the interior of British Columbia near Vernon. I was never too sure why they picked on Kohse. I knew he was German and all, but they never bothered anyone else in his family. His mother and father and a number of brothers and sisters had all come out from Germany after Fred had moved to Victoria. Perhaps it had something to do with the fact that he worked in hotels or maybe because he had boats. Who knows?

In any event, I was left to look after the boathouse. I was living on it, but there wasn't much business. Pretty soon, I was down to the point where I didn't have any money left. I realized that I was going to have to go into something else to make my living. I closed down the boathouse and sold the little engine that I had repaired to Parker's Machine Shop, which was located right next door to us on the waterfront. I got five dollars for it.

Kohse's half-brother Otto, who was about my age, and I went to work in a logging camp at Port Renfrew for awhile. Then we went down to Chehalis where we did the same thing. I was doing contract falling and bucking at this time; Otto ended up running the steam donkey. I only stayed a short while in the camp in Chehalis, then I returned to Victoria. Otto stayed and never moved back. He married a girl who grew up next door to our home down there.

But this time, I didn't stay in Victoria long. Tom Colley and I went up to Ocean Falls where our friend Jack Smith was working. Jack was a first-rate mechanic. They had him rebuilding the engine on a pile driver that someone else had taken apart and not been able to fix. I got a job running a gasoline-powered engine that hauled two flatcars on a track that ran from the dock up to the dam site about a mile away. I was hauling sacks of cement for the dam, which was going to raise the level of the lake twenty-five or thirty feet, and provide more power to the pulp mill. Tom Colley worked as my brakeman; he threw all the switches on the rail line for me and would hook up and unhook the cars.

There was a crew of Japanese that loaded the sacks onto a set of empty flatcars on a siding alongside the ship. I would hook onto the load and haul it up to the dam site. Then I'd return with the empty cars from the previous trip. When I got back to the dock, I would put the empty cars on the side track and pick up the next set of loaded cars from alongside the ship. The Japanese would then move the empty cars over onto the other track and load them.

One day we ran into some trouble with the Japanese crew. For some reason or other they decided to change the way we were working. And they didn't bother to ask us about it. When we came down with a set of empty cars and Tom tried to switch them onto the usual track, the foreman of the crew came running up and tried to stop him.

"You have to take them down the other track," he said.

"What the hell for?" I asked.

"I have decided that we will switch it around the other way," the foreman replied.

"Nothing doing," I said.

I ran the empty cars down against the loaded ones that they had on that track. I had no idea what they were up to; I didn't much like the fact that they had simply made the decision without asking anyone.

Apparently, the Japanese foreman didn't like the fact that I wasn't going along with his plan. In fact, he got real mad! He suddenly rushed at me, his fingers like claws trying to get at my eyes. I knocked him flat. Behind him there were eight or ten others from the crew, and they started coming at me one after the other. I knocked each of them down as they came. Tom Colley was standing there with a coupling pin in his hand, ready to offer assistance, but he said that he never saw the need. He stood there laughing at the way they came at me one at a time and got knocked down.

"They were going down like bowling pins one after the other," he said later. "You didn't seem to need any help at all."

The thing was that they all seemed to want to grab me, so they were coming in wide open. I was small and quick, and I had done a bit of boxing as a kid. I would just pop them before they could get their hands on me. I was lucky that they didn't come at me in a group, I guess.

It wasn't too long before the foreman could see that they weren't getting anywhere, and he called his men off in Japanese.

"You watch out! We'll get you!" he said in English.

I never thought too much about that threat, but it wasn't long before the Japanese acted on it. We worked very late one day. It was about one in the morning when I was making my way home. It was a dark night and the rain was pouring down like it does at Ocean Falls. I had just passed the shed where Jack Smith was working on the pile driver. For some reason he was still at work. I was too tired to go in for a chat, so I called out a greeting and continued on my way.

In the darkness just beyond the shed two Japanese jumped me. They came at me from each side from out of the shadows of two piles of lumber that I had to pass between. I knocked one of them down, but the other grabbed me from behind. I reached back, grabbed him around the neck and bent down and threw him over my shoulder. Luckily, Jack had heard the commotion and come running. He got there just in time. The one that I had knocked down first was pulling a long knife out of his belt as Jack approached. As he started at me from behind, Jack was able to blind-side him. He kicked the knife out of his hands and it flew off into the darkness. With the odds evened up, my attackers decided that they'd had enough and disappeared into the rain.

It didn't take long for the word of that attack to spread. The next morning, all of the workers in the mill and on the construction site had heard about it. No one went to work that morning. Instead, everyone got together on the wharf—there were about two thousand men milling about. There was a lot of talk about going down and "cleaning out Jap town." I didn't feel that I needed anyone to fight my battles, but it had gotten right out of my control. Apparently there had been an earlier incident where a group of Japanese had beat a fellow unconscious. They had him on the dock with a large stone tied around his neck. They were going to toss him into the water. Ironically, it was the Japanese foreman that I had been fighting with who had talked them out of it. But that incident had not been forgotten, and now a lot of the men wanted some action. All the bosses from the mill and dam site were there trying to talk the men into going back to work. It was a tense situation. The confrontation lasted about two hours. Finally, tempers cooled a little. It was agreed that if anything else happened, then action would be taken. Finally, everyone went back to work.

I guess the word also got back to the Japanese pretty quickly. I ran that engine hauling cement for another month or so and never had any more trouble at all.

Jack and Tom and I all quit our jobs at Ocean Falls at the same time and went back to Victoria. Tom got a job with the Pilot Office that had started up after the Empress Boathouse went out of business. He was running a pilot boat out to meet the ships entering the Strait of Juan de Fuca. Jack Smith started repairing cars for people. I went to work for him. I would take motors down and help him put them back together. I learned a lot about engines from Jack. He could do just about anything there was to be done as far as motors were concerned. He could make parts, pour bearings, you name it.

At this time, I was living with Fred Kohse's parents. They had a house on the corner of Humboldt and Douglas streets right across from the Empress Hotel. It was a nice big two-storey house set back from the street about fifty feet with a border of small cedar and fir trees around it. The Kohses were excellent people; they treated me just like one of the family.

In the summer of 1915, Jack Smith and I went down to Washington to help Jack's father, who was starting up a sawmill that had gone bankrupt. It was located over at Lake Whatcom, about ten miles from Bellingham. We worked there for a couple of months—or at least I did. After we'd been there about a week, I had learned everything that needed to be taken care of. After that, Jack was seldom around. He was always off in Bellingham living it up, leaving me to look after the job. Jack was the kind of guy who liked to take life pretty easily; he was hard to tie down to a regular job.

"I think I'll go down and sign up for the army," Jack said to me out of the blue one day. It seemed like not a bad idea.

"Well, if you're going to sign up, I guess I will too," I said.

The next day we went to Bellingham and registered. There was conscription on then in the United States. The first thing they wanted to know was why we hadn't registered sooner; the war had been on for almost two years by this time. We told them that we had been way up north in Canada and did not even know that there was a war on. They seemed to accept that and we registered.

We didn't get called up right away. Jack went back up to Victoria for awhile. He wanted to see his family before he went to war. He had a wife and young daughter. I went to work in the Navy Yards down at Bremerton, pouring concrete in a dry dock they were building. I did that for a couple of months, then I got a better job with one of the contractors on the site. All I had to do was keep an electric pump going during the night, and I was making twice as much money as I had been pouring concrete. I liked that job.

THE WAR

IN MARCH OF 1916, I got my orders to report to Camp Lewis for basic training. The funny thing was that my brother August had been drafted at about the same time, and he was, there at Camp Lewis while I was. The thing was, neither of us knew it until years later. August had been handlogging back up at Blind Channel on West Thurlow Island on Johnstone Strait when he had received his conscription notice. All during basic training, I was right there in the next barracks to him. We were both in the 91st Division of the 361st Infantry. I was in Company G and August was in Company H.

Basic training was no problem for me. I was young and fit and already knew how to handle a gun. When we first went out on the firing range, a lieutenant came and began to show me how to use the strap on the army rifle to help keep the gun steady.

"I've been shooting since I was eight years old," I said. "I've never used a strap yet and I think I'm better off without it."

"OK, you go ahead and try your way and we'll see how you score," he said.

I took some shots at the stationary target and scored well; right away I was near the top of the Company.

"You shoot whatever way you like," the lieutenant said.

The men who were the best shots were issued automatic rifles.

I got mine and was assigned a first and second carrier to haul ammunition for the rifle.

We only got about three months of training. They were sending men overseas as fast as they could. As far as I was concerned, I didn't need a lot of training. I was already an experienced rifleman; I only needed training in how to march and how to get along in the army.

Just a couple of days before we were to leave for New York, I came down with the mumps and was held up in sick bay. I was supposed to catch up with the 91st Division, but I never did. Instead, I was transferred to the 81st Division and went overseas with them later on.

I went over to Europe on a troop ship in June. The trip took four or five days. We landed in the south of England, where we camped for about a week before making the crossing to France.

My experiences in the war in Europe were pretty tame compared to what some men went through. I didn't really get involved in any of the real fighting until very near the end of the war. You'd have to say I was lucky again.

To begin with, we were sent to an area in the south of France where there was not a lot of action. We could see the German lines with field glasses from our observation post. They were dug into a line of trenches about five miles long. They had a cannon back there and were firing at our line of trenches—not very often, just enough to keep things interesting. One side would fire a shot, and then, after awhile, the other side would fire one back.

At first I had some trouble getting along with our second lieutenant. He always used to pick on me. Whenever he needed someone for KP, and there was no one else around to pick on, he would use me. He always seemed to be able to find something wrong with my uniform or my kit. I didn't have any idea why he did it, but I got pretty tired of it after awhile.

One day he put me on an observation post. During the day, the men were allowed to move back from the front-line trenches, and the observation posts watched for any enemy activity. I was on that post all day. It was fall by this time and when it got dark, I knew I should have been relieved. I hadn't had anything to eat. After nightfall the observation post was not really needed anymore anyway, because the men would be back in the trenches again.

I knew that deserting a post was a very serious offence as far as the army was concerned, so I stayed on that post. I was thinking that I'd be relieved at any minute. The worst thing about it was the fact that I knew that there was really no reason for me to be there now that the trenches in front of me were manned. There were all kinds of men who would be aware of an attack before I was.

I stayed there until after nine o'clock. Still no one came to relieve me. Finally, I put my rifle over my shoulder and started for headquarters. I was steaming! The second lieutenant had his headquarters in the basement of an old building that was all shot to pieces. I marched right into his office and asked him just what the hell he thought he was doing!

"I've been on that post since early this morning, and now it's after nine o'clock and I haven't even had anything to eat," I said, not bothering to be the least bit polite. I really cussed him out, calling him just about every name I could think of. I suspect I might have shot him if he had started anything! I was really mad and I think he knew it.

"Oh, I'm sorry," he said. "I forgot all about you."

"That's the damn trouble with you," I countered. "You don't think about anybody but yourself." I wasn't only mad about being left out on the post, I was also angry about the way this guy had been treating me all along. I was definitely going to get my licks in.

"Have you had any supper?" he asked, trying to sound concerned.

"Where the hell would I get anything to eat out there?" I replied. Then the second lieutenant sent me over to the mess with orders for the cook to make me something to eat.

After I left headquarters, I wondered about whether I would be court martialled for deserting my post, or for insurrection. I was uneasy about it for a couple of days. But nothing ever came of it. In fact, the second lieutenant quit picking on me altogether after that. He never found anything wrong with anything I did again. After awhile, I even tested him on it. I went on parade with a dirty gun. It didn't make any difference—he passed it anyway. From then on he was my friend. Perhaps he was grateful that I had not made a complaint to his superior officer. Anyway, I was happy simply to be left alone.

The war went on. Nothing much changed. We shot our cannon at the Germans, and they shot theirs at us. Days became weeks,

weeks became months; winter passed into spring, spring into summer, summer into fall, and back to winter. The war went on, but for us it was not too bad. We weren't getting killed or doing much killing.

It was in about September of 1918 that we were finally relieved of our position in the south of France and transferred up to Verdun. We spend a week or so in barracks there. The Germans were firing "Big Bertha," their largest cannon, at a railway station which was about a mile behind our position. For all of the time that we were there, every fifteen minutes, like clockwork, they fired at that station. The shells for "Big Bertha" were sixteen inches in diameter and six feet long. What a rumble they made when they landed! That went on the whole time we were there. I guess they never did demolish the station, because they were still firing at it when we left.

We finally moved out to the front lines. Early in November, my platoon was sent out on a day patrol to try to feel out the enemy position in the area where the rest of the army was to advance the next day. We went a couple of miles and came up to a strip of timber that was probably a mile long. Before we had gone very far along the edge of the woods, the lieutenant stopped the patrol and ordered my corporal to take his squad and scout out the woods.

We had only gone a couple of hundred yards into the bush when the corporal stopped us.

"I think we'll just stop here and wait," he said. "We'll let enough time pass and then we'll go back and report that we saw nothing."

This didn't sit well with me. I didn't feel like just sitting there.

"We were ordered to go down to the end of the timber," I said. "I'm going to go down there. If any of the rest of you want to come along with me, that's fine."

Only one man chose to come with me. That was my second carrier. It was funny because he was the last person I would have expected to act bravely. I figured him for a coward because he never spoke up on anything. He was just a very quiet guy. So he and I went all the way to the end of the timber, but we didn't see a thing. When we came back, we joined up with our squad again and went back to where the platoon was and reported seeing nothing.

Early the next morning, before daybreak, our line started

advancing. The area that we were going through was covered by a thick, heavy ground fog. You could only see about fifty feet. There was lots of firing going on but we sure couldn't see much. The Germans were retreating in front of us. They were mostly firing with their artillery. One of the first shells to come over landed pretty near under the feet of our first sergeant. It looked like it blew all the flesh off his legs right up to his hips. We thought he was finished right then. He looked really bad. I was not more than twenty feet from him when it happened. I sure didn't think he would live, but he did. The first aid unit that came along behind us got to him pretty quickly, and we heard later that he was going to be all right.

We were in the second line and were not allowed to fire lest we hit one of our own men. I got fed up with that pretty quickly.

"I'm going up to the front," I told my corporal. "I don't like the idea of someone shooting at me and not being able to shoot back."

Once again my second carrier decided that he would go with me. We were under fairly heavy machine gun fire, but because of the fog we couldn't see anyone to fire back at. Finally, we got up to a place where the firing was pretty regular and I could use the automatic rifle. I started to shoot just by using the sound of where the firing came from. It seemed that every time I shot, the firing from that direction would stop.

We were advancing a few steps and then dropping flat on the ground. Once, just as I was dropping, the grass right under my nose was torn up by machine gun bullets. If I had fallen a split second earlier, I would have been dead. My luck was still with me.

Soon a barbed wire entanglement appeared in the fog in front of us. My second carrier had the wire cutters, so he went forward to cut the wire. A shell landed about ten feet from where he was crouched. Luckily it landed in an area of soft dirt, so it didn't do him any harm. It sure gave him a shock, though. He ran back and flopped down beside me.

"My God! That was too close for me!" he said.

I took the cutters from him and went up and cut our way through the wire.

And that's where I was at eleven o'clock on the eleventh of November, 1918 when the war ended. The word came up to us just after I had passed through the barbed wire. My carrier and I were the only two in our area who had made it through. I was also surprised to see that our second lieutenant was right behind us and would have been the next through. He turned out to be a pretty brave fellow. The fog had started to lift only a few moments before we heard of the cease-fire. Within ten or fifteen minutes the landscape had cleared. We were able to see what we would have been facing had the war not ended when it did. That fog was probably the only thing that saved our lives! We would almost certainly have been killed or wounded if it had lifted half an hour earlier. We were just coming up to a knoll where the Germans were well dug in. We would have been sitting ducks for them as we would have had to cross to an open field to get to their position. The Company just to the right of us was not in the fog. There were sixty men lying dead in the field that they had crossed.

As soon as word of the cease-fire got around and the shooting had stopped, the Germans came out of their trenches and we all shook hands. Everyone was happy that the fighting and killing were over.

The Germans couldn't understand why we had been advancing. They had been told that an armistice was about to be signed. Most of them were just trying to avoid being killed. That was why, as soon as I shot at a gun position in the fog, the firing stopped from that position. Whoever was there quit shooting and retreated. We had to tell them that we did not know that the armistice was coming. All we had heard were rumours, and there were so many of those going around in the army all the time that we had not paid any attention to them.

We found out later that our officers knew that the cease-fire was coming, but they had decided not to tell the enlisted men. It wasn't so bad for our Company because we had no one killed, and only one wounded. But it was hard to make sense of when you looked at the sixty bodies laying in the field next to our position. There was no need for it.

I've always said that I have been a really lucky guy throughout my life. But I guess no one is lucky all the time. Right after the fighting in Europe ended, I made a decision that turned out to be an unlucky one.

All of the Allied countries were having a shooting competition between teams of their best marksmen. Each nation had a team of twenty men. The contest was in rapid-fire shooting, which involved firing up to fifteen shots per minute with an army 303 bolt-action rifle.

Fifteen shots per minute was about the most you could manage with that rifle. You had the gun already loaded with a clip of five shells when you started. Then you had to load two more clips as you emptied them to get the fifteen shots in. You were firing at a stationary head-and-shoulders target at two hundred yards.

I was ranked ninth in the American army of two million men who were overseas. Naturally they wanted me on the team. The only problem was that at the time my Division was slated to be the second to go home. And I sure did want to go home! If I went on the team, I would miss going home with my Division. They told us that the shooting team would be sent home on the first boat after the contest was over. But that would still be later than if I stayed with my Division. Or so I thought. Anyway, I wanted to go home and be done with the war so badly that I decided not to shoot on the team.

Then I got unlucky! My Division ended up not going home second—we were the second-to-last to be sent home! And the American shooting team easily won the contest—and they were home six months earlier than we were! Bad luck.

I spent another seven months in France. Most of that time we were in a small village where we did a lot of work to repair some of the damage done in the war. We rebuilt stone fences and whatnot. By the time we left, that little village had never looked so good.

For the most part, the rest of the time we spent overseas was just sheer boredom. We did a lot of useless drills and went on parade for some visiting dignitary or other far more often than was necessary. It was all done just to keep us in line.

About the only thing that relieved the boredom for me was a few boxing matches that I was in. And then even that was spoiled by an officer.

Back when we were kids, August had bought a couple of pairs of boxing gloves from the Sears and Roebuck catalogue, and we used to box each other and some of the other kids who lived nearby. While we were quite small, we got used to fighting with our fists without hurting each other. Later, when I worked in the logging camps, I always carried two pairs of gloves along with me. We would do a little boxing in the bunkhouse in the evening, just for the sport of it.

I never cared who I boxed with. I was pretty small; I only went one hundred and thirty-four pounds, but I could box with anybody. I never did get knocked out. I was small, but I was very quick and I was strong for my size.

I had had one or two boxing matches in the army and they knew I was pretty good. After the war, when we were still in France putting in time, they had some boxing matches. I entered and won a fight. A few days later, my sergeant arranged another fight for me, and I won again. Then, a little while later, the second lieutenant who was in charge of our platoon came up to me in the barracks after breakfast.

"You're going to box a man tonight," he said.

"Oh, am I?" I said. "Is that an order?"

"Yes," he replied.

"Well, I'll tell you what," I answered. "I'm not going to box anyone tonight."

"Why not?" he asked me, as if he couldn't imagine why I wouldn't want to do whatever he told me to do.

"I don't mind boxing," I said. "But I'm not going to do it when you order me to do it."

And that was the end of that. I didn't like that officer much anyway. And I sure as hell didn't like the idea that I was there to box at his pleasure. If he had asked me to box, I would have fought for sure. But I wasn't going to be ordered to do something that had nothing to do with the army. That was the end of my boxing. I never put the gloves on again.

Finally our orders came through and we marched out of that village and all the way to the coast, where we got a ship home. We landed back in the United States somewhere south of New York. Within three or four days we were discharged. We got sixty dollars, a train ticket home, our regular uniform and an honourable discharge. And that was the end of the army for me. I went back home to Chehalis and went back to falling and bucking trees in the logging camps.

A LETTER FROM KOHSE

I WAS WORKING as a faller out of a camp at Quinalt Lake, about twenty-five miles out of Hoquiam, Washington when I got a letter from Fred Kohse in Victoria. With the war over, Fred and his family had been allowed to move back to the coast. In his letter he said that he'd run into a fellow who was looking for someone to help run a boatload of liquor down south. He wanted to know if I would be interested in the job. The guy who owned the boat wanted someone who was good with engines, and Fred had recommended me.

Prohibition had been around for awhile in Washington by this time. There were an awful lot of people against it. That included just about everybody that I knew. Although I was never one to drink much—I had seen what it did to my father and wanted no part of it—I resented the fact that the government was the one telling me not to take a drink.

Anyway, there was still a good deal of liquor around in spite of the Volstead Act. In the country, there were people running illegal stills, making moonshine. And in the northern part of the state, it was a pretty easy thing to bring good liquor in from Canada where Prohibition was not in effect.

I had been thinking about trying to get into the liquor-running business even before Kohse wrote to me, but I just wasn't too sure how to go about it. I was very handy with engines—I seemed to have a knack for things mechanical—and liked the idea of working on the water after my years up the Johnstone Strait. Funny enough, even though I didn't spend any time near the water until I was almost grown, I had always felt at home on the sea.

I couldn't see anything wrong with hauling liquor. It seemed like everyone knew that the law would be changed eventually. And the rumrunning seemed like a much smarter idea than moonshining.

So, when I got Kohse's letter down there in Quinalt Lake, I didn't spend too much time pondering the possibilities. I think I got that letter on a Saturday and I left the camp Sunday morning. I stopped by Chehalis just long enough to say hello to Gus and drop my logging gear and pick up some things.

The day after I was back in Victoria, Kohse took me down to the wharf to meet the fellow who owned the boat. His name was Harry. He was a tall, raw-boned fellow in his early thirties. He wore a thin, neatly trimmed moustache which he was constantly running his finger over, as if he was never sure whether it was still there or not. He talked like he was an old hand at this business, but I was not all that impressed. He never seemed to look me in the eye. All he wanted to know about me was how good I was in a mechanical way. I told him I was pretty handy. Then Kohse went into the story about the little engine of his that had never worked, how I broke it down and put it back together and managed to get it running perfectly. This seemed to convince him.

Harry offered me $500 to pilot his boat to San Francisco and back. I would be the captain and he'd be my mate. I looked the boat over. The *Rose Marie* was a bit small for a trip like that—only twenty-eight feet long with a seven-foot beam—but she looked to be seaworthy enough. There were holds aft where the liquor would be stored. The forward cabin was just big enough to contain the engine, a bunk and a bit of a galley. Behind that was the pilothouse. The deck at the stern was open. The little boat was powered by a two-cylinder, ten-horsepower gasoline engine which would make about six knots. I fired it up and it seemed to run all right. While I was having a look around, Harry indicated that he'd made the trip before, but didn't seem keen to talk about it.

When it came right down to it, the *Rose Marie* was not the

boat I would have picked to run down the coast, and Harry wasn't the fellow I would have chosen to make the trip with, but it was a chance to get into the rumrunning and the money was right. I wasn't long in deciding to go.

After I made arrangements to meet Harry the next morning, Kohse and I left the wharf and walked over to Johnson Street and into a saloon. I asked Fred to fill me in on what he knew about my new boss. He told me that it was true that Harry had twice set out to take a load of booze down to San Francisco, but that he hadn't made it either time. It seems he had a rather coincidental bit of bad luck. On the first trip, Harry and his partner were down off Aberdeen, Washington when the engine broke down. They were lucky because a fish boat came along before they had drifted too far. It towed them into Aberdeen. Luck stayed with them, and they were able to get rid of their load of whisky there. Then they got the engine fixed and made their way back to Victoria.

On the second trip to San Francisco, the engine again quit just off the coast near Aberdeen. This time they were not so lucky—or at least they had a bit of bad luck thrown in with the good. No one came to their rescue, and they drifted a long time. Still, they were lucky to drift towards shore rather than out into the Pacific. The bad luck was that they drifted right in over the bar at the entrance of Aberdeen Harbor. Crossing that bar can be a rough experience under power in good weather conditions. The onshore winds pile up some fearsome waves over the shallows. Harry and his mate went over it in a storm. The breakers were so heavy that they tore two planks off the side of the boat. Fortunately the tide was high enough that they did not ground on the bar, but washed right over. Although they were again able to get rid of their cargo of liquor safely, Harry was badly shaken up by the ordeal. According to Kohse, Harry's main interest now was in finding someone who could keep the little engine running long enough to get beyond Aberdeen, Washington! I was his man.

The next morning we got all the supplies that we would need for the trip. We loaded a two-week supply of tinned goods on board. We also carried a couple of drums of gasoline and, according to Harry, enough oil to take us to California nonstop. We stopped at the Customs office and cleared from Victoria to Mazatlan, Mexico.

About four o'clock in the afternoon we passed out of the harbour. It was the eighth of November, 1920.

We ran out past William Head and into Pedder Bay. There was a wharf on the north shore with a cabin close to the beach and a house further back. From the cabin we loaded one hundred and ten cases of liquor packed in straw in gunny sacks. We managed to cram these into the hold of the little boat. We then put the hatch covers back on and wrapped them in canvas, and tied them very securely so that no water would get in and they would not come off in rough water.

We cleared Race Rocks about ten o'clock that night. Once out into the Strait of Juan de Fuca, we ran into a strong westerly. The waves started to pile up and it got quite rough. We were also bucking a bit of a tide and not making a great deal of headway for awhile.

I had done all of the steering so far. Harry seemed to be watching me closely to reassure himself that I knew what I was doing. Or so I thought! I didn't bother to bring up the subject of his two previous attempts at this trip, but did ask him a few questions about his experience on the sea. He said that he'd been on boats nearly all his life. He told me that the *Rose Marie* was the first one he'd actually owned. He said that he had big plans for this rumrunning business, though, and that, if I worked out, I could make a lot of money.

About the time we were opposite Sooke Harbour, I told Harry to take the wheel for awhile. I thought I would check and oil the engine, and then catch a bit of rest. I knew that, with only the two of us, we would have to take fairly short watches and sleep in snatches on a trip this long. I set a course that would put us well off Cape Flattery and gave Harry the compass bearing.

Then I went below into the little cabin. On the *Rose Marie* the galley, berths and engine room were all combined into one tiny cabin. I oiled the engine and made sure that everything was running smoothly. Then I lay down on the bunk. I had not eaten since early afternoon, but I had no appetite. The sea was pretty lumpy. It would take a few days to get my sea legs.

I lay on the bunk for about an hour and a half, but I didn't really get any sleep. I just sort of dozed off a bit. (I never did learn to sleep on a boat, even years later.) After awhile, judging by the motion of the boat, it seemed that the wind had died off and the sea calmed considerably. I got up and oiled the engine again—it seemed to be needing it about once an hour or so. Then I went up into the pilothouse.

"How're we going?" I asked.

"Just fine," Harry replied. "The wind has shifted; it's following us now."

I stepped out on deck to have a look around. I could hardly believe my eyes! There, straight in front of us, were the lights of Victoria! I went back inside and grabbed the wheel from Harry.

"You damn fool!" I shouted at him as I swung the boat back on course. "You've turned us completely around! We're almost back where we started from."

I didn't stop there. I used a few choice cuss words to let him know what I thought of his abilities as a navigator. He didn't say a word. I went back on deck for a moment and had a look at what lights I could see. I judged that we were out in the middle of the Strait, due south of Race Rocks. We'd only lost ten or twelve miles, but the worst of it was that I now wondered if I could count on any help at all with the navigation. It would be a very long trip if I had to do it all myself!

I didn't stay in my black mood for too long. With just the two of us, it didn't seem to make much sense to hold a grudge. But I did need to know what I was dealing with. After an hour or so, I began to ask Harry some pointed questions about his sea-going experience. The truth came out. It turned out he had spent two years as a cabin steward on a trans-Atlantic steamer before he came out to the West Coast. When he arrived in Victoria, he had invested his savings in the *Rose Marie*. Harry intended to get rich in the rumrunning business; his lack of experience was not a factor that concerned him. He'd spent a couple of months running the boat around in the Gulf Islands and had made his two ill-fated trips down the coast. That was it!

Well, now I knew! I guess I could have swung the boat around and headed back to Victoria, but that thought never even crossed my mind. I had signed on to take the *Rose Marie* to San Francisco and that's what I intended to do. But I did have a major problem that I hadn't expected to face. How the hell was I going to do all the steering all the way to San Francisco? Even if things went right, that trip would take nine or ten days! I decided that I'd have to learn to catnap pretty quickly.

I stayed behind the wheel all the way out the strait. I passed

Cape Flattery a good long way offshore, giving a wide berth to the reefs there.

About noon the next day the engine started to act up. One cylinder began to misfire off and on. Then, about four in the afternoon, that cylinder quit altogether. I went down to have a look at it. It looked to me like the problem was in the exhaust valve which was open, but stuck tight. This motor was the kind with a big scoop out of the top above the valves. You have to have a special wrench to get at it. Luckily, I had the wrench to get the valve loosened and out as well. All this time, the little engine continued to run on one cylinder. We were making so little headway that I knew Harry couldn't get us into any serious trouble.

We were now out in the open Pacific and I had not yet got my sea legs. I was not feeling much better than that engine. When I was up top were I could see out, I only felt lousy. Down below with the exhaust fumes and all, I felt quite miserable. The sound of the water running over the rolling hull didn't help at all. I found out later on that no matter how much time you spend on the inside waters, the swell out there in the open is a different thing altogether. Most people take two or three days to get used to it. But I never did!

It looked to me like the problem with the engine was that the valve stem fit too tight. When the engine heated up, it expanded until it froze up. I got out a file and sat and filed the stem lightly all over. Then I sandpapered it until is was really smooth again. I put the valve back in its place and screwed the spark plug back in. Once it was all back together, the second cylinder began to fire again. It worked fine after that. We never had any more trouble with the engine for the rest of the trip.

I went topsides and spent fifteen or twenty minutes out on deck in the fresh air. That seemed to put me right. After an hour or so, I began to feel like life was worth living again. I didn't feel good; just better than I had down below. I never did feel good on that whole trip.

About nine that evening, a southeaster started to blow. It came up out of nowhere in less than half an hour. We were bucking straight into it, and it just kept getting stronger and stronger. Pretty soon we were not making any headway at all. The waves were breaking over the bow of the *Rose Marie*. Although it didn't rain, we could hardly see due to the heavy spray that constantly lashed the windshield. Not that there was much to see—the night was black as tar. Every now and then we would get a glimpse of swirling green foam as a breaking wave crested over the bow. It was all I could do to keep the nose into the wind and hang onto the wheel. Harry had jammed himself into the other corner of the wheelhouse, but didn't look comfortable at all.

The wind blew like the devil for about three hours, and then died just as suddenly as it had come up. By dawn there was not a breath of wind. In a few more hours the sea had calmed. I gave the boat a good going over and was pleased to discover that the *Rose Marie* had come through our first storm unscathed. When I was tending to the engine, however, I realized that we were going to run short of lubricating oil—the motor was using a lot more than Harry had bargained for. We were going to run out long before we reached San Francisco.

We made our way down the coast in calm seas. About midmorning, I pointed out to Harry that we were passing by the mouth of Grays Harbor at Aberdeen. He seemed relieved. We were running five or six miles offshore along there. Later in the day, as we were coming up to Cape Disappointment and the mouth of the Columbia River, I calculated that we had used almost half our supply of oil.

"We're going to have to go into Astoria to get oil and gas," I told my boss.

"Oh, no!" he said in alarm. "You can't go in there. I ain't going over that bar!" Apparently his previous captain had told him that the bar at the mouth of the Columbia River was worse than the one they had drifted over at Aberdeen.

"Well, I'm going in there just the same," I said. "I'm not about to run out of oil and have no engine and drift halfway to Japan. As I see it, I'm in charge of the running of this boat and I'm going into the Columbia and that's all there is to it."

Harry was madder than the devil and we had quite a few words about this. Finally, he got so angry that he went below to the bunk and wouldn't come up. I guess his experience up at Grays Harbor had been pretty frightening because he sure was terrified of doing it again.

I didn't really know anything about the bar at the Columbia, but I knew that we had to have more oil. As we approached the mouth of the river, I could see that there was a large swell running over the bar. But there was no wind to speak of and under power we had no difficulty getting through. After we were safely inside, Harry came back up into the pilothouse. We didn't talk much until we docked at Astoria, five or six miles up the river.

We tied up at the first wharf that offered gas. For some reason the fellow who ran the station was suspicious right away.

"What have you fellas got on board?" he asked me as soon as he'd got the hose into the gas tank. "If you're carrying liquor, I can get you $125 a case."

I didn't say anything one way or the other, but took Harry aside and asked him how much he was going to get down in California.

"One hundred and twenty-five dollars a case," he replied.

"Well then, why don't we just let it go here and save ourselves the trip?"

"Oh no," Harry maintained. "I'm supposed to take this load to San Francisco and that is what I'm going to do. I couldn't sell it here, it's 'in bond'."

Well, that liquor was no more in "in bond" than I was! It couldn't have been "in bond" for any U.S. port because of the Prohibition laws anyway. But at the time I was not too sure of the laws, and I still felt that Harry was the boss as far as the liquor went, so I didn't press him on it. We got our gas and oil and set off on our way. As things turned out, Harry was fortunate enough to live to regret his decision not to sell in Astoria.

Before casting off, I asked the fellow at the gas dock if there was enough water for us to head straight out toward the mouth of the river, or if we would have to follow the channel that ran up the north side. He asked me how much water the boat drew. When I told him we only drew four feet, he said we'd have plenty of clearance on the tide.

It was about three in the afternoon when we cast off our lines from the wharf. From Astoria downstream the Columbia River is two or three miles wide. We headed straight out towards the point on the south side of the river mouth. We started off all right, but after awhile we seemed to be slowing down a bit all the time. First I thought that we were bucking an incoming tide. Finally we seemed to have stopped altogether. I looked over the side and could see that we were grounded on a sand bar. The water must have gotten shallower very gradually because we didn't even feel the boat come to a stop. It turned out that the tide was not rising at all, but falling.

When the tide went out, we were left high and dry in the middle of a patch of sand that extended for a mile in either direction. The boat keeled over until it lay on its side. You could see the mark in the sand where the keel had first touched nearly half a mile back. The track got deeper very slowly until the boat finally came to rest. If there had been a foot more tide at the time, we would never have known that that sand bar was there.

There was nothing to do but wait for the rising tide and hope that the boat would right itself again. We passed the time debating whether the fellow at the gas dock was bitter about the fact that we would not sell him our cargo, or just stupid. I was never sure. One thing though, once it got dark, we kept a close eye out for anything that might suggest a boat approaching our sandy berth, fearing we might be hijacked. The six hours passed uneventfully.

When the tide came back in, the *Rose Marie* righted herself smartly enough, and we set off again. There was a big swell running in over the bar, but no wind to speak of and we were soon through it and headed south. At this point, I was feeling that I had things pretty much under control. I now knew what the little engine needed to keep her running. I knew the boat was sound; I knew we now had lots of supplies to finish the trip; and I knew that I could not count on my boss for any help in anything that mattered. All I had to do now was stay awake for another five or six days! And that proved to be my downfall!

AFTER THE WRECK

THERE WE WERE—shipwrecked—soaking wet, and sitting on the sand in the middle of the night watching as the *Rose Marie* was pounded to pieces in the surf. Our cargo of good whisky was washing out to sea. And someone was sure to find us when day broke.

I sat for a time wondering how the hell I would get myself out of this mess. It is funny, but I don't recall ever thinking that I was lucky to be alive. I was still too angry.

The night was moonlit and fairly bright. But the only sign of life that we could see came from a lighthouse that looked to be ten or fifteen miles to the south. This would be the light at Cape Blanco.

It wasn't too long before the cold brought me to my senses. I began to think practical thoughts. I decided that we should at least attempt to save what liquor we could. I figured that we could sell whatever we could salvage to someone in the local area, and the trip would not be a total disaster.

I told Harry to wait on shore while I made the first trip back onto the *Rose Marie*. In the darkness it was hard to tell just how much the boat had broken up already. As soon as one of the big waves started to recede down the beach, I followed it and climbed back on board. Before the next breaker hit, I was able to get the hatch cover off the aft hold. Then I crouched in the lee of the pilothouse while another wave washed over me and the little boat. I could feel the tremendous force of that wall of water as it smashed against the hull and cabin. Something had to give. Planks and timbers creaked and groaned and split. I knew we did not have much time to salvage what we could of our cargo.

Between waves I grabbed a sack of liquor and jumped off the *Rose Marie* and ran up the beach above the high-water mark. I called to Harry and we got to work. It was not a pleasant task, but it gave us something to do. We would climb on board between waves, let a breaker roll over us, then grab a sack of liquor each and try to get ashore before the next wave hit.

In the next hour or so, we managed to get about seventy cases ashore. By then, most of the planks had been torn off the bottom of the boat, and the rest of the cargo had washed away. It got to the point where there was not enough of the little boat left to hang onto anymore and we were in danger of being washed out to sea.

Now we were faced with the problem of what to do with the liquor. I had a good walk around to try to find someplace to hide it. We seemed to be somewhere in the middle of a long stretch of sand about four hundred feet wide. Behind that was a fairly wide slough. It seemed impossible that we could hide the liquor in the sand. Anywhere we dug would show up because the dunes were well packed by the sea and wind. I knew that there were sure to be people snooping around before long. By the time those waves finished beating on the *Rose Marie*, there was bound to be lots of evidence of our shipwreck on the beach.

Then I came up with the idea that if we walked across to the slough, it would look like we had taken the liquor over and put it into another boat and taken it away. We dug a trench along the trail that we would walk to the slough, and buried the liquor. Then we walked back and forth along the trail until the sand was well packed down and you could not tell where we had been digging. That seemed to be the best that we could do.

It was now about four in the morning. There seemed to be no point in just sitting there shivering in the cold, so we set off down the beach in the direction of the lighthouse.

When we had walked a mile and a half or so, we could make out a patch of light in some trees at the edge of the beach ahead of us. At first, it looked to be quite close, but it turned out to be another mile or so down the beach.

When we finally got there, tired and wet, we found four men spearing salmon from the creek that ran into the slough. They had a big fire burning along the bank, a most welcome sight. These fellows told us that they were farmers who lived nearby and we told them of our shipwreck. Harry let me do most of the talking. I don't think he was too keen to talk about how we ended up on the beach.

When the farmers asked about our cargo, I told them that it was liquor bound for Mexico, and that it was all washed out to sea. But they just laughed. One of them, a big, ruddy-faced fellow with a red beard, said that that was too bad because if we had anything to sell, they would be glad to help us out. Well, I figured that we had to take a chance with someone, so I told them that we had managed to save about seventy cases. They seemed very pleased to hear this. They said they could come down that evening and load the cargo in a wagon and haul it out of there for us. We agreed that this would be fine. Harry and I warmed and dried ourselves at the fire and ate some food that they gave us. The farmers continued to fish until after daylight and then went off home. We made arrangements to meet them at the same spot that evening. After they left, we slept for awhile around that fire. Although I was exhausted—I'd had maybe ten hours' sleep in five days—I only slept for a couple of hours. Then we headed back down the beach to our cache.

It was mid-morning when we got back to where we had wrecked. The beach was crawling with people. The farmers had warned us that there would be folks out because they came to fish for salmon in the slough. But we were amazed by the number of them. I suspected that our partners had not been as quiet about this thing as they had promised to be. People were running up and down the beach picking up bottles that the tide had washed ashore. There were pieces of the *Rose Marie* strewn for hundreds of yards along the beach. We had only been able to salvage about seventy of the hundred and ten cases, so quite a few bottles had washed ashore. Many had broken free of the gunny sacks they were packed in. The sandy shoreline meant that most of them made it to the beach unbroken.

The waves breaking on the beach were now no more than two feet high. It was strange—during the two days that we spent there after that, the waves were always about the same. The heavy breakers that smashed our boat to pieces must have come from a storm a good distance offshore. We had not felt the large swell as long as we were well out from the beach. But in the shallows, the waves really started to pile up.

It was sad to see the carcass of the *Rose Marie* lying now a few feet above the water's edge, a forlorn monument to the ocean's power. The tide had gone out, leaving her high and dry right where she had grounded. But there really wasn't much to see; all that was left was about twelve feet of keel with the engine bolted to it. Both ends of the keel had broken off. The rest of her was scattered far and wide; a good part of it was now being brought back to haunt her as the tide came in again. Gas tanks, an oil drum, a hatch cover, and lots and lots of shattered planks and ribs and whatnot littered the beach. It was not a pleasant experience to sit and watch the scavengers pick the bones of our little boat, but I did not want to get too far away, fearful that someone would discover our buried treasure. But, with the crowd of people tramping all over the sand, no one noticed our well-worn path.

We stayed there until late afternoon. By then the beach was remarkably clean. What the beachcombers hadn't taken, the sea had reclaimed. The keel and engine of the *Rose Marie* sat alone.

We headed back down the coast for the rendezvous with our farmer friends. We waited by the river, but no one came. After dark, we retraced our steps to the wreck site. But no one showed up there either. By this time we were not only angry, we were also very hungry. We'd had nothing to eat since the early morning.

And we had nothing all the next day as we again waited on the shore. But at least we were able to have a fire, thanks to the matches that the farmers had left with us. Only a few people came to pay a brief visit to the site. As soon as they saw that the beach was clean, they hurried off. No one seemed to want to have anything to do with us. And no one though to bring us any provisions!

That night we again made our way down to the river. This time the farmers showed up shortly after we arrived. They had an excuse for their absence the night before. It seemed that they had decided that the best way to get the liquor was to bring a team of packhorses down to the edge of the slough directly behind where we were shipwrecked. One of them owned the farm located right back of there. They said they planned to ferry the liquor across the slough in a small boat. The only problem was that when they got the horses down to the slough, they had got stuck in some quicksand. The farmers had spent the rest of the night trying to get them out. Or so they said.

I didn't know whether to believe the story or not, but we didn't seem to have a lot of options, so we made new arrangements to move the liquor the next night. At least they brought us some grub.

The next night, we again waited for our friends to show up at the appointed time. And again they did not show. Finally, about one o'clock in the morning, the four arrived with a big old wagon drawn by a couple of workhorses. We loaded the liquor and slowly made our way off the beach and down a small dirt road to the main highway. We were headed for the red-bearded fellow's farm where we were going to store the liquor until its sale could be arranged. He said it would be safe enough in his barn.

We travelled a couple of miles on that road and were just cresting the top of a small rise when the sun began to show itself from behind the hills to the east. We could now see a village a half mile down the road. The red-bearded fellow who owned the wagon stopped and said that we would not take the load through town in the daylight. He said that we would have to stash it again until nightfall. I thought that he was crazy. The place consisted of no more than a store, a little hotel and four or five houses close by. It wasn't much more than a crossroads kind of place.

"Look here," I argued. "The booze is all covered with canvas. What is there to worry about?"

"Oh, I couldn't take the chance. I have to live around here, fella, you don't!" he said, more angrily than seemed necessary. "Anyway, we can hide it just in here—the place is deserted—and get it tonight."

I didn't like what was happening, but there wasn't much I could do at this point. We followed the farmers off the road into what seemed to be an abandoned farm. They seemed to know where they were going, which made me more uneasy still. They ran the wagon into a grove of small cedar trees and began to unload the liquor behind a large cluster of bracken. When the wagon was empty, the four farmers promised that they would meet us there shortly after dark and climbed into the wagon.

"Hold on there," Harry said. "We might as well catch a ride into town with you."

"One of us will have to stay here and watch over this," I warned, hoping that Harry would catch on and not let the farmers know that we were going to leave it untended. But no such luck.

"Oh, to hell with that," Harry answered. "I'm going into that hotel in town and get a decent meal and some sleep."

I was as tired as I had ever been in my life, my arms and legs ached and my stomach was again crying out for food. I decided that if Harry didn't care enough to make some kind of plan, I wasn't going to worry about it either. I think that we were both so tired and hungry that nothing else seemed to matter right at the moment. So we both climbed up on the wagon and rode into town. I made a point of saying that I would just get a bit to eat and then go back, but I don't think I could muster enough enthusiasm for it to fool anybody.

Just after daybreak the farmers dropped us in front of the little hotel. They said they lived a mile out of town on the other side. Once again they promised to meet us at nightfall. At the hotel we each got a room and a big breakfast and then went off to sleep. I slept all day without stirring. That night I woke about nine o'clock. I started to jump out of bed, thinking we were going to be late for the rendezvous, when I noticed I could hear voices through the thin walls of the room. I recognized Harry's and the husky voice of the bearded fellow, but I could not make out what they were saying. I guess I was still pretty groggy, because I dropped off to sleep again without finding out what was going on. It was eight the next morning when I woke again. I had slept for twenty-four hours!

I found Harry in the hotel's dining room. He explained what was going on. Or at least what was supposed to be going on. That afternoon, the bearded farmer was to take Harry to Bandon, Oregon, about twenty miles north, where he claimed to have arranged a buyer for the liquor. The deal would be made and they would return before nightfall, and the exchange of money and liquor would be completed.

Right after lunch, Harry and his escort set out for Bandon. Having nothing better to do, and beginning to get very suspicious about our friendly farmers, I set out to inspect our cache. I stayed off the road and hiked all the way through the woods, staying out of sight as much as I could. When I arrived back at the cedar grove, I was not all that surprised to find that the liquor was gone. The only evidence that it had ever been there was the flattened grass behind the bracken, and a few pieces of straw from the packing. I did a bit of looking around and soon found a trail that led over a small knoll to another narrow dirt road. Bits of straw were scattered all along the trail. In the dirt, I could see where they had loaded a wagon and headed off with our liquor.

As I walked back over the knoll, I passed a hazelnut bush. A bit of brightness caught my eye in the grass under the bush. I reached down and pulled out two bottles of Highland Cream Scotch whisky. I went a little farther down the trail and sat down in a patch of sunshine. It was nice and warm for the time of year. I was feeling pretty low right about then. I had nothing to do but sit there and think about what a waste of time this whole trip had been. A short while after I sat down, I suddenly heard someone coming through the brush off to the left of where I was sitting. I just stayed very still. In a moment, a short fellow in a plaid lumberman's jacket came out onto the trail fifty feet from me. He went directly to the hazelnut bush and looked under it. Then he bent and began to search around in the grass with his hand. He looked puzzled and got back to his feet and started up the trail towards where the liquor had originally been hidden.

Before he saw me, I said, "Who the hell are you, and what do you think you're looking for?"

The guy just about jumped out of his boots at the sound of my voice.

"Huh...well...," he stammered. "My name's Bill Carling and I'm looking...I'm...I'm looking for some cattle that are missing from a farm up the road."

"Like hell you are!" I said hotly. "You're a damn liar. You're looking for two bottles of whisky that are not there any more because I've got them. You stole that whisky from me!"

At that, the fellow just turned and headed off into the brush the way he had come. I knew that I should have followed him to see where he would lead me, but at that point, I just didn't care about that load of liquor anymore. I sat there in the sun for a bit and then I walked the main road to the hotel.

Harry arrived back from Bandon at six o'clock. Before I could say a word, he proudly told me that he had arranged to sell the seventy cases for $125 a case and that the buyer would be down as soon as it got dark. When I told him that we had no liquor to sell, he refused to believe me. I suggested that he go check it out for himself. He could see from my manner that I was serious and was soon ready to listen to my story. But even after I explained to him that the liquor was gone, he didn't want to believe that we'd lost it. He tried to convince himself that perhaps the farmers had moved the cache for some good reason. It was only after the time that the buyer was to have shown up came and went that Harry began to understand that the whole thing was a setup.

Now we were really in a fix. The two days we had wasted trying to sell the liquor had used up most of our cash. Now we didn't have enough to get us back to Victoria. We had about twenty dollars between us. Harry said that he would wire his girlfriend in Victoria and she would send him money that he had left with her. Harry's girlfriend owned the Blue Mouse Café right across Douglas Street from Eaton's department store. We went on up to Bandon and Harry wired for $300. That's when we found out that the money could only be wired to Marshfield, a town further north. We went by boat up the South Fork of the Coquille River and then caught a bus to Marshfield, which was located right beside the town of North Bend on Coos Bay. There was quite a little harbor there, where good-sized ships could come in.

By the time we got to the telegraph office in Marshfield, it was six o'clock. The money had arrived, but, unfortunately, the man had already closed the safe and it was time-locked, so we would not be able to get at it until the following morning. There was nothing that we could do, so we got a room at the hotel and had a bite to eat. Then, as it was still early, we spent the last of our cash to see a show.

The next morning, we were at the telegraph office just after it opened at eight o'clock. Harry went in to get the money while I waited just outside. As he went in, a fellow in a grey suit and a black fedora walked in right behind him. Another fellow dressed almost the same stepped up beside me and put his hand on my shoulder.

"You're under arrest," he said. He showed me a badge which identified him as a federal agent.

"What for?" I asked. When he said that the charge was rumrunning, I was ready for him.

"Oh, is that so," I said. "I'll have you know that we were not rumrunning. That cargo was bound for Mazatlan, Mexico and we were shipwrecked."

"We'll see about that," he said.

Meanwhile, inside the telegraph office the other agent arrested Harry just as the clerk was about to hand him the money.

"I'll take that," he said to the startled clerk.

"Like hell, you will," the clerk replied and tossed it back in the safe and slammed the door. I guess the Prohibition agents were not the most popular guys in town. The agents knew that they could do nothing because the money had never come into Harry's possession, so they led us off to the Marshfield jail.

When they began to question us, I again demanded to know what evidence they had to arrest us. They knew all the details of our shipwreck and that we had liquor on board.

"Sure we had liquor on board," I said indignantly. "You check with the Customs office in Victoria, and you'll see that that shipment was bound for Mexico. We were shipwrecked on the coast south of here and then we were pirated. We haven't done anything illegal at all."

They were very reluctant to believe this, but finally left us alone for about an hour. When they came back, they said that they had checked our story with Victoria and that it was true. They also said that they still knew that we were rumrunning. However, they knew that they couldn't prove it. They would have to let us go, but they weren't going to do it until the sheriff from Bandon came up to authorize it, because it was he who had ordered our arrest. We spent the night in the city jail. I had spent nights in a lot worse places, especially recently, so did not complain too much.

The next morning the sheriff arrived from Bandon, and we went over our story once again. We explained how we had been shipwrecked, how we had managed to save seventy cases of the liquor and how it had been stolen from us. Of course, we said nothing of our attempts to sell the liquor, saying only that we had hidden it to protect it until we could arrange a way to complete our journey to Mexico. They had no choice but to accept our story. The funny thing was that the sheriff then offered me a reward of $250 if I would stay and help catch the people who stole our liquor. Pirating was a very serious crime in those days. Naturally, I wanted no part of that. I made some excuse about having to get back to work as soon as possible, and politely declined his offer.

All we really wanted to do by this time was get as far away from that part of Oregon as fast as we could! As soon as we were out of jail, we went back to the telegraph office and collected the money that Harry's girlfriend had sent. Then we got a bus north. We rode the bus only until we came to a town that the railway passed through, then we caught a train. I stopped off in Chehalis to see Gus. Harry continued on to Seattle and home to Victoria.

And that was the end of my first experience in the rum trade. Not a very successful venture! Harry gave me $100 of the $300 that his girlfriend sent. I never did see him again after that. I think he must have gone into another line of work. Judging by his luck in the rumrunning up to that point, that would certainly have been a good idea! I had little to show for the trip but some stories. I lost a few clothes and some tools, but in the end, considered myself lucky to have got out of the whole mess with my skin.

WORKING FOR KOHSE

I WORKED OUT of Chehalis for awhile after that. I went back to falling in a logging camp over near Aberdeen. I needed to get some money coming in again. I lived in the camp during the week and came home to stay with Gus in the house out on Coal Creek on the weekends.

Shortly after I got settled in, I went to see the girl that I had been going with before I went up to Victoria. Jessie lived with her family on a farm east of town. I drove out there on a Sunday afternoon in Gus's car. At the house I was met by her two brothers, who told me that Jessie was out. They also let me know that she had been seeing a farmer from Idaho. I wasn't angry about that or anything. I'd been gone for better than two months and I hadn't given much warning when I left or said whether or not I was coming back. So it wasn't like she owed me. But the rest of the family all liked me, and they urged me to come back when Jessie was home. I did go back once more a week or so later. But Jessie would not even come out of the house to see me. She stayed in her room, in spite of the pleading and threats put on by her brothers.

So for the rest of that winter I was just logging again. The money was pretty good and I was saving some.

In March of 1921 I got another letter from Fred Kohse. This time he wanted me to operate a boat for him running loads of liquor across the Strait of Juan de Fuca to Washington State. This sounded a lot more sensible than trying to haul it all the way down the coast, so I quit the logging again and was soon back in Victoria.

Kohse and his wife and son were back living on the boat house in Victoria harbour. His mother and father were still living in the same large house on the corner of Douglas and Humboldt streets. They asked me to stay with them, so I rented a room and took most of my meals there. The old folks were really wonderful people and treated me like one of their own children.

Fred had made a couple of liquor trips across the strait before he got in touch with me. He and Billy Garrard were working together. I knew Billy from before the war as well.

Billy Garrard was married to Kohse's sister. He was about twenty-six at this time and had just come back from university. He seemed to know a lot of important people in town and enjoyed going out a lot. He seemed like kind of a funny guy to be in the rum trade, just back from university and all, but I guess he liked the money all right. He and his young wife lived pretty high on the hog. I liked Billy; but I found his wife to be just a bit too stuck up. She always seemed like the company was not quite good enough for her. But Billy was a very pleasant fellow and we got along just fine.

Kohse and I had a talk and agreed that I would take his place and operate the boat. Fred didn't want to get out of the business, but he didn't enjoy the actual trips very much. The agreement that we came to was this: of whatever we made for the delivery of the liquor, Kohse would get a one-third share for the boat, and I would get two-thirds for doing the hauling. I would then split my share with Billy, who helped me load and unload.

When we started out we were doing the hauling in a small boat of eighteen feet powered by a one-cylinder, five-horsepower engine. It would do just about five knots. We were taking the liquor to a dropoff point about five miles north of Anacortes. We would load the liquor right from the wharf in front of the Consolidated Exporters office on Wharf Street at the foot of Fort. In those early days there was no problem exporting liquor to the United States as far as the Canadian government was concerned. There was a $19-a-case duty on it, but that never bothered anybody.

We were able to carry seventy-five cases of liquor in that little boat. We received $11 a case for the hauling. We would generally set out from the wharf in Victoria harbour about ten o'clock in the morning. By the time that we crossed Haro Strait into American waters it would be dark. We would arrange to meet our contact about eleven o'clock at a remote stretch of beach north of Anacortes. Then we'd turn straight around and head home. If all went well, we'd be back in Canadian waters by dawn, and back at the dock in Victoria by ten in the morning. It was twenty-four hours or more with no sleep, but other than that, there wasn't too much to it. The American Coast Guard cutter *Arcata* was our only worry. It had a top speed of twelve knots, but did very little patrolling that far north, concentrating instead on the area around the mouth of Puget Sound.

In that first month or so we made five or six trips without incident. My share amounted to well over $1,000! I'd never made money like that before and quickly made up my mind to stay in the business. Almost right away I decided that the way to make a success of rumrunning was to have a fast boat. I knew that it wouldn't be too long before the government in the United States made a greater effort to cut off the supply of illegal liquor coming in from Canada. It had even been in the papers before I left Chehalis.

After I had been hauling for Kohse for awhile, I began to think about having a boat of my own built. I figured I would need something about thirty-five feet long with a narrow beam of about six feet. I had lots of time off and soon got the idea of making a scale model of the boat I wanted. I got to work and carved a model on a scale of one inch to the foot. I really enjoyed designing my own boat. After that I designed all of the boats that I used in the rum trade, and a couple of others as well. And I was very well pleased with all of my boats but one. It seemed that I had a good eye for designing a high-speed hull because all of my boats were fast.

I worked on that model for several months. When I had it just the way I wanted it, I took it to a Japanese boatbuilder who had a shop on Chatham Steet just above Government. Tomotaro Yoneda agreed to build the boat from my model. He worked with his father, who was about sixty years old; both of them were excellent carpenters and shipwrights.

Just about this same time Kohse made a trip down to Tacoma and bought a round-bottomed speedboat that was thirty-two feet long and had a seventy-five-horsepower engine in it. It made about fifteen knots. With this boat we were able to deliver larger loads and more of them. We could now carry about one hundred ten cases.

With the new boat we could also leave later in the afternoon. Normally we would go up to East Point on Saturna Island and then run straight across to the other side. We didn't have very much to worry about in those early days. Often we would be half-way down the American shore before it got really dark. We also went on nights when the moon was so bright that you could read a newspaper by its light. But as I say, we were not very worried about the Coast Guard at that time. That would change soon enough, though.

It wasn't too long before we had something else to worry about. Word got out pretty fast about the easy money to be made in the rumrunning. For awhile there it seemed like everyone in town wanted to get involved with it. Early on, the American government simply did not have the resources to enforce the laws that they had passed under the Volstead Act. So the risks were relatively small. That, combined with the fact that the economy in Canada was still recovering from the effects of the First World War, made the rum trade a very attractive business. And if you wanted to split the profits, the risks could be minimized even more. A lot of the Canadian boats that got involved simply hauled the liquor out into the strait where they met Americans who then ran it over the border and past the Coast Guard to any number of ports in Washington. The Canadians were taking practically no risk at all. Or so they thought! But the easy money and quick profits naturally attracted a few bad apples to the trade. A few hijackers began to prey on the easy pickings.

Discovery Island lies almost directly east of Victoria, just off Ten Mile Point, the southeastern tip of Vancouver Island. It is the most southerly of the Canadian Gulf Islands. The protected bays and channels of the Chatham group of islands, of which Discovery is the largest, along with its proximity to the international bound-ary, made it an ideal rendezvous point. It became a very popular spot during the rumrunning years.

Before I was ever in the business, there was a fellow and his wife who used to anchor their boat at Discovery and sell beer to American boats that came across the strait. But once the trade in

hard liquor picked up, there was no call for the beer anymore—
there was not enough money in it compared to the stronger stuff.
The man and his wife then built a small lodge on the island and
offered good, home-cooked meals to people who were there waiting
to pick up or deliver a load. They built floats out into deep water so
there was room to tie up right in front of the lodge. The woman was
an excellent cook and it was a nice spot to pass the time.

Most of the American boats that were into the rumrunning
made their pickups at Discovery Island. It was while I was still
operating Kohse's second boat that I quit making my pickups at
the Consolidated Exporters wharf and got all my liquor brought
out of the harbour. I did not want to be connected with the liquor
business any more than was necessary. It was just a lot easier if I had
a load brought out to Discovery from either Victoria or Vancouver.

On one trip Billy and I were tied up at the float at Discovery
Island waiting for a shipment when a boat identical to Kohse's
pulled into the bay. The only difference between the two boats
was that the other boat had twenty-five horsepower more than we
had. The hull of that boat was painted completely black. The two
men in it were rough-looking characters, both of them were hawk-
faced and raw-boned. I didn't like the looks of them at all,
especially when they began to ask all kinds of questions about the
price of liquor, but didn't seem interested in buying any.

As the afternoon wore on these two characters just hung
around the floats. When Billy and I came down from the lodge
after having some lunch, we found them tossing empty bottles out
into the water and shooting at them with revolvers that they carried. There were several other fellows taking part in this sport as
well. It was a competition to see who could bust a bottle first. I
went and got the Luger revolver that I carried on the boat and
joined in the game. I was a good shot, and on that day maybe a
bit lucky. I hit the first three bottles that I shot at. After that I quit,
figuring that I'd leave well enough alone!

Later that afternoon our load arrived from Victoria and, as
soon as it was stowed, we set off for Anacortes. As we headed up
the east side of Vancouver Island, I noticed that the black-hulled
boat had pulled out of the bay about a mile behind us and was
also headed north. We knew that they could outrun us, so I kept a
close eye on them. When we got to D'Arcy Island, I kept to the
east side and the other boat went up the other side. I looked for

them when we got to the north end of the island but they had disappeared. Which was just as well for us, as it turned out.

When we were back at Discovery about a week later, we learned that the black-hulled speedboat belonged to the Eggers brothers from Seattle. The Eggers—Mickey, Happy and Ted—turned out to be about the most notorious hijackers to work the inside waters of the Pacific Northwest. I guess that they picked up enough information by hanging around the floats at Discovery to know that a big shipment was due in further north in the Gulf Islands. Why they followed us I was never sure. Perhaps they thought they might pick us off before going after the big haul but then decided against it. I always liked to think that the little demonstration of my shooting skill probably helped them change their minds.

In any case the very next day the Eggers boys surprised Tom Avery of Vancouver on the *Pauline* and relieved him of more than one hundred twenty cases of liquor. Shortly after that they hijacked the *Erskine* at D'Arcy Island and towed it right across the strait where they disabled the engine and stole the cargo. It was about this time that everyone involved in the trade began to arm themselves. The threat of violence did have one side effect that was beneficial from my point of view. That was to scare off some of those who weren't serious about the business. It was getting to the point where there were just too many people in it. The resulting competition was bound to drive down the delivery price. I'd been around guns since I was very young and had gotten used to carrying one when I was trapping up the coast, so it never bothered me. But I was just as glad that I never had to use it on another man. It turned out that we hadn't heard the last of the Eggers brothers or of violence in the rum trade!

MOONBEAM

I HAD OPERATED Kohse's new boat for only a couple of months when he decided that he wanted a greater share of the profits. He wanted forty percent for the boat, leaving sixty percent for Billy and I to share. I could have cut Billy's share to keep my own up, but I refused to do that. I always gave an equal share to whoever helped me. So after almost two years of working for Kohse, I quit. Billy decided that he wanted to work with me on my new boat, so he quit too.

The new boat was only about half built at this time. But being out of the actual hauling for awhile gave me lots of time to work on it. Yoneda was only doing the boatbuilding; I had to install the engine and all of the other hardware on it. I began to work on the boat all of the time. It was actually not such a bad time to be without a boat. It was summer and with the long days and short nights the rumrunning business generally slowed right down anyway.

At the time I had enough money to pay for the construction of the boat, but I didn't have the cash to buy the engine. I needed about $300 to buy the kind of engine I wanted. I made a trip down to Chehalis to see my sister's husband's brother, who was a good friend of mine. (I didn't care for my sister's husband at all, but his brother and I got on very well.) I asked him if he thought he could lend me $300 for a short while. He said that he sure could. He gave me the money and refused to let me pay him any interest on it. (Once I was back hauling liquor, of course, it did not take me long to pay off this debt.)

When I'd borrowed the money, I went up to Seattle and spent a couple of days looking at different engines. I wanted to get an engine with lots of power. I was determined to have a boat that could haul a load at speed. It was obvious to me that speed was the way to stay out of trouble in the rumrunning.

A funny thing happened while I was there in Seattle. One evening I went to a show somewhere down along First Avenue. There was a fortune teller on the stage offering to predict the future of anyone who wanted to write a question on a piece of paper. Just for fun I decided to give it a try. I asked if I would be successful in the business that I was involved with, and signed my initials on the slip of paper. When he came to my question, the fortune teller's answer was that I would be very successful in the "adventure" that I was going into. I never did really believe in fortune tellers, but much later on I came to realize that that fellow had hit the nail right on the head. My career in the rumrunning business was a success—and it was definitely an adventure!

In Seattle I ended up buying a six-cylinder, eighty-horsepower Marmon car engine. I had it shipped back to Victoria. It seemed to be the most powerful engine that I could find at that time. The Marmon engine had a Bosch magneto on it with double ignition in each cylinder. That was the only car engine that I had ever worked on that had two spark plugs per cylinder. (All of the airplane engines that I was to use later on had double ignition.) I'd never put a motor in a boat before and the job took me about three weeks.

Once I'd got the engine installed in the new boat—I named her the *Moonbeam*—Billy and I took her out in the harbour to see how she would go. At first the engine was only running on one set of spark plugs. I was disgusted with the speed she was making. For an eighty-horsepower motor it was pretty disappointing. I went down below and started playing with the ignition wires, trying to get a connection that would fire both sets of plugs. I kept working the wire around making different contacts in the magneto. I finally hit the right spot and the boat suddenly shot ahead— it was at least a third faster when both sets of plugs were firing. With the Marmon engine the boat made seventeen or eighteen knots at top speed. At the time that was plenty fast enough as the American Coast Guard cutters could only do twelve.

I worked on the boat right into the early fall of 1923. One day Pete Peterson and Carl Melby came up from Seattle to see me. I had hauled for them when I had been working for Kohse. They came up because they had heard that I was building my own boat. They wanted me to haul for them as soon as I had it ready to go. I had always been good about keeping to their schedules and had never missed a dropoff. When I got the new boat going, it ended up that I had pretty much the same group of customers as I had when I was working for Kohse. I didn't really lose anyone. (Kohse wasn't too pleased about this, but we were still on friendly terms. He did his own hauling for awhile after that—he even took his wife with him on a few trips that I knew of—but he wasn't in the business for very much longer. As soon as the faster boats took over, he quit the rumrunning. Soon after that he sold his boathouse and moved up to Kelsey Bay on the northern end of Vancouver Island where he bought a farm.)

Carl Melby was known as the "gentleman bootlegger" around the Seattle area. I always enjoyed doing business with him because he was as honest as could be. This was more than could be said for his partner. Pete Peterson was Carl's brother-in-law. He was a bit of a character. He was one of those guys who didn't feel he'd had a good day unless he knew he'd got the better of someone. No matter what the deal was he always tried for an edge.

Business must have been good for Carl and Pete because I hauled two or three loads for them during the first month that I had the new boat in the water. I could carry seventy-five cases on the *Moonbeam*. This was fine with Melby and Peterson because that was all they could handle at one time. They each had a big touring car that they used to haul the loads to Seattle. Peterson had a big black Cadillac; Melby, a dark green Studebaker. They had extra-heavy springs installed in the rear ends of those cars so that they wouldn't show the weight.

We'd make arrangements for the dropoff when they came over to buy the liquor at Consolidated Exporters. We used a lot of different dropoff points, anywhere from down around Port Angeles right up to north of Anacortes. Even though we often just pointed out the spot on a chart, I was always able to find the exact location where we were to meet. They would be waiting there in the pitch black night. Sometimes on the first trip to a new spot we would exchange signals with a flashlight before I would bring the *Moonbeam* in close to shore. But most of the time I would just know where to land in the dark. It was safer that way.

Then we would load the liquor into the dinghy and haul it to shore. After the last load was in, Peterson would hand me the money for the haul. It was always dark so I wouldn't count the money there. And this is where the problem was. When I got back home and counted it, the sum was always $30 or $40 short. This happened every time until I finally got fed up with it. I met Carl and Pete in Consolidated Exporters one day and said, "Look, boys. There is only one way that I will continue to haul for you and that's if Carl handles the money."

Peterson pretended to be shocked at this and argued that that wasn't the way that they did business, but I held my ground.

"That's the way it's got to be," I said. "I'm tired of being short-changed every trip."

I had to hand it to old Pete, he didn't give up easily. We must have spent a good two hours in the back room at Consolidated working out that little problem. But I finally got my way. Quite a bit later on Carl Melby told me that Peterson had been shorting him on the other end as well. By the time they got to town, Peterson's load would always be half a case or a case short. After I spoke out about being shorted on my end, Carl knew what was happening. I guess the only reason he put up with it was because he was married to the guy's sister. But my problem was solved, at least; once Carl started handling the money I was never short again.

It was around about this time that the United States government started to put more pressure on the Canadians to get tougher laws to prevent rumrunning. I guess the Canadian government was of two minds about the whole business. On the one hand, they had to preserve good relations with the U.S., but at the same time they were reluctant to lose the tax dollars that were being generated by the rum trade. But, after a lot of talk, they made a kind of half-hearted attempt to put a stop to the most obvious aspect of the business. The government announced that they would no longer allow small vessels to clear Customs for distant points that they were obviously not going to reach. (This was the kind of thing that we had done when Harry and I set out for Mazatlan on my disastrous initiation into the trade.)

I say that this was a halfhearted measure because it really had no effect on slowing things down in the rum trade. After that, shipments were simply consigned to some upcoast port in British Columbia that did not have a Customs office. Bowen Island was a favourite spot. The liquor being shipped out of Victoria might be consigned there, but of course it never arrived. I'm sure that if the records for that period were examined, places like Bowen Island would show a per capita alcohol consumption that far exceeded human capability!

Actually we had a good laugh about the whole business. I remember when Carl Melby brought a clipping from the *Seattle Times* over to the Consolidated Exporters office one day. "Puget Sound Booze Fleet Doomed by U.S.-Canada Pact" it said. Wishful thinking! The report went on to say that liquor smuggling would be too dangerous for most of those now involved in it because Canadian Customs officials would notify American Prohibition agents of all shipments of liquor leaving Canadian ports regardless of their purported destinations. Well, the American agents may have been notified, but they still had to catch us! And there was a lot of water and a lot of coastline out there. I didn't envy them their job.

In fact, the only real change the new law made was that different boats would be used to clear the liquor through Customs. These craft, usually slow-moving fish boats, would haul the cargo out to places like Discovery Island, East Point on Saturna Island, or D'Arcy Island. Once there the cargo would be transferred to a faster rumrunner. I was already picking up all my loads outside the harbour anyway, so it didn't really bother me at all.

Consolidated Exporters hired three fish boats to carry the shipments out of the harbour. They would get clearance for somewhere like Bowen Island or Bella Coola and slowly chug their way out of the harbour. Most of the time they would meet me at Discovery Island and we would transfer the load to the *Moonbeam*. The fish boat would wait out there until the next morning just in case I was not able to make contact with the buyer on the other side. Then they could take the load back into the warehouse and say that they had engine trouble or something and I wouldn't have to worry about hanging around all day with a load on. We actually had to do this only once or twice.

This system worked really well. It meant that there was never any record of the *Moonbeam* hauling any liquor at all. And it spread the work around. The fishermen were happy to get the work because we were busiest in the winter months when their business was at its slowest. Consolidated hired three boats and used them in rotation so that they each got about the same amount of work, but there was always someone else to call on if one of them couldn't make it. The three men who did the hauling out of the harbour for us were Joe Fleming, Charlie Bright, and a fellow I knew only as Griffith.

The *Moonbeam* was a good little boat. She was fast for the time and seaworthy enough for her type. I hadn't had her too long when, in the fall of 1923, she was put to the test by the weather.

We started out from Discovery Island in the early evening. I would normally run the boat at about ten knots. When we left there was just a light west wind blowing. We were heading to a dropoff point about a mile east of Port Angeles, so we were running due south. By the time we were halfway across the strait, the wind had begun to pick up. We could see a heavy cloud bank moving in, blocking out the stars one by one in front of us. Before long the waves began to build pretty good and I had to cut my speed. I wasn't worried about this because I always allowed for extra time on the crossing.

By the time we were nearing the American shore, the wind was really howling. The waves had built to almost twenty feet, and a stinging spray was being whipped across the water. I could feel the boat bending and twisting as the huge seas buffeted her. The exhaust from the engine went out the side on the *Moonbeam*, and with the pounding she was taking, the pipe started to come apart and the fumes were coming into the boat. It was so rough that I didn't dare try to fix the problem then. We managed to make it to our rendezvous in a small bay without the pipes coming completely apart, although we had to breathe some pretty foul air for the last part of the trip.

Once we got rid of the liquor, I got everything put back together, but I had no intention of going back out in those seas. The wind continued to roar and the seas outside the bay were enormous.

"I'm not going back out in that storm," I told Barney Sampson, who had picked up the load. "I don't care if the Coast Guard gets the boat. It's too rough out there!"

"I know the caretaker at the government wharf at Port Angeles," Barney said. "He'll put you up until the wind dies down."

It was now about midnight. We eased our way out of the bay and, staying as close to shore as we dared, we made our way slowly down the coast and into the harbour at Port Angeles. Close in the waves were not nearly so bad and we were now heading straight into the wind, but it was a slow mile. We came into the harbour without any lights—I didn't even have lights on the boat at this time—and eased up to the far side of the government float where the smaller boats tied up. Sampson was there to meet us with the caretaker.

"Look, boys," he said. "Be real quiet. The *Arcata* is tied up on the other side of the float!"

At first I thought he had to be joking, so I went to check. Sure enough, not fifty feet from where the *Moonbeam* was moored, sat the Coast Guard cutter *Arcata*! Talk about being between a rock and a hard place! I thought about heading back out to sea, but the wind crashing and rattling the rigging on all the boats around me drove that out of my head in a hurry. There were no lights on the *Arcata*, so we could only hope that the crew were all asleep, and that the wind would die down so that we could make our escape before morning. There wasn't too much else that we could do.

The caretaker took us up to his little house on the wharf where he made us bunk down in his bed. He insisted on staying up to keep an eye on things. He was a funny old character and treated the whole episode like it was a fine opportunity to play a great practical joke on the Coast Guard. Billy went straight off to sleep, but I was too nervous and sat up and drank coffee with the old fellow.

This was my closest contact with the *Arcata* so far, but it wouldn't be my last. Everyone in the trade came to know, at least by reputation, the boat and her captain, Lorenz A. Lonsdale, known as "Grandad." The *Arcata* was a tug, eighty-five feet long and steam-driven, with a top speed of twelve knots. She was top-heavy and not meant for the open ocean. On the deck was mounted a semi-automatic, one-pound cannon. The gun had a range of four thousand yards and was highly accurate to about five hundred yards.

Lonsdale, formerly the master of several merchant ships that sailed the Pacific Northwest, was integrated into the Coast Guard when the rumrunning trade first got started. He was just a little fellow, only five feet tall, but he wasn't long earning the respect of his adversaries. Although the Coast Guard was nearly always at a disadvantage when it came to speed, anyone with any experience in the business learned to give the *Arcata* a wide berth because they knew that her master was not the least bit timid about using that one-pounder if a vessel chose to ignore his request to stop for inspection.

I sat up with the caretaker for about an hour and a half that night while he told me stories about the Coast Guard and the rum trade. I had heard most of the stories before, but I enjoyed the old fellow's company just the same. And he seemed pleased to have someone to talk to. He didn't seem the least bit concerned that we were keeping him out of his bed that night. Sometime after two o'clock I went to lay down. I dropped off to sleep almost as soon as my head hit the pillow.

About four in the morning the caretaker woke us up.

"The wind has died down a bit," he said. "I think you can make it out now."

We went back down on the float and quietly untied the *Moonbeam*. We eased our way out into the darkness, keeping a close watch on the *Arcata* for any signs of life. The wind had dropped below gale force, although it was still blowing about thirty knots. But it was manageable, especially considering that our only other option was having breakfast with "Grandad" and the crew of the *Arcata*! It was a rough trip back to Victoria. The wind died right off just before daybreak, but the water was very lumpy all the way across. Fortunately, I didn't have any more trouble with the exhaust.

SHORE PATROL

AS I SAID, the Coast Guard didn't give us very much trouble at this time because all they had were a couple of those slow cutters like the *Arcata*. The shore patrol, as we called it, gave us a better run for the money. In the spring of 1923 they had hired a new chief of Prohibition enforcement in Seattle and he turned out to be a pretty tough cookie.

Carl Jackson came from Wyoming and was a big, good-looking fellow and a bit of a cowboy. He brought a record for two-fisted toughness with him from the cattle country to the east, where he had also been Prohibition director. The newspapers in Seattle gave him big play. Carl Melby would always bring the clippings to show me. We began to suspect that Jackson might be serious when he started to talk about hiring a lot more agents and even building a fleet of small, fast boats to patrol Puget Sound.

Jackson didn't get the boats right away, but he did hire more men. It wasn't too long before we found that we had to be a bit more careful about choosing our dropoff points. We had to keep moving them around all the time. Most of the people who I was delivering for had some contacts in the police departments in various cities. Quite often we would be tipped off if the Prohibition agents were going to pull a raid because they would usually take a couple of cops along. There were plenty of people who just didn't believe in the Prohibition laws, even on the police forces, so a guy didn't have to be a crooked cop to help out the bootleggers and rumrunners. If Melby or one of the others heard there was going to be a raid on one of our dropoff points, they'd call Consolidated Exporters to let me know and we would hold off making the trip until another delivery spot was set up.

We weren't always tipped off, however. I remember one trip when I was going to make a drop at a bay five miles south of Anacortes. (This is the same bay that the ferry docks in today.) At the time there was nothing there but a road down to a nice beach. We had made several previous deliveries to the same spot.

On this particular night I pulled into the bay and waited for the signal from Melby's party on shore. In a minute or two a series of flashes told me the coast was clear. I dropped my anchor about one hundred and fifty feet from shore, and Billy and I heaved about thirty cases into the skiff. I always stayed on the boat until the last load was ashore. I watched Billy row in until he disappeared into the darkness of the shoreline. Then I got out the night glasses and picked him up again just as he hit the beach. Melby and Peterson were there quickly to help him unload. They were carrying the last of the cases from that first load up to the cars parked at the top of the beach when all at once lights came on from all over the place and about a half-dozen cops jumped out of the woods that bordered the shoreline.

Somebody shouted "Halt!" but, of course, nobody paid any attention. Melby and Billy ran one way with two of the policemen in hot pursuit, while Pete Peterson ran the other. The problem was that the ambushers had got a little bit over-anxious and had turned on their flashlights too soon. If they had waited until Melby, Peterson and Garrard were right up to the cars, they would have had them surrounded. As it was there was a stretch of beach between the good guys and the bad, and the boys managed to get a head start.

The cops were firing at them with handguns, but in the darkness any hit would have been pure luck. Billy and Carl made it to the woods and simply ran as hard as they could. Pete Peterson went the opposite way. As soon as he got a ways into the woods, he climbed a tree. Pete was packing a few extra pounds and not in very good shape. I guess he knew that he was not going to outrun anybody for very long.

During all of this excitement, which only lasted a minute or two, I had done nothing but watch. Suddenly one of the cops started firing at the *Moonbeam* with a rifle. I pulled up the anchor and was getting ready to move out of range. But I soon realized that the fellow with the rifle was either not very keen to hit me or was one hell of a poor marksman. Even though he took fifteen or twenty shots, the *Moonbeam* was unscathed. I had to believe that he really didn't want to hit her.

Then there was a lot of shouting from off in the woods in the direction that Carl and Billy had taken, and the fellow with the rifle went off to investigate. There wasn't much I could do, but I didn't want to take off until I was sure Billy wasn't going to be stranded. I hung around for fifteen or twenty minutes, carefully watching the shoreline for any signal. Then I started up the engine and left. I headed back over to Discovery Island and sent what was left of the load back to Consolidated Exporters with Joe Fleming, who had brought it out. I heard the complete story a few days later.

In the chase through the bush Carl was running along a couple of paces behind Billy and the cops were twenty yards or so behind them, still firing their revolvers and shouting for them to stop. If they were taking any kind of aim at all, they must have been shooting to hit them in the legs because somehow or other Carl managed to take a bullet in the sole of his left foot. The bullet went through the sole of his shoe and lodged itself in the bottom of his foot. Luckily, the policemen gave up the chase very shortly after that, just before Carl couldn't stand the pain any more and had to stop. When he and Billy stopped and pulled off the shoe, they found that the bullet had not completely penetrated his foot. It was stuck in the muscles right in the centre of the ball of his foot. Billy was able to pry it out with the blade of his pocket knife. (Carl kept that slug in his pocket for a long while after that and used to brag about the tough leather soles on the expensive shoes that he bought!)

Melby and Peterson had an agreement that if they ever got separated in a raid, they would each try to make their way to a certain place as soon as possible. Billy and Carl kept off the road when any cars came by and walked all the way up past Anacortes to the designated spot. When they arrived, they were surprised to find Peterson sitting there in his Cadillac waiting for them. It turned out that once the cop who was firing at the *Moonbeam* took off into the woods, there seemed to be no one left on the beach. The agents who were chasing Pete had passed right by the tree he'd climbed and were further off in the woods in hot pursuit of a phantom. Peterson decided to take the chance. He climbed down out of the tree, got into his car and sped away. He took a great deal of pleasure in the telling of that story! I listened to it many times over the years!

Although Melby phoned to let me know everything was OK the next day, I didn't learn all of the details of the escape until Billy arrived back in Victoria a couple of days later. He had taken the bus up to Vancouver and caught the ferry home. All we really lost in the whole deal were the thirty cases and the skiff. As soon as Melby got back to Seattle, he called the cops to say that his car had been stolen. The next day he drove up to Anacortes to claim it at the police station.

Melby had a fix in with some high official in the Anacortes area. He could get almost anything done there. One time he got caught with a truckload of liquor in Mount Vernon. They arrested him and impounded the truck. Carl was out within an hour, and the next day he got the truck back with the liquor still in it! This kind of thing wasn't all that unusual. I remember dropping off an order of sixty-five cases at a little wharf just southwest of Dungeness Point one night and there was a policeman there to help us unload!

The shore patrol gave us a hard time on another run we made for Melby and Peterson that winter. This time it cost me an anchor and a $500 fine. I pulled in close to shore a couple of miles south of Deception Pass on the west side of Whidbey Island. For some reason I cannot remember, I did not wait for any signal, but just went in and dropped my anchor. Before we had even started to unload, the blasted shore patrol opened up on us with their guns. I yelled to Billy to go forward and raise the anchor while I started the engine. Bullets were flying left, right and centre, and in his panic Billy just cut the anchor line instead of pulling it in. Anyway we got out of there in a hell of a hurry.

That was another trip when the fish boat had to take the load back into the Consolidated Exporters warehouse. While we were at Discovery Island I had a look at the hull of the *Moonbeam* but could not find any signs that she'd been hit. When we went back

into the harbour later that morning, George Norris, who was head
of Customs, came down to examine the boat. He had been tipped
off by the U. S. Prohibition Office. I told him to feel free to have a
look around, as I was confident that he would not find anything.
Needless to say, I was a bit surprised when he dug a lead slug out
of the stern. It was the kind of square slug that the shore patrol
used to fire out of their shotguns.

On the evidence of that slug Norris impounded the *Moonbeam*. I argued that the bullet could have come from a .22 rifle or
something that had ricocheted off the water, but old George would
have none of that. I let them keep the boat for a couple of weeks
because it was a period of the full moon and the nights were too
bright for hauling anyway. I knew that I could beat the charge.
They would never have been able to get a conviction on that little
evidence, but it could have kept the boat tied up for several
months at least. So, after a couple of weeks when the orders
started to come in again, it was simpler just to pay the $500 fine
and go back to work.

I was pretty busy that winter and ran the *Moonbeam* hard. We
were regularly making three, four or even five trips a month. The
money was coming in at a good clip. Now that I was running my
own boat the split was a third for the boat, a third for me and a
third for my mate, Billy Garrard. But there were a lot of expenses
as well. The boat required a fair amount of upkeep on top of the
regular expenses of gas and oil. Even back then we joked about
how a boat was mostly just a hole in the water that you put your
money into. There was always something unexpected to pay for.

One night when we were heading for a dropoff over near Anacortes, a light wind from the north very suddenly turned into a
gale. Within the course of twenty minutes it was blowing about
forty knots. We were OK as long as we were in the lee of Orcas
Island, but when we got out in the open it got pretty wild. We
were taking the seas from the starboard quarter, and there was a
lot of water on the deck. Unfortunately some of it leaked through
to the engine compartment and wet the ignition system. More unfortunate still was the fact that the engine stalled when we were
right in front of Sinclair Island. We were immediately being driven
towards a sheer rock wall that rose straight up out of the water. I

dropped the anchor right away, but knew that it wouldn't hold for long against that wind. For awhile I really thought that we were going to have to abandon the *Moonbeam*. There was nothing that we could do. For fifteen or twenty minutes the wind gradually pushed us closer to the cliffs. The thunder of the waves beating against that wall was deafening. We were close enough that the boat was surrounded by a sea of greenish-white foam, the backwash of the pounding surf. Then suddenly the wind died as quickly as it had come up. We were left bobbing up and down in the big swells not more than a hundred feet from the bluff. Lucky, I guess.

It was about seven in the evening. I knew that there were some people living on the other end of the island, so I got in the skiff and rowed ashore. I found a rough road and followed it to a small harbour where there was a fish boat at anchor. I talked to the fellow who owned it and explained our position. I offered him $50 to give us a tow. He was happy to oblige.

We ran the boat around the island, picked up the skiff and then took the *Moonbeam* in tow. That was the only time I had to make a delivery under tow. But everything went fine. We made our connection, and dropped the liquor off at about midnight. Then we towed the *Moonbeam* five miles south to a ship-repair dock in Anacortes. I paid the fisherman and he headed home about four in the morning.

As soon as the shop opened I made arrangements to have the ignition fixed. We sat around the dock and passed the time of day with a couple of oldtimers who came down to have a look at the *Moonbeam*. It wasn't very long before a couple of Coast Guard officers showed up as well. They wanted to know how we had got there. We told them we had drifted for a long ways before a fish boat finally towed us in. I maintained that we had broken down way up the strait off of Saturna Island and that the wind had driven us south. They couldn't do anything but take our word for it, although they did give the boat a good looking over before they went on their way.

I had no lights on the boat at the time—they were not required in Canadian waters but they were in the U.S. According to American regulations you had to have running lights, and a copy of the Marine Rules hanging in the pilothouse. The fine for violation of this was up to $500. While the work was being done on the engine, I went to the chandlers and bought the Rule book and the things I needed to install the necessary lights. By the time the mechanics were finished fixing the ignition, Billy and I had the lights all set up. We did not get a mile out of Anacortes when the Coast Guard cutter appeared and signalled us to stop. I was happy to comply. A young officer came on board and had a quick look around. As soon as he saw the running lights, I could see disappointment written all over his face. I tried my best to be friendly, but the fellow didn't want to chat at all. He didn't stay long.

MORE POWER, MORE SPEED

IN THE SPRING of 1924 Carl Jackson got his way, and the United States Customs department announced construction of ten, seventy-five-foot cutters to patrol the waters of Puget Sound. The ships would be powered by twin two hundred fifty-horsepower Sterling engines and would be capable of about eighteen knots. That was just about the speed I could make with the *Moonbeam*. This began to make me nervous.

Just about this time the Bosch magneto on the Marmon engine was beginning to go haywire on me. It seemed to be getting weaker and weaker. I kept narrowing the gap on the spark plugs until they would hardly fire. I had run that engine pretty hard. I guess it was just wearing out. When the announcement came about the new boats for the Coast Guard—that news even made the papers in Victoria—I decided that I had to have more power in the *Moonbeam* if I was going to keep out of trouble.

I always read the boating magazines and I had seen several advertisements for a three hundred-horsepower Fiat airplane engine. It sounded like just the ticket for the *Moonbeam*. I went down to Seattle and bought one of those engines for $500. (I didn't have to pay any duty on it when I brought it across the border because there was no type of engine like it being built in Canada at the time.)

It took a bit of doing to adapt that Fiat engine for use in the boat. When it arrived, there was just a shaft about a foot long out the front of it where the airplane propeller went onto a spline. I had to get a special coupling made to connect it to the propeller shaft in the boat. Joe Parker and I made the coupling in Parker's Garage, which was just up at the end of Raymond's Wharf where I tied up most of the time.

That Fiat engine was direct drive—there was no clutch, no neutral, no reverse, just straight ahead. When you started the motor, the propeller turned and off you went. I had to always make sure I was pointing the way I wanted to go before I started.

The *Moonbeam* became something of a curiosity around the Victoria harbour when I first put that engine in it. It was about the fastest boat around at the time. Sometimes there would be fifty or sixty kids lined up along the edge of the wharf when I took off. They got a real kick out of watching me fire it up and go. I guess part of the attraction was that they all knew that I was in the rumrunning, although that was something that I never talked about at all. (Funny thing was that years later I would run into a grown man and he would start telling me how great it was as a kid watching me take off in the *Moonbeam*.)

There was no flywheel on that Fiat motor either, so, while we were making the coupling for the shaft, we also had to make a ratchet to go on the shaft behind the motor so I had some way to start it up. I had a four-foot steel bar that went onto the ratchet and I used that to turn the shaft and kick the engine over.

That wasn't the best way to start a three hundred-horsepower engine, but I got pretty good at it. It got the better of me once, though. I was cranking the bar over and came right up against the compression of the engine and I guess I wasn't quite ready for it. I had the bar right in front of me when the engine backfired. It kicked that bar right back at me. Before I knew what hit me, the full power of the engine drove that bar right back into me. It split my thumb from the rest of my hand, tearing the muscles right away from the joint. Fortunately I had my chest right up against the bar so that it pushed me rather than hit me. I'd have been split wide open if I'd been a bit farther away from it. As it was I was tossed like a sack of wet straw back against the wheelhouse wall while the bar went down and slammed into the deck. It broke right through the one-inch floorboards and bent that one-and-a-quarter-inch steel bar about eight inches out of line.

The blow to the chest drove all of the wind out of me. That three hundred-horsepower engine sure had a wallop to it! I just stopped breathing altogether. And I couldn't seem to get started again. No way. I got up off the deck and walked around, but nothing seemed to work. I even tried to squirm and shake myself to get things going again—trying to give myself a bit of a kick start—but I just couldn't get any air in my lungs.

Billy was with me at the time and he was dancing around beside me, pounding me on the back because he could see what the trouble was. I guess I'd lost all my colour. I was beginning to think that I was going to choke to death. I was starting to turn blue when I finally got a bit of a breath.

It was fifteen minutes or so before I was anywhere near back to breathing normally. I checked out my hand and it wasn't bleeding at all, so I just bandaged it up nice and tight. I rested for about a half an hour and couldn't find anything else wrong.

"You'd better go see a doctor," Billy said. "You're as white as a ghost."

But I didn't feel too bad, and we had a load of liquor to deliver, so I decided against that idea. I got the bar back on the ratchet and cranked the engine over and off we went. It was kind of funny about that because everyone who saw me for the next couple of weeks remarked about how pale I looked and kept asking me if I felt all right. But I really didn't feel that badly. For a long while after that I was very careful about starting that engine, though.

That Fiat, like all airplane engines, was made to run at pretty near top speed all the time. This wasn't so good in the rumrunning because we spent a good deal of time just idling along in the darkness as we eased our way into a rendezvous point. We always wanted to keep as quiet as possible so as not to attract attention, so we often ran very slowly for the last mile or so. The trouble with this was that the engine would not be running hot enough to burn off all the oil and the spark plugs would get fouled up really fast. After nearly every trip I would have to clean them. This was no small job because there were two plugs on each cylinder on that engine as well.

I thought I'd solved the problem when I bought a plug cleaner in Vancouver. The machine had a high-powered blower and you loaded it with sand and then put the plug in and it blew the sand up through the plug. It took the carbon build-up off the plugs all right, but the trouble was that it also took the glaze off the porcelain on the top of the plugs, and after a few cleanings they would start to short out through the porcelain. This was not the answer.

I kept on thinking about that problem for a couple of months. Finally I figured out that the solution lay in reducing the oil pressure. I figured that the engine was pumping twice as much oil as was going through the bearings, so that it was going through the bypass valve back into the base of the engine. I tried to find a way to reduce the oil pressure. First I tried different springs on the valves, but that didn't work. Then I got the idea of boring a hole right through the valve to see if that would reduce the pressure. I wasn't too sure this would work, so I started out by drilling just a tiny hole. When I fired up the engine, the oil pressure had dropped from sixty to forty pounds at idle but went right back up to sixty when I sped up. I was very excited about this discovery.

I increased the size of the hole in the valve and tried the engine again. Again the oil pressure dropped at slow speed. It took eight or ten tests before I got the hole the right size, but eventually I got the pressure down to fifteen pounds when I was running as slow as I could. At about half-speed the pressure jumped back up to sixty pounds and stayed there. I had solved the problem! No more fouled spark plugs.

This solution worked perfectly. I used it on all of the airplane engines that I used later. For quite awhile it seemed that I was the only one on the Coast who was able to use airplane engines in boats without constantly having problems with them. Of course, I didn't let on how I had solved the problem. People in Vancouver, Seattle and other places were trying to find out what it was that I did that was different, but I never told anyone. I wanted to keep any edge that I could get. Only Billy Garrard, Tom Colley and Joe Fleming knew what it was I was doing. There was a Japanese fellow from Vancouver who tried everything he could think of to find out. He would come over to see me and talk about this and that and the other thing for maybe an hour or so, and then he'd finally get around to the subject of airplane engines. I'd just play dumb and go along with him. I'd go on about how much power those Fiat engines had and how much trouble they were! But I never gave away my secret. After five or six visits he gave up and stopped coming to see me.

With the new motor in it the *Moonbeam* could make about thirty knots, maybe a little better. The torque from the propeller was so great and the boat so narrow that it ran at about a fifteen-degree angle at top speed. It looked a little odd, but at least I didn't have to worry about the Coast Guard and their new cutters so much anymore.

At least I didn't worry too much about them catching me. I still had to worry about them getting close enough to fire their damn guns, though. The Coast Guard cutters were pretty well armed by this time. They had a one-pound cannon mounted on the bow and usually a couple of machine guns as well. If you weren't careful, they could catch you by surprise. Just as we did, the Coast Guard ran at night without lights if they were looking for a rumrunner. (Technically they were breaking the law, but no one took them to court.)

I got caught by surprise one night just west of Port Townsend on my way back from a delivery. I was just cruising along at about ten knots when I happened to look behind me and saw what at first appeared to be a fire on shore. I got out the night glasses to have a better a look. Needless to say, I was shocked to see that what I had thought was a fire on shore was, in fact, the phosphorescence in the water being pushed up by the bow wave of the *Arcata*, which was steaming towards me at full speed!

As soon as I took the *Moonbeam* up to full throttle, my own wake gave me away and the *Arcata* took a shot at me with the one-pounder. Fortunately we were on the outer edge of their range of accuracy and they didn't hit us, but I didn't like the sound of that gun! One of those shells would have been the end of the *Moonbeam*! They fired on us several times, but I was soon out of range. It was a wonder that old "Grandad" didn't kill someone with that gun. He normally fired a warning shot across the bows first, but if you didn't stop, Captain Lonsdale had no hesitation about aiming for a direct hit. He hit a rumrunner out off of Port Townsend one night and seriously wounded one of the crew. The Arcata rushed the fellow in to port before going back out to confiscate the boat and cargo. I always did my best to keep a sharp eye out and try to stay out of range of those one-pounders.

In the spring of 1924 hijacking probably posed more of a threat to the rum trade than did the Coast Guard. The Eggers brothers raised a lot of havoc for awhile there. In March they commandeered the *Kayak* at anchor in Peter's Cove at the mouth of

Bedwell Harbour. "Feathers" Martin and Joe Edwards were up from Seattle, patiently waiting for a load that was coming down from Vancouver. Under the cover of darkness the Eggers managed to get on board the rumrunner and take over. Heavily armed, they prepared to ambush whoever made the delivery.

The *Hadsell*, operated by Fred Davidson and Adolf Ongstad, arrived just after daybreak. Milo Eggers, armed with two pistols, forced Martin to stick his head out of the hatchway and signal to Davidson that the coast was clear. As the *Hadsell* approached, Milo crept out and lay prone on the deck. When the Vancouver boat was just a few feet from the *Kayak*, he jumped to his feet and started firing. Seventeen shots riddled the wheelhouse of the *Hadsell*. Davidson went for the loaded Winchester rifle that stood in the corner but was hit in the shoulder and the ankle before he reached it. He collapsed in the cabin while Ongstad wisely rushed out on deck, his hands raised.

The Eggers took off in the *Hadsell*, quickly transferred the hijacked cargo into their own boat, the *M-197*, which they had hidden nearby, and headed for American waters. The *Hadsell* was simply abandoned.

Not too much was heard of the Eggers for awhile after that. I think the hijacking got too dangerous for them because people started to arm themselves. They turned to robbing banks and headed down the coast to California. Then in the fall of 1924 two of them, Milo and Happy, were arrested in San Francisco. A few days later brother Ted attempted a dramatic rescue as the other two were being taken to an extradition hearing in the Justice building. He darted out from behind a pillar, squirted ammonia into the eyes of the federal marshall escorting Milo and Happy, and started firing his gun. The marshall clutched at his eyes and fell back. The bullet intended for him struck Ted's brother Happy. Although the other two escaped, Happy's outlaw career ended; he died there on the floor of the Justice building.

But the Eggers weren't the only ones raising havoc in the rum trade about that time. Late in September of 1924 I was on my way back from making a drop near Anacortes when I saw a boat that looked to be drifting, out in the middle of Haro Strait. It was a fish boat, about fifty feet long. At the time I didn't think too much of it—in those days you tended to mind your own business unless someone asked for help. But, as I was later to learn, that boat was the *Beryl G*, a craft that was the scene of one of the bloodiest murders of the day. It was several days later that the story first appeared in the newspaper and quite a few months before the whole story was finally told.

William Gillis and his seventeen-year-old son dropped the anchor of their fish boat, the *Beryl G*, at Sidney Island. On board they still had about half of a large cargo of liquor that they had bought from one of the big warehouse ships that sat just beyond the territorial limit off the west coast of Vancouver Island. (There were a number of these ships that worked the outside waters of the coast. The *Malahat* was probably the most famous, or infamous.) Gillis also had the cash that they'd received from the sale of the other half of the load. They were making contacts with fast boats from the American side who were running the liquor across the international boundary. Pete Marinoff, who owned a "near beer" brewery in Olympia, owned one of the boats that bought from the *Beryl G*. His boat picked up one load of sixty-five cases and ran it over to the other side. When it returned for a second load, the *Beryl G* was nowhere to be found.

Sometime during the night of September 24, Bill Gillis and his son were hijacked, robbed and brutally murdered. Their bodies were ripped open with a fish knife, weighted down with anchor chain and tossed into the sea. They were never recovered. The *Beryl G* was stripped of her cargo and cast adrift in Haro Strait.

This was the first actual killing reported in the rum trade in the Pacific Northwest. It raised quite a fuss and was in the news for a long while. After an intense police investigation on both sides of the border, three men were arrested in various places in the United States: one in New York, one in Texas, and one, I think, in New Orleans. I figured that they knew who did it for a long time; it just took time to track them down. They were brought back to Victoria to be tried. It turned out that a fellow by the name of Stromkins, who was hired just to take the hijackers out to the boat, agreed to testify for the Crown. The other two, Owen Baker and Henry Sowash, were convicted. They were hung at Oakalla prison outside Vancouver on January 14, 1926.

In the summertime when the days were long and the nights short, there was very little liquor moved. The people in the bootlegging business in Washington State would stock up for the summer months. Except for the odd trip to points directly across Juan de Fuca Strait around Port Angeles or to Whidbey Island, we'd only make a delivery in an emergency, or if there was a stretch of bad weather when we knew the moon and stars would be blocked out. The nights were too short to make trips down into Puget Sound.

It was nice to have the summers off. We used to take it pretty easy. A group of us rented a cabin up the Gorge just above the Gorge Bridge. Billy Garrard and his wife Emma, Phoebe and Phyllis Day and myself would take the cabin for two or three months. It wasn't a big place, but it was right on the beach. And the Gorge was a great place to be in the summer. In those days the water was clean and warm, perfect for swimming. I could anchor the *Moonbeam* right out in front of the cabin.

We would have a lot of fun with the boat during the summer. I made a surfboard and would tow the girls around on it. They got to be pretty good. One First of July there was to be a celebration out at Cordova Bay, and one of the organizers asked me to come out in the *Moonbeam* and give a demonstration using the surfboard. I said I'd be happy to do it. They had a fellow all lined up who was supposed to be an expert surfboarder.

I ran the boat out to Cordova Bay on the morning of the holiday. I pulled in to the wharf they had set up and was introduced to the fellow who was going to put on the demonstration. He seemed a little apprehensive. The first thing he said to me was, "Now, don't go too far out."

"Okay," I replied.

"And don't go too fast," he added quickly.

I didn't say anything to that. But I wasn't too impressed with this fellow. I took off and hauled him out about one hundred yards. Then I did a quick circle at about half-speed. I looked back and he was still there, so I opened it up. The guy didn't stay on the board for a hundred feet after that. I picked him up and took him back to shore. I asked him if he wanted to have another go at it, but he wasn't interested. Then the girls got on the board and put on a show. The crowd really liked that. We had three girls on it at once. And they never fell off.

We used to take the *Moonbeam* out to Saanich Inlet and go fishing as well. Sometimes we'd stop the boat and go for a swim or have lunch right in the middle of the fishing. We'd just let the lines sink without bothering to pull them in because the water is so deep out there that you didn't have to worry about getting caught on the bottom. After we started up again, it seemed that we always caught a fish or two right away.

I didn't always go swimming with the rest of them when we were out there. I wasn't really much of a swimmer. I just didn't seem to have the right kind of body for it. With some people, if they just relax in the water, they'll float. Me, I sink like a stone.

I remember when I first tried to swim. It was when I came down to Victoria from up the coast and was living down on the boathouse with Kohse. The boys used to swim right off the wharf and I wanted to learn.

"There's nothing to it," Jack Smith said. "You just make up your mind that you're going to do it and just keep swimming and you'll make it."

I decided to try it. I dove into the water and began to try to swim alongside the float. I was making the right strokes, but the further I swam, the deeper I sank. Except I didn't really even know that I was sinking. I was just swimming as hard as I could. Finally Jack hooked onto me with a pike pole and pulled me out. I thought I was doing all right, but he told me I was headed straight for the bottom and that I wasn't making any headway at all.

When we had the cabin up the Gorge, I used to stay close to shore and practice swimming where I knew that I could put my feet down and touch bottom. I thought that I was getting pretty good and finally decided to swim out to the raft that the others were lying on. I walked out as far as I could and then pushed off and swam for all I was worth. The distance was not much more than one hundred and fifty feet. I just managed to get there and dragged myself up on the float. No sooner had I stretched out in the sun, than one of the others, Phoebe, I think, said that she needed a drink and was going in. The rest decided to follow.

I rested for a short while to get my breath back and then started to swim in. I didn't think I was ever going to make it! I swam for what seemed like a long time. I began to feel myself starting to sink and put my foot down, but the bottom was nowhere to be found. I swam on and the same thing happened—I started to sink and felt for the bottom, but found nothing. I had no intention of calling out for help, so this scene repeated itself four or five more times before I finally made it to where I could stand. What a relief!

Years later I realized that I had a body that just wanted to sink. We were down in California at Palm Springs when somebody said how you couldn't sink in the hot springs because of all the minerals in the water. Well, I went out there and took a few strokes and then let myself float. And I sank right to the bottom! I just sat there on the floor of that pool for awhile before I swam to the surface. My friends couldn't believe it. None of the rest of them could do it.

The group of us that lived on the Gorge used to go out to another friend's cabin on Cordova Bay to swim and lie on the beach. I would anchor the *Moonbeam* out in the bay and ferry everyone ashore in the skiff. Sometimes we would stay out there for two or three days at a time.

Cordova Bay is a long, open-faced bay that offers little protection from the east or southeast. But in the summer the breezes are nearly always offshore. Everyone said you never had to worry about a southeaster in the summer months. I would sometimes leave the boat anchored there and not worry about it.

Then one fine day I was in town at the Consolidated Exporters offices when a freak storm blew up. In a matter of minutes it was blowing about forty knots. The wind was from the southeast. Billy and I jumped into my car and rushed out to the bay. By the time we got there, four-to five-foot waves were crashing onto the beach. There was a small crowd of people gathered, watching as the *Moonbeam* was pushed closer and closer to shore. The anchor simply could not hold in the sandy bottom against the force of that blow. By the time we arrived the boat wasn't much more than a hundred feet from the beach. And if she was pushed aground, she would be nothing more than driftwood by the time those breakers finished with her.

Billy and I pulled the skiff down the beach. We managed to make it through the surf by timing the waves before jumping in. We did all right for the first little bit, but it was really wild. The waves were very steep and breaking all around us. In no time we were soaking wet. Even rowing as hard as I could, it was difficult to keep the flat-bottomed skiff pointed in the right direction and nearly impossible to make any headway. We finally got to within ten feet of the *Moonbeam* when disaster struck! The crest of a big wave broke right over the top of us, filling the little boat to the gunwales.

Billy was a strong swimmer, and when he saw that we weren't

going to make it in the skiff, he dove into the water and tried to swim for it. We weren't more than fifteen feet from the *Moonbeam* at the time. The force of the incoming waves, however, was too much for him, and he was driven back. In fact, he arrived back on the beach before I did in the half-sunk skiff.

Next we grabbed a small rowboat that lay on the beach above the tideline. Again we made it through the surf by following a receding wave. The rowboat was much easier to handle in the waves; it's steep chine offered little resistance to the waves. It took only a few minutes to reach the *Moonbeam*; by this time it was almost on the shore. Billy jumped on board and held the bow line while I stowed the oars on the rowboat and then climbed out also. Then we just released the small boat and let the wind carry it ashore. There were enough people there that we knew someone would haul it back to its place.

"As soon as I get the motor started, you pull up the anchor," I shouted to Billy.

I dashed into the pilothouse and cranked that engine over. Luckily she started right off. As soon as I put a little slack in the anchor rope, Billy hoisted it up onto the deck. He then made his way back and into the protection of the wheelhouse. We ran the boat down to the south end of the bay behind Cormorant Point where there was protection from the wind. We anchored there and played cards for a couple of hours until the wind died down. Then we went around and into the safety of Victoria Harbour. After that experience I decided that there was no such thing as "never" when it came to the weather around this part of the world.

LOSS OF THE *MOONBEAM*

TOMMY TOMSON WAS a good friend of mine. He worked for the B.C. Pilot Association. At this time during the twenties there were two rival associations that competed for the right to pilot ocean-going ships when they came into the waters of the Strait of Juan de Fuca and Georgia Strait. Whoever got to a ship first had the right to pilot it. At the time both of the associations had slow boats. Tommy Tomson wanted to try out the *Moonbeam* to see if he could then talk his group into building a faster boat.

We talked about it a number of times. I told Tommy I'd take him out anytime he wanted. He said that he'd let me know when a ship was coming into the strait and we'd go out to meet it.

A couple of weeks later he came down to Raymond's Wharf late one evening to tell me he'd just heard that a ship was on the way in. I was a little hesitant because I'd been out on a delivery the night before and I hadn't refilled my tanks yet.

"How far out are we going to have to go?" I asked him. "I don't have too much gas."

"Oh, we won't have to go much beyond Race Rocks," he assured me.

I knew that I had lots of gas to go that far, so we set out right away. When we passed the Rocks, there was still no ship in sight. We kept going. We were pretty near halfway to Cape Flattery and still hadn't seen any sign of the ship that we were trying to connect with. It was a clear night, so I knew we hadn't missed it.

"This is as far as we can go, Tommy," I said finally. "We'll never make it back to the harbour as it is."

"Head for Sooke. There's a fellow that lives at the fish traps west of there that has a telephone," Tommy said. "I'll call the office and have some gas sent out."

We headed in towards the lights of Sooke. Even in the dark I had no trouble finding the fish traps about five miles west of the entrance to Sooke Harbour. We were lucky. We ran out of gas within a hundred feet of the outside piling of the trap and were able to coast in. Tommy took the skiff and went in to phone for more gas, while I stayed on the boat.

It was about two hours before a couple of fellows arrived with some gas. And then they only brought two, four-gallon cans. They were not used to feeding three hundred-horsepower engines and figured that would be lots. I wasn't sure that we'd make it back on that much, but we headed off anyway. That was the thing about my boats—they were fast, but they burned an awful lot of gasoline. About halfway between Race Rocks and Victoria the tanks were dry again. We drifted and waited for the pilot boat that had brought the gas to catch up with us. Finally we saw it coming. It was closer to shore than we were, so we started signalling it with a flashlight. I don't know what those two fellows were doing, but they just cruised right on by us. We even lit some paper in a cardboard box and tossed it overboard, but they didn't even see that.

Fortunately, the dispatcher in the office at the Pilot Association was watching and figured out what was going on. As soon as the boat hit the dock, he sent them out again with more gas.

In spite of the fiasco that trip turned out to be—I never did hear what happened to the ship we went in search of—Tommy Tomson was very pleased with the way the *Moonbeam* ran and was keen to get a faster boat for the association. He convinced the rest of his company that they should hire me to design a boat for them.

I came up with a design for a forty-foot, V-bottomed boat very similar to the *Moonbeam*. I put another three hundred-horsepower Fiat in it. (They now came with a clutch and reverse, but cost a heck of a lot more.) That boat would cruise at eighteen or twenty knots and had a top speed of nearly thirty. I had the boat built in the Yonedas' shipyard on Chatham Street. Funny thing was, the opposition pilot group was having a new boat of their own built right alongside ours. They had it designed in Seattle, but for some reason didn't follow the design all the way. One of the pilots figured that he knew better. He cut off part of the stern so that it came to more of a point. This was a real mistake as it ruined the lift that the stern should provide. They put a two hundred-horsepower Sterling engine in that boat, but it would only make about twelve knots.

The boat that I designed was christened *Association*. Eventually the two rival groups of pilots joined to form the B.C. Pilot Association. That boat was around for years, but I finally lost track of it. In more recent times I've tried to find out what became of it, but no one seems to know.

For a couple of years things went along pretty smoothly in the rum trade. I worked steadily through the fall, winter and spring months, averaging four or five trips a month. During the summer I took it pretty easy. I had my share of close calls, but always had enough speed to stay clear of any real trouble.

The *Moonbeam* was a good boat, but I began to realize that I needed something bigger. I had customers who wanted me to deliver a hundred cases or more rather than the seventy-five that I could now handle. The rumrunning was just the same as any other business, I guess; you had to satisfy the customer or he'd soon find someone who would. I had no shortage of customers, that's for sure. As time went on, more and more of the people in the trade got caught and spent some time in jail. But on the distribution end, there was always someone to take the place of anyone who got sent away. The demand for the goods didn't let up at all. I had people wanting me to haul for them all the time because they knew that I had never been caught. Finally I made up my mind that I had to have a new boat. I designed a forty-eight footer with a nine-foot beam. Once again the Yoneda boatyard on Chatham Street did the actual construction and I installed the engines and did the finishing work.

The new boat was only a month or so from completion when I was invited down to Seattle to a party at Pete Peterson's. I was going to spend a few days down there, so when I left I told Tom Colley and Billy Garrard that they could use the *Moonbeam* while I was gone. Tom had a Coastal Pilot ticket and was a very good engineer. He had made several deliveries with me by this time. I told them that if an order came in from one of my customers, they should deliver it and I wouldn't charge them anything for the boat. We were making most of our landings about ten miles south of Bellingham then, and they both knew the area well. I went off to Seattle to enjoy myself.

Peterson and his wife put on a pretty good party. There were all kinds of people there, including some pretty high-ranking officials in the police department. These were the guys who were able to keep Pete and Carl out of jail from time to time. The Petersons had a nice home in a fashionable area of Seattle. The place had a large living room and dining room. They had a small combo in the corner to play dance music. The music started at about nine. At midnight a buffet dinner was served and then everyone danced again until four or five in the morning. Everyone seemed to have a really good time.

I caught a cab back to the hotel I was staying at just as the sun was coming up. Later that afternoon Peterson and Melby came by and picked me up. They drove me around town, showing me the sights—and showing me all the big shots that they knew.

We ended up at dinner at a posh restaurant downtown. As soon as we sat down, Peterson bought a round of drinks and ordered expensive cigars for us all. I never did smoke so he was wasting his money on mine. A little later on, while Pete was off visiting someone at another table, I happened to mention to Melby that his partner was very generous with his money. Carl just laughed.

"You just wait," he said. "Watch what happens when the big bill comes around at the end."

We had a very fine meal and a few more drinks. Just when things were winding down, I noticed that Peterson got up and went off to talk to the manager of the place. This was just before the bill arrived. Naturally Melby got stuck with the check.

"It happens every time," he said as he handed the waiter a $100 bill. "Old Pete is quick as lightning to pay for anything that costs a dollar or a dollar and a half, but when the real money is spent, he's always somewhere else."

I always had the feeling that Melby would not have had Peterson for a partner if he were not married to his sister.

I spent another day or two in Seattle just looking around, and then caught the CPR boat back home.

The morning after I arrived back in Victoria, Tom Colley showed up at my room in the Kohse home at about 7:30. He woke me up with some very bad news.

"Geez, I'm sorry, Johnny," he said. "But this is all we've got left of the *Moonbeam*." With that he handed me a flashlight. Except for the sorry look on his face, I might have thought he was joking. Tom sat down and told me the story.

An order had come in to Consolidated Exporters from one of my regular customers. They wanted seventy cases delivered to a spot about ten miles north of Anacortes. Both Tom and Billy had made the run before so they took the order.

They had just cleared the last of the San Juan Islands and were out into Rosario Strait when a Coast Guard cutter appeared from the south and began to fire on them with their machine gun. Somehow the cutter got within range before they even saw it.

It was later on that I came to realize that it was probably my night vision as much as anything else that kept me out of the hands of the Coast Guard for all the years I was in the rum trade. There never was a time when anyone else who was with me ever saw another boat at night before I did. I could point out a boat travelling without lights half a mile or a mile before Billy or anyone else would be able to see it. On the other hand, no one that I ever met could pick out a light better than Tom Colley. He'd say "There's a light," and I wouldn't see anything. Maybe five or ten minutes later, sure enough, there'd be a light right where Tom said it was. He figured he'd developed the skill in all the years with the Pilot Association, running out into the strait looking for the lights of ships heading in.

Anyway, on this occasion the Coast Guard had the *Moonbeam* in their sights before Tom and Billy realized they were there. It was right after those first shots were fired that the boys made a serious mistake of judgement. Instead of swinging around and heading back into Thatcher Pass and outrunning the cutter in the San Juan Islands, which they should have been easily able to do, as they had almost twice the speed of the Coast Guard, they headed straight across the channel towards the American shore. The first few shots were over the bow—warning shots—but once the cutter saw that the boys were going to outrun them, they aimed for the *Moonbeam*. A number of bullets found their mark; at least one hit the engine and it started to miss and backfire and quickly lost power. The boat slowed to half-speed—about the same speed that the cutter could make. In fact, the cutter was slowly gaining on the *Moonbeam*, firing all the time. Tom and Billy were very lucky that they weren't hit.

The distance across the channel there was about three miles. About halfway across, a second cutter appeared from the north and joined the chase. Both cutters kept the *Moonbeam* under a constant barrage of machine gun fire. Only the darkness prevented them from putting the boat out of commission sooner. Billy told me later that he winced every time he heard the thwack of another bullet digging into the hull, expecting the boat to explode into flames with every hit. It was amazing that the *Moonbeam* kept running at all.

When they came to a spit of land on the American shore, Tom simply ran the boat up onto the beach. As soon as they hit the shore, Tom and Billy jumped off the bow and ran up into the woods. In the darkness the men on the cutter did not see them leaving because Tom told me he could hear them shouting as he ran through the bush.

"We've got you now, you sons of bitches! We've got you now," they shouted, as they continued to fire on the boat.

Fortunately, Billy was familiar with the area where they had landed. There was a children's summer camp very near where they beached the boat. A short distance through the woods they found a dirt road that led them to the coastal highway. They now had a bit of good luck—fifteen minutes after they hit the highway the night bus came along. It was only about 11 p.m. They flagged the bus down and were soon on their way to the border. They spent the next day in Vancouver and caught the CPR ferry back to Victoria that night.

It was a sad tale to hear so early in the morning, but I was thankful that Tom and Billy hadn't been hurt or captured. I was especially sad to lose the *Moonbeam*; she'd served me well. I never saw her again, nor heard anything about her except rumours. There was never anything mentioned to me about it. I expected a visit from the Canadian Customs people, but nobody ever showed up. Actually, the boat was registered in Billy Garrard's name because I was still an American citizen and the boat had to be sixty percent Canadian-owned. But no one bothered Billy either. In any case, around Victoria everyone knew that the boat was mine. I did hear a rumour that the Coast Guard were thinking of using the boat as a cutter, but apparently they decided that she was a bit too light; nothing ever came of it.

I lost a Luger revolver that I'd had for a long time when I lost the *Moonbeam*. I never did carry a gun on the boat after that. I was not worried about being hijacked anymore. I made up my mind that I would always have enough speed to keep clear of trouble. I also decided that no one else would ever run one of my boats again either.

MISS VICTORIA

FORTUNATELY, WHEN THE *Moonbeam* was lost, the new boat was almost completed. I spent about a month finishing her off. I wanted to put two of the three hundred-horsepower Fiat engines in this boat. At the time, however, I only had enough cash to buy one engine. Those engines that had been $500 when I put the first one in the *Moonbeam* were now $3,000. I think the fact that they were being used in the rumrunning had driven up the price. The good news was that they now came ready to install in a boat, with a clutch and gears and all.

When I had first decided to build the new boat, I knew I would not have the cash for both engines. I went down to Tacoma to see Pete Marinoff and asked him to loan me the $3,000. I had been hauling for Pete for quite awhile by this time. He was one of my steadiest customers. He said sure, the loan would be no problem.

But then, when I lost the *Moonbeam*, I wasn't able to do any work for him for a spell, and he had to get someone else. I didn't see him for awhile after that, and I began to wonder if he would still want to lend me the money. One day I ran into him at the Consolidated Exporters office, and I mentioned that I was just about ready to install the engines.

"Oh, yeah. You wanted to borrow some money, didn't you?" he said. "How much was it?"

When I told him that I needed $3,000, he reached into his pocket and pulled out a roll of money. He calmly peeled off thirty $100 bills and handed them to me.

"Pay me back when you can," he said. "I'll have some work for you when you get the new boat going."

This was good news to me. I liked Pete—and not just because he lent me money. He was a good guy.

Pete Marinoff was short and dark and spoke with a bit of an eastern-European accent. He owned a "near beer" brewery in Olympia, but made his real money bootlegging the good liquor that we were bringing into Washington.

I liked Marinoff because he shared my enthusiasm for fast boats. For awhile there he had a fleet of seven speedboats that were kept busy making runs from Discovery Island and East Point down to Seattle and Tacoma. And he didn't mind getting in there and doing some of the hauling himself. It was said that he'd had more run-ins with "Grandad" and the Coast Guard than anyone else in the trade. He'd certainly lost his fair share of boats and cargoes.

In fact, at the time that he lent me the money for the new engine, he was verging on bankruptcy. That morning he asked me to stick around until he finished his business at the Consolidated Exporters office, and then we went up the street and had a cup of coffee. He told me he was anxious for me to start hauling again, because he needed someone he could rely on to deliver a load. He'd had a real run of bad luck.

Within the past month he'd lost one boat and two cargoes to the Coast Guard. "Grandad" Lonsdale had spotted him off Marrowstone Point in Admiralty Inlet when he was carrying a load of eighty-five cases in the M-855, his black-hulled forty-footer that was powered by two Liberty engines. He turned and ran the other way when the *Arcata* opened up with the one-pounder. The M-855 could do forty knots and would have been easily able to outrun the cutter except for the fact that they soon saw another Coast Guard cutter blocking their exit from the north. Marinoff was forced to dump the valuable cargo into the saltchuk and watch it sink beneath the waves.

In that instance the only satisfaction that "Grandad" had was knowing that he'd cost Marinoff a few thousand dollars. A week later, however, he was luckier still. The marksman on the *Arcata* managed to put a one-pound shell right through the transom of one of Pete's boats under chase. This time Marinoff was not on board. The direct hit blew the transom to bits, but the engine wasn't damaged, so the skipper kept it at speed and ran it up on the beach. He and his helper beat it into the bush and got away, but the boat and cargo were lost.

Losses like these in so short a time would hurt anyone's business. However, Pete told me that the Coast Guard was still the least of his problems right then. He was far more worried about the competition for control of the liquor business in the Seattle area. It looked like Roy Olmstead, a former Seattle policeman, was determined to have the whole thing for himself.

Roy Olmstead was the youngest lieutenant in the Seattle Police Department in 1920 when he realized that he'd never get rich at what he was doing and set out to change that. He went after the quickest, easiest money he could find, and was soon heavily involved in rumrunning. It wasn't too long before he was caught unloading a large cargo of liquor from a tug at Brown's Bay. Naturally he was thrown off the police force. But he soon discovered that this just left him more time to devote to more profitable ventures.

It wasn't long before Olmstead was running far more liquor into Washington than anyone else. By 1924 they say that it was a very poor month when he didn't gross $200,000. He even bought his own ship and started buying his liquor down in Tahiti where he could get it duty free. The ship then sat off the coast and small boats were used to bring it in as needed.

It was about that time that he decided he'd put the competition out of business. Olmstead started undercutting everyone else's prices by twenty-five percent. He could do this because he was not paying duty on his liquor.

And he was not above resorting to strongarm tactics, either. That morning in the coffee shop Pete Marinoff described an incident that had taken place only a few days before, down at the Seattle docks where one of his boats was taking on fuel. Someone had pushed a full, forty-five-gallon drum of oil off the dock down onto the deck of Pete's boat, a drop of about fifteen feet. Fortunately it missed the fellow with the fuel hose, but it still made quite a hole in the deck. Marinoff didn't know who did the actual pushing, but he was very sure about who had given the orders to do it.

Marinoff was a hardworking and determined man, and he managed to survive the rivalry with Olmstead. I had a lot of respect for him. He gave me that loan when he could probably least afford it and never asked for any interest on it. Of course, he was interested in seeing me get my boat on the water, so there was some benefit to him as well. I paid him back in about six months anyway. Pete was able to stay in the business right up until the end of Prohibition. I hauled for him a good deal. I think he may have gone to jail for a short spell at one point, though.

Now Roy Olmstead was a different type of character altogether. I had about the same opinion of him that Marinoff did. At the time that he was still buying some of his liquor from Consolidated Exporters, I had taken a few loads over for him. It was nothing but trouble. When I delivered the first load, the fellow on the beach who was supposed to pay me for delivery had some excuse about not being able to get to the bank. I didn't buy that, but the end result was that he didn't have the money, and I didn't want to haul the liquor back to Victoria. The fellow said he'd have it for sure on the next delivery. I took one more load down and was forced to listen to the same story. I didn't bother to say anything this time. I just waited until they called with another order. Then I phoned the head office of Consolidated in Vancouver and told them that I wouldn't haul another load until the delivery money for all three shipments was in Victoria. A number of phone calls went back and forth. Olmstead claimed that the money would be there for sure this time, but I held out. They moaned and groaned a lot, but I finally got my way and the money was sent.

And that was the last load I delivered to Roy Olmstead. It just wasn't worth the trouble. I never lost a cent on the deal, but a lot of other people never got paid. I think it was shortly after that that Consolidated cut him off as well. I heard that he owed them $280,000. And it wasn't too long before the Coast Guard caught up with him too. He ended up doing four years in the federal penitentiary on McNeil Island down south of Tacoma.

Anyway, back to the new boat. With the help of Pete Marinoff's loan I was able to buy the two, three hundred-horsepower Fiat engines that I wanted. I mounted them side by side and sent the drive shafts out through the bottom of the boat and attached them to a strut made of a six-inch metal plate. The strut was bolted through a heavy beam on the inside of the hull. I then welded a metal fin onto the strut to protect the propellers from being damaged by driftwood.

I named the new boat the *Miss Victoria*. She could do about thirty knots with a load on. I had decided to make this boat a bit more comfortable than the *Moonbeam*; I put a stove in and a couple of bunks. I made one major mistake, though. I built the cabin the full length of the hull. As soon as I started hauling with the *Miss Victoria*, I found out that this was not a good idea as it made the loading and unloading a lot more work. This was especially bad because it increased the time that it took us to drop off a load, and the time that we were at the rendezvous point was the riskiest time of all. The cabin was also a little too high for my liking; I thought that it made the boat too visible, even though I painted it a dark grey like all my other boats. Although it was nice to have more room inside the boat, the inconvenience in the loading and unloading far outweighed the advantages gained with the full cabin. I only made a few deliveries with the *Miss Victoria* before I had the shipyard start building a new boat.

The *Miss Victoria* had lots of power, though. Those two Fiats really pushed her through the water. I had Tom Colley with me on one trip down to drop off a load of liquor near Edmonds when I learned just how much power was in those engines. We were on our way back, right out in the middle of the strait about halfway between Port Townsend and Victoria, when all of a sudden there was a queer sound coming from the back of the boat.

I had no idea what was going on—both engines were running normally—but something just sounded funny. I sent Tom back to see if he could find out what was causing the strange noise.

I always built a watertight bulkhead fore and aft of the engines in my boats. That way, if you hit something and started to take on water, there was a good chance of keeping the engines running. The sound appeared to be coming from the compartment at the stern. Tom took the hatch cover off and took a look inside. Even in the dark he could see that there was about a foot and a half of water in the back end of the boat. He figured that somehow or other a bit of driftwood had been rammed through the hull.

Without really thinking about it, he stuck his hand down into the water to feel around for what had caused the leak. Before he knew what hit him, the propeller sliced his middle finger into three pieces right down to the first joint. It was a wonder he didn't lose his whole hand.

He shouted at me and I immediately shut the engines off. First I bandaged his finger as best I could; then I went back to survey the damage and try to figure out what had happened. There wasn't much to see and nothing to be done about it out there. I could feel the propeller blades where they had come through the hull, but other than that I didn't know what the heck had happened.

We ran the rest of the way home on one engine. That turned out to be a trip where we needed repairs to the crew as well as the engine. I dropped Tom off at Raymond's Wharf where he had left his car and he went off to the hospital to get his finger stitched up. I then took the boat straight over to Foster's by the Point Ellice bridge so that I could get it up on the ways first thing in the morning.

When I had the boat out of the water, it was easy to see what had happened. The weld on one side of the strut that held the shaft had broken. The thrust of the propeller was powerful enough to bend the shaft until it was right up against the hull. I guess the shaft bent slowly enough that the propeller just ate its way through the planking of the hull a little bit at a time. I would have thought it would have dug in and bent or broken the prop, but it did not. In fact the propeller blades were not bent out of shape at all. They simply cut a neat hole exactly the size of the blades right up into the hull.

The problem was solved easily enough. We had to put four new planks in the aft of the boat, put in a new shaft, and weld the strut again. This time I made sure the welds were good and strong.

Tom's finger healed up good as new as well.

Driftwood was a real hazard in the rumrunning. In fact, it probably represented as much of a danger to our safety as did the Coast Guard with their guns. Anytime you run a boat at high speed at night in the waters of the Strait of Juan de Fuca and Puget Sound, the risk of hitting a piece of floating debris is great. The confined waters and strong tide-rips tended to gather anything floating on the surface in certain areas, and back in those days, there was an awful lot of good wood floating around out there. There were no beachcombers or log salvagers, and no one was cutting firewood on the beach. There were spots in back eddies where there would be acres of solid driftwood. The stuff was packed so tight that it looked like you could walk right across it. Naturally we avoided those areas, but you couldn't avoid it all.

Billy Garrard and I were on our way back from making a delivery down near Seattle one night when I felt a little bump near the stern just as we were coming past Trial Island. It wasn't much of a knock at all, but right away the boat slowed to about eight knots. I gave the engines a bit more throttle, but the boat did not go any faster.

I figured that there must be a bit of driftwood stuck on one of the props, so I reversed the engines to try and kick it off. Then I revved them again, but that didn't work. The *Miss Victoria* would only make eight knots. I ran her slow the rest of the way into the harbour. It was three in the morning when I tied her up at Raymond's Wharf.

The next day I put the boat up on the ways at Foster's. When it came out of the water, it was easy to see what the problem was. There was a piece of fir log about eight inches in diameter and about five feet long stuck right up against the struts that held the propellers. It always amazed me how that bit of log got jammed in there. It must have come right in under the bows and run all the way back there without turning endways. And it hit the struts dead on—exactly the same length of log was sticking over at each end, so the force of the water couldn't flip it off. The log was a bit rotten and the fins that I had welded on to protect the props had dug into the soft wood and helped to hold it in place. In fact, it was wedged in so tight that I had to take a crowbar and pry it off.

Not only had my reversing and speeding-up the engines been unable to dislodge the log, but it had caused a more serious problem as well. With the boat up on the ways I discovered that the nails in the planks in front of each prop were protruding about half an inch out of the wood. In trying to dislodge the log I had really poured the power to it and I guess the suction created between the propellers and the back of that log was so great that it had lifted the planks off the bottom of the boat. When I slowed the engines the planks had popped back into place, leaving the nails sticking out. The force was so great that it had straightened the nails where they had been clenched on the ribs inside the hull. I had to renail and clench three planks. I often wonder what would have happened if I had given the engines full throttle with that log under there. Would it have torn the planks right off the bottom of the boat?

Running a fast boat in the dark was dangerous, but that was simply one of the risks we took. (It was also one of the advantages that we had over the Coast Guard. Some of the captains of their cutters would not take the chance of damaging their ships, so they wouldn't open the throttle after dark.) I went through a lot of propellers, and I always kept a supply of props and shafts on hand. The shaft would often be twisted out of shape when the propellers kept turning after hitting a log. It seemed that every second or third trip I'd have the boat up on the ways straightening a propeller or putting in a new shaft. I could usually straighten a prop out four or five times if it was not bent too badly, then I'd have to toss it away. We never even tried to straighten a shaft.

I spent a lot of money on propellers and shafts. And a lot more on boats and engines! I guess that was why I never did get rich in the rumrunning. I was making real good money for the day—a hell of a lot more than the average Joe—but I was pretty good at spending it too. And I never spared any expense when it came to my boats. I always figured that the better shape my equipment was in, the less chance I had of getting caught and being put out of business. And my record would never prove me wrong about that.

CLOSE CALLS

I USED THE *Miss Victoria* for just about a year while the new boat was being built. Apart from the inconvenience caused by the full cabin when we were loading and unloading, she was a good vessel. I was never really that comfortable with her though, because I felt that the cabin stuck up a bit too high and made her too visible from a distance. Still, nobody ever did catch us. But we did have a couple of close calls.

One night I took a load over to Whidbey Island with Tom Colley as my mate. We had made several deliveries to the same area, south of Point Partridge where the out-of-use fish traps were. I always travelled very slowly when I approached a delivery spot in order to be as quiet as possible, and to be able to watch exactly what was going on around me. That way I never rushed into a situation that I later regretted.

On this evening the sky was overcast and there was no moon. It was very dark, especially in close to the shore where there was a background of tall fir trees. I made a pass fairly close in to our delivery point and had a look through the night glasses. I could just make out the silhouette of one of the seventy-five-foot Coast Guard cutters tied up against the pilings a little bit north of where we were planning to make our drop.

I had no idea whether they were lying in ambush for me or

just tied up for the night. They certainly weren't showing any lights to give their position away! I must have been feeling particularly lucky that night, or very brave—or maybe I was just more foolhardy than usual! Anyway, instead of heading straight off home and waiting to hear from the customer to arrange another dropoff spot, I decided to try to make the delivery in spite of the presence of the Coast Guard. I slowly made a wide circle offshore and came into the rendezvous point from the south. I made the approach as close to the shore as I could get. I kept the night glasses on the cutter the whole time. For some reason I thought that maybe they hadn't seen us. I think I was also intrigued by the possibility of making a delivery right under the noses of our adversaries.

Whatever my motivation, it turned out to be anything but a good idea. I came up to the delivery spot and was just about to drop the anchor, still watching the cutter closely through the glasses. I guess part of my bravado came from the fact that I knew I could outrun them in a chase. Tom was up on the bow waiting for my order to drop the hook when I saw the Coast Guard boat pull away from the pilings and start to come in on us. I quickly swung the Miss Victoria around and headed back down the shoreline. I nearly threw Tom overboard when I gunned the engines, but he knew what was going on and stowed the anchor and made his way back into the pilothouse. We ran in close to shore for about half a mile. The dark background of the shoreline must have worked to our advantage this time, because the cutter did not even fire a shot at us. We soon outdistanced them and headed back across the strait.

When we got back to the other side I decided not to stash the load out on one of the islands as I had done a number of other times when I could not make a delivery for one reason or another. Instead I went right into the harbour to Raymond's Wharf where I moored the Miss Victoria. Percy Raymond was a good friend who let me tie my boat up at his wharf anytime I wanted.

Raymond's Wharf was located down at the west end of Belleville Street and was built on pilings about one hundred and fifty feet out into the harbour. A large warehouse stretched across the outer end of the wharf. Cement that was brought by freighter down from Bamberton in Saanich Inlet was stored there. A second building ran along the west side of the wharf right back to shore, where it joined the back of the building that housed Joe Parker's machine shop.

What I liked best about Raymond's Wharf was the fact that, when my boat was tied up on the west side, it could not be seen without going right down onto the wharf. That side of the wharf was hidden from the street by the warehouse and by trees and bush that grew along the shore beyond Parker's. That way nobody knew whether I was in or out unless they went to some trouble to find out. And that's the way I liked it.

On the east side and right up against the shore, just above the high-water mark, there was a small shack built between the pilings under the wharf. The shack was about twelve feet square and had a small porch on it about four feet wide. Some time earlier I'd asked Percy if he ever used this shack. He said he didn't and that if I ever needed it, I was welcome to use it. It was here that I decided to store the one hundred twenty-five cases of liquor that Tom Colley and I had been unable to deliver to Whidbey Island.

It was about two o'clock in the morning when we got back to the harbour. The tide was high, so we simply took the *Miss Victoria* right in next to the shore and loaded right onto the platform on the front of the shack. Although the east side of the wharf was plainly visible from the street, there was no one around at that time of the morning, so I didn't worry too much about being seen. In half an hour Tom and I had the cargo stowed. We said goodnight to each other and made our separate ways home. I walked; it was only a couple of blocks to the Kohses' where I was living.

About eight o'clock the next morning Percy Raymond phoned me at home. He was kind of excited.

"You'd better get your butt down here right away," he said. "Somebody's broken into the shack and the door's wide open and there's a case of liquor sitting on the porch in plain sight!"

I managed to calm Percy down soon enough. I told him to go into his office and stay there, and that I'd be right down. I assured him that, if anything went wrong, I would take full responsibility for it. Then I went out and jumped in my car and drove down to Belleville Street. All of this took perhaps five minutes.

The first thing I did when I got to the wharf was go to the shack and put the case of liquor that was sitting on the porch inside. A quick count told me that about fifty cases were missing. It looked like the robbers were unexpectedly interrupted. Somebody must have happened along and scared off whoever was stealing the liquor. Maybe a car or truck drove down onto the wharf. In any case they simply dropped that last case and beat it.

I had a look at the door of the shack. The padlock had been pried off. The staples that had held the padlock were still in good shape, so I went down to my boat and got the lock off of it and used it on the shack. Then I went to see Percy in his office. He was still pretty upset.

"Geez, Johnny," he said. "I was scared as hell when I saw that case of liquor just sitting there out in the open. I could lose my business over something like that!"

I assured him that it wouldn't happen again. I wasn't too worried. Only about fifteen minutes had passed from the time Percy called me until I had the new lock on the door of the shack. I already had my mind on other things. I wasn't bothered much by the stolen liquor; Consolidated Exporters always made good for anything that I lost in transit, no matter how it happened. I was more curious about who had stolen the liquor.

That night I moved the rest of that liquor out of the shack and filled the load out with fifty cases from Consolidated Exporters. I made the delivery to a new dropoff up near Anacortes. Billy Garrard went with me.

I wasn't too long figuring out who had hijacked that liquor from me. I had no reason to distrust the people working for me, but Tom Colley was the only one besides myself who knew that cargo was there. I had also noticed that Joe Fleming's boat was tied up at the float in front of the Empress Hotel when we came in during the night, but was not there in the morning. It was not like Joe to be off anywhere so early at that time of year.

I talked it over with Billy, and we just couldn't figure how it could have been anyone else but Joe and Tom. We guessed that they'd be trying to sell it on the black market. There were a number of bootleggers operating in Victoria at the time. I wasn't particularly friendly with any of them, but I knew who most of them were. We went to see Jimmy "The Joker" Price out at the Six Mile House. Jimmy was known to sell the odd bottle from time to time. We told him what had happened and who we suspected had the liquor. I put out the word through Jimmy that I wanted to know if Tom Colley or Joe Fleming tried to sell any liquor. Then we waited.

Nothing happened for about ten days. Then I got a call from Jimmy Price. Tom had offered him ten cases of booze at a real good price. Jimmy had agreed to buy the liquor and made arrangements to pick it up. Billy and I took over from there.

The delivery was to be made at midnight in Cadboro Bay just south of the yacht club at a spot where Beach Drive comes quite close to the shore. Billy Garrard had been to university with several fellows who were on the Victoria police force, and he was still friendly with them. He managed to borrow a policeman's uniform, telling his friends that he was going to play a practical joke on another fellow. This was very close to the truth.

At the appointed hour Billy, disguised as one of our city's finest, was hidden in the bushes along the shore, flashlight at the ready. Tom and Joe soon approached the beach in a skiff loaded down with whisky. The tide was a good ways out. Billy waited until the boys had unloaded most of the liquor and piled it neatly above the high-water mark. When they were just on their way back up the beach with the last of the load, he stepped out of the bushes and, turning the flashlight on our two friends, announced that they were under arrest. Tom and Joe immediately dropped what they were carrying and headed off in different directions. Joe went straight for the skiff and was soon rowing furiously back out to sea. Tom ran down the beach and disappeared into the bushes. Billy made no attempt to follow either of the culprits. When they were out of hearing, he had a good laugh, then loaded the ten cases into his car and drove off.

Meanwhile I was in the *Miss Victoria* on my way to Joe Fleming's boathouse out on Discovery Island. I figured that I would find the other forty cases there. Joe had told me that he had built a hidden compartment into the boathouse so that he wouldn't have to worry so much about being robbed, as there was often no one around out on the island. The boathouse had only three walls, the fourth side being open so a boat could be driven in. The back wall was false and made to look exactly like the outside wall.

Although I knew that the secret compartment was there, I didn't know how to get into it. Joe had told me that there was a plank that he could lift out and that he could then swing a section of the wall out on hinges. But he'd sure hidden it well! I'll be damned if I could find it. I searched for over half an hour and was unable to find a loose plank or anything else that would allow entry. Finally I decided that Joe would be coming back soon and I left empty-handed.

As it turned out I left none too soon—I was just coming around the end of Discovery Island when I passed within fifty feet of Joe heading back out in his boat. We were both running without lights and neither of us ever acknowledged that we'd seen the other.

A couple of days later Billy and I took the ten cases out to the Six Mile House and gave "The Joker" a really good price on them for helping us out. I never did recover any more of that load. But we certainly enjoyed the fact that we were able to put one over on the thieves who had robbed me. The hardest part was keeping it to ourselves. Billy had a tough time keeping quiet every time he saw Tom and Joe for awhile after that. He wanted to tease them about how fast they'd run off into the darkness. I was kind of frustrated about not being able to find my way into the back of Joe's boathouse, and I wasn't too friendly to either Tom or Joe for awhile. But I got over it, and both of them worked for me again. I guess I had to carry part of the blame—the temptation of that liquor sitting there right in the harbour was just too much. I never kept any more liquor in that shack—much to the relief of Percy Raymond.

And that wasn't the only load of liquor that I lost after I had stashed it when I couldn't make a delivery. But Consolidated Exporters always bore the losses when that kind of thing happened, so I never let it get me down.

MISS VICTORIA II

THE NEW BOAT was ready in the fall of 1928. I named her the *Miss Victoria II*. This boat was thirty-six feet long with an eight-foot beam. I put a twelve-cylinder, four hundred-horsepower Liberty airplane engine in her. With that engine she could carry a load of one hundred twenty-five cases of liquor and still make around thirty knots.

I sold the *Miss Victoria* to a fishing company that operated a cannery over in Bellingham. They planned to use her as a scout boat during the herring season on the West Coast. They figured she'd pay her way by being able to scoot around and find the large schools of herring, allowing their boats to get to the best fishing grounds before their rivals'.

It was funny about those airplane engines. When I bought the first Fiat, it had cost me $500. The next two Fiats that came equipped with a clutch cost $3,000 apiece. And I paid $4,000 for that Liberty engine which had reverse and everything. I guess you'd have to say that the rumrunning was stimulating the economy in airplane engines. The fact was, the engines that they were selling through the boating magazines were really not being used in airplanes anymore. Somebody was buying them up real cheap, making the necessary adaptations for boats, and making a bundle on them selling them to the rumrunners.

But nobody complained too much about the price. Those engines gave us what we needed: speed and power. I always tried to get the best speed that I could with a load on. I figured it wasn't much good to design a boat that could go fast empty, if it slowed right down when you loaded her up. Not in the business I was in—it was when you were still carrying a load that you were in danger of going to jail, not after you had dropped it off. So I built my boats for maximum speed with a load. (Later on I found out that I was actually doing better than the professional designers down in Seattle as far as getting speed out of my boats when they were hauling cargo. There were a few boats around that could keep up to me empty, but when it came to carrying a load, I could run away from them.)

After my experience with the full cabin on the last boat, the *Miss Victoria II* had an open cockpit at the back of the boat. I could now store the cargo out in the open, which made loading and unloading a good deal easier. Most of the time I never even bothered to cover the load. Nearly all of our hauling was in the dark, so I figured it didn't matter too much.

The cabin on the *Miss Victoria II* was again very low, not more than two feet above the level of the deck. I wanted the boat to offer as low a profile as possible. I had a hatch on the top of the pilothouse that I could open. I would stand on a box and my head and shoulders would stick out the top and I then could see all around.

I always drove with my hand on both throttles so I could shut the engines off quickly if we hit anything. I have mentioned the problem of driftwood before. It was a constant menace. There was just no way to avoid hitting debris travelling in the dark at the speeds we were. I simply tried to minimize the damage as much as possible. As soon as I felt or heard something hit the bow of the boat, I'd shut the engines down. Sometimes I'd be lucky and there'd be no damage; at other times, the propellers would be bent even after the engines were turned off. And it didn't take a very big piece of driftwood to bend a prop.

I got used to it, I guess. And after awhile I'd just expect to pull the boat out of the water after every third or fourth trip. The biggest problem I had was finding a machine shop that could keep up to me. Usually when I needed a job done, I needed it done on fairly short notice. I liked to have my boat ready to go when an order came in.

At first I used Joe Parker, whose shop was right up above Raymond's Wharf. He was a good mechanic; in fact, he was the one who made the coupling for the drive shaft on that first Fiat engine for the *Moonbeam*. Joe was reliable; if I needed a part, I would tell him when I needed it, and he would have it ready by that time. But unfortunately he went out of business after a time.

Next I tried Ramsey's over on Wharf Street. I'd take something there and ask them if they could have it finished in two days, and they would say they could. Then I'd come back on the second day, and the part would be lying in the very same spot that I had left it, and it hadn't even been looked at. It might take a week to get the job done. I didn't put up with that for long. After that I tried Hafer's shop which was almost right next door. They were good for awhile, but before too long the same thing was happening there.

Finally someone told me to try Bert Foster's shop over near the Point Ellice Bridge. He turned out to be the best one for me. If I came in with a bent prop or a twisted shaft and he had a boat up on the ways, he would put that boat back in the water and pull mine out and fix it. He understood that I needed my work done in a hurry. I suppose that I paid extra for that kind of service, but I did not mind that. As far as I was concerned, getting the job done was the important thing. (Speed was essential on some jobs—like drilling out and plugging bullet holes before the Customs men came down to check my boat!)

One of my early trips with the *Miss Victoria II* was also one of the most unusual deliveries I ever made. I received an order from Consolidated Exporters to take a load out to a rendezvous point near Barnes Island, about halfway between Anacortes and East Point. The strange thing here was that we were to make the delivery to a U.S. Coast Guard cutter! The story was that this cutter was not in use on the weekends. Apparently though, the captain was still allowed to take the boat out for his own personal use. A couple of bootleggers from Everett had persuaded the captain of that cutter to bring a load in for them. I guess the Coast Guard didn't pay all that well! When Consolidated first called me about it, I said no way. I figured it could only be a trap. But when the guy placing the order assured me that he would send someone over to Victoria to run out with us, and that he would guarantee that the captain would be alone on the boat, I agreed to make the run.

The delivery was made on a Sunday night. The bootlegger's man showed up at Raymond's Wharf in the early afternoon. I came down to the boat about four to find him waiting. We picked up the cargo out at Discovery Island in the early evening. When it was good and dark, I headed up Haro Strait and around the northern end of San Juan Island. The weather was good: heavy cloud cover and only a light breeze. Our rendezvous point was just west of Barnes Island, a small island in Rosario Strait between Orcas and Lummi islands.

We made contact with the seventy-five-foot cutter about eleven o'clock. I stopped the *Miss Victoria II* a good two hundred yards away so I would have a chance to run if necessary. Billy and the bootlegger's man rowed over empty on the first trip to check the boat out. When he was sure there was no one but the captain on board, Billy flashed a signal to me, and I moved in a little closer. We transferred the hundred and ten cases without a hitch. When he'd dropped the last load, Billy came back with the money and we were on our way. Even though everything went like clock-work, I never did feel comfortable while we were that close to that cutter. It just didn't feel right.

I always tried to schedule my runs when there was not too much of a moon, or when the weather was not so good. That was why we did so much more hauling in the winter months than in the summer. I liked the nights to be as dark as possible. And the worse the weather was, the better I liked it. I always felt safer knowing that "nobody in his right mind would be out in weather like this!" In the wintertime you did not expect to see too many other boats if you were travelling in the middle of the night. And the general rule was to simply stay clear of any that you did see— mind your own business and hope that the other guy did the same. On a winter's night any other small boat that was cruising those waters was almost certainly doing one of three things: it was hauling liquor, it was looking to hijack someone else who was hauling liquor, or it was a Coast Guard cutter. In each case steer-ing well clear was the only sensible thing to do. Any other course of action was liable to get you shot!

The Strait of Juan de Fuca could be a really wild place as far

as the weather was concerned. Because you had the currents coming into a fairly narrow channel from the wide-open Pacific, you
got some pretty good tide-rips when the current changed direction. Combined with a good blow from the west, the tide-rips
could really stand the waves on end. The only good thing about
the tide-rips was that you could pretty much predict where they
would be at certain stages of the tide and generally avoid them.

Another funny thing used to happen when the tide was coming in and there was a big swell out in the open ocean. The swell
would roll right down the strait. You might hardly notice it out in
the middle of the channel, but close to shore it would toss up
some fearsome waves. When the current was running out, the
swell would be killed farther out in the strait and would not get
down to where we were making our deliveries.

One night I had to take Griffith along on a trip. For some
reason or other Billy could not make it at the last minute, and
Griffith, who was hauling the liquor out to Discovery Island for
Consolidated Exporters, said that he would come along.

There was only a slight swell when we were crossing the
strait. We were headed for Dungeness Spit, just east of Port Angeles. There was hardly any swell on the way over, but the tide was
just finishing its run in, so when we got close to shore we could
see that the waves were piling up.

I anchored where I usually did and got the night glasses out
to see what I could see. Right away I saw the flash of light from
Carl Melby who was there to meet us. But I also saw something
that worried me a bit. Huge breakers were pounding onto the
beach, their foaming, white crests forming a series of unbroken
lines rolling along the shore. I warned Griffith about the breakers,
but he was confident that he'd have no trouble. He'd been a fisherman along the West Coast for a long time and didn't seem
bothered by this at all. Still, when he set off with the first load, I
told him that if the breakers were too heavy, not to go in. It was
still early and we could afford to wait awhile.

I watched him as he headed for shore. We were only about a
hundred yards from the beach. Within a couple of minutes Griffith
was into the breakers. What a ride he must have had! At first I
could see him each time the skiff rode up the back of one of
those huge waves. I watched as he struggled to control the little
boat. Then he would just drop from sight as another swell rose up

behind him. Suddenly he just disappeared altogether!

I scanned the surf with the glasses but did not get another glimpse of my man or the skiff. I shouted to Melby and his men onshore, but, of course, they couldn't hear me over the din of the sea. I could see that they were shouting back at me, but I couldn't make out what they said either. There was nothing to do but wait.

So I waited. And waited. Once in awhile I would yell to those on the beach, but I could never understand their replies. I watched through the glasses, but couldn't see anything that told me what was going on. Even with the night glasses I could barely make out Melby and his men when they were at the top of the beach because of the dark backdrop of forest that grew right to the shoreline. And when they went down near the water, they were hidden behind that huge surf.

After about three hours, about an hour and a half after the change of tide, the waves began dying down. Finally I could see someone starting out toward me in the skiff. When he was about halfway out, I could see that it was Melby. I figured that I had lost Griffith for sure. I helped Carl over the side and we went into the pilothouse before he began to tell me what had happened. He was soaked from head to foot.

Melby and his men had watched helplessly as Griffith struggled to keep the flat-bottomed skiff headed towards shore. They could see that he wasn't going to make it as the force of the waves continually tried to spin the little boat sideways.

The skiff was never intended for use in seas like that. It was only eleven feet long and I'd built it with a flat bottom and a long, sloping prow so that it was easier to land on the beach. The prow stuck out enough that, by the time you grounded on even a shallow beach, you could step right off onto dry land rather than into the water.

Griffith was about a hundred feet out when he and his cargo were spilled out as a wave broke right over the skiff. Fortunately he was washed ashore quite quickly; it would have been suicide for anyone to go in after him. Unfortunately he was unconscious when they dragged him out of the water. They carried him up the beach, rolled him over a log and got most of the water out of him. He came around after five minutes or so. They now had him in a small cabin up in the bush trying to warm him up.

The skiff washed up onshore about the same time that Griffith did. The only really good news was that all of the liquor was washed up onto the beach as well! And not a bottle was broken! That was the good thing about landing on a sandy beach.

Melby and I loaded the skiff and took a second load in. The waves were still tricky but they seemed to be dying out. We got the rest of the cargo ashore in two trips and then went up to the cabin. Griffith was feeling pretty good by this time—he'd had a few shots of whisky to settle him down—so we decided to be on our way. The tide was going out and the waves looked to be only about two feet high. We dragged the skiff down to the water and climbed in. I was doing the rowing. The oarsman's seat in the skiff was backwards to what it is in most rowboats, in that the oarsman faced the seas and pushed with the oars rather than pulled. Griffith was sitting in the bow of the boat, his back to the waves. Suddenly I saw a huge breaker forming ahead of us. I just had time to shout, "Here we go again!"

That breaker completely upended us! We went straight up the face of it and Griffith flew out of the bow right over my head. All of a sudden I was falling straight down into the water. I knew the skiff was coming down on top of me so I got my arms up and kept my head down. I just managed to squirm out from under it as the force of that wave drove us head-over-heels up the beach. When the frothing green water receded we were left high but definitely not dry, fifty feet from the water's edge.

God knows where that wave came from, but it appeared to be a rogue. We righted the skiff and dragged it down to the water, ready to try our luck again. Once they saw that we were all right, Melby and his men had a good laugh over our antics. The funny thing was that, when we put the boat back in the water, the sea was almost calm. There was not another wave that amounted to anything at all.

The longer I spent on the ocean, the more convinced I became that only a fool would try to predict it all of the time. The best you could do was to respect it and be careful!

I ran the *Miss Victoria II* for about two years. It must have been a good boat because I sure never had any trouble with it. She was fast and she was reliable and I guess that's about all you could ask for in a boat—at least if you were in the rum trade.

I made one trip down into Puget Sound when I had a bit of trouble with that Liberty engine, but that's the only time I can remember anything ever going wrong with the *Miss Victoria II*. We made a delivery to a spot about three miles north of Edmonds one cold, rainy night in November. We had no trouble with the delivery, but after we'd unloaded and been paid, the engine didn't want to start again. I worked and worked on it, but couldn't even get it to cough. I had some harsh words for that motor after awhile, but nothing seemed to work. We'd made the delivery at midnight. By three o'clock in the morning I was beginning to get worried. There was really nowhere much to hide around Edmonds and the sound was not all that wide there. Two or three of the cutters could box a boat in well enough to get some good shots off with their one-pound guns, even if the boat was twice as fast as they were! And the fact that we were empty wouldn't stop the Coast Guard from impounding the boat if they caught me. I'd have to fight them in court to get it back and that could take months or even years!

It was almost dawn when I finally decided that it had to be the spark. I took all twelve plugs out and set the points closer together and cleaned them up a bit. Sure enough, when I put them back in, that Liberty came to life. It would have been light if the weather hadn't been so socked in by the time we set off up the sound. Luckily there was no wind that morning because I really opened up the throttles. We were back in Victoria in time for an early breakfast at the Poodle Dog Café.

I was never unhappy with the *Miss Victoria II*. It was a damn good boat. But once again I found myself needing something bigger. There were more and more people after me to haul for them all the time. As time went on nearly everyone who had been in the rumrunning for any length of time got caught for one thing or another. I never did, and my reputation for reliability grew. It got so that I could make deliveries to two or three different people on every trip if I could haul enough cargo. I decided I had to have a larger boat.

I sold the *Miss Victoria II* to the Reifel Brothers in New Westminster. They had a big distillery over there and were also involved in the rum trade. I had met George several times and he seemed like an honest fellow. I knew that he had a lot of land at the mouth of the Fraser River. He used to take his friends out there to hunt ducks and geese. That land is now a bird sanctuary if I'm not mistaken. George's brother Harry had a beautiful, big yacht that I would sometimes see cruising in the Gulf Islands during the summer months.

After the deal was completed, the Reifels sent a mechanic over to pick up the boat and run it back to Vancouver. The fellow had been in the U.S. Army and had worked on Liberty engines during the war. He seemed to know everything there was to know about the Liberty engine. He told me how many parts there were—nine hundred and sixty some-odd pieces. He claimed that he knew every nut and bolt.

The boat was tied up at the float over at Bert Foster's boatyard when the Reifels' man came for it. I had my new boat up on the ways. When I asked him if he wanted me to give him a hand starting the Miss Victoria II, the fellow looked at me as if I was something that had just crawled up out of the sea.

"You don't have to worry about me," he said with a know-it-all smile. "I've started more Liberty engines than Henry Ford has cars."

I watched him swagger off down to the wharf, and then went back to work on the new boat. Five minutes later there was a muffled "bang" from the direction of the float. I looked up to see the "expert" stagger out of the smoke-filled pilothouse. The Miss Victoria II was on fire! Everybody that was around ran down to the float, and we soon had the fire out. There was very little damage done to the boat—I'm afraid the pride of that mechanic suffered more—there was some burnt paint in the engine compartment and a lot of oily soot on everything, but no real harm.

I then showed the considerably humbled mechanic where to set the controls, and started the boat for him. After that he took it out of there just as quickly as he could. That fellow may have known all about taking those Liberty engines apart, but he needed to learn a few things still about starting them. And that was the last I saw or heard of the Miss Victoria II.

KITNAYAKWA

SO ONCE AGAIN I was doing the finishing work on another boat. This one was forty-five feet long with a ten-foot beam. In order to be able to carry the larger loads that I intended to haul, I put two of the four hundred-horsepower Liberty engines in her. I wanted to be sure that she could carry two hundred cases of liquor and still make over thirty knots.

I named this boat the *Kitnayakwa*. I took the name from a river up in northern British Columbia. It was an Indian word and its only significance to me was that it was a word that I thought people would have a hard time remembering if they only saw it once. No sense making it easy for anyone to be able to identify your boat. ·

The *Kitnayakwa* was built in the shipyard on Chatham Street where I'd had my other boats built. The shipyard was about three blocks from the water. When each boat was ready to be launched, I had them put onto a truck and hauled to a dock and hoisted into the water with a derrick. When the *Kitnayakwa* was ready to go, I got permission to use the derrick at Naden, the Canadian Navy base in Esquimalt. This boat was bigger and heavier than the others and that derrick was the only one that I felt safe using.

I always enjoyed the launching process. I liked to ride with the boat as it was lowered into the water. I would have everything primed and ready to go. As soon as the slings were off, I would step on the starter, rev the engines and go. It was a big thrill to take that first ride in a new boat. There was always a feeling of anxiety mixed with the excitement of the moment. You never knew for sure whether the boat would perform the way you expected it to. For someone like me who was basically untrained, there was always a good deal of anticipation involved. But I must say, my designs never let me down.

With those two Liberties in her the *Kitnayakwa* was a real powerhouse! Even at idle those big four hundred-horsepower engines fairly rumbled. With this boat I put the exhaust under the water to keep it quieter. There was no starting exhaust above the water, so once in awhile the expansion chamber would get filled up with fumes if the engine didn't catch right away. The expansion chambers on the exhaust were made out of twenty-gallon tanks. When the engine did start, those gases would explode—you could feel the boat bounce up about two inches! Sometimes I worried that those tanks would explode!

I bought all my propellers from Coolidge Propellers in Seattle. As I said before, I went through a lot of them, so I got them right from the factory. Coolidge had been making only one type of prop for quite awhile. Then, shortly after I built the *Kitnayakwa*, he started producing another model. He claimed they could get more power on tug boats with it. I decided to get a set to try them out.

I put them on the *Kitnayakwa* and took it out for a run in the harbour. Up to about twenty knots the new props seemed to be more effective than the old ones. But when I opened up the throttles, all of a sudden the boat lost speed. I gave it more power still, but it would not go any faster.

. I came back in and put the *Kitnayakwa* up on the ways. I was kind of shocked by what I saw. The blades on the propellers, which were far narrower than normal, were all bent right forward. They were simply not strong enough to stand the power of the Liberty engines. On the tugs I guess the blades were far bigger in proportion to the power of the engines than the ones I had bought. Anyway, that was the end of that experiment. I soon had the old blades back on.

On one of the first trips that we made with the *Kitnayakwa,* the guys who were supposed to pick up the load did not show up.

The rendezvous point was at a wharf down about seven miles south of Seattle. I really didn't want to haul that load all the way home and then back again. I was delivering to one of my regular customers, so I was quite sure that the delivery would still be made. Something must have come up that caused them to miss the pickup, that's all. Billy and I sat around down there until almost dawn, but still nobody showed up.

Finally I made up my mind to cache the load under the wharf there. The place was used a lot during the day, but I was counting on nobody looking too closely underneath it. The tide was quite low when we were there so we simply dropped the sacks into about six feet of water under the wharf. I knew the tide would not drop too much farther. I figured that that was the best I could do.

By the time we had done all of this and were heading home, it was broad daylight. We were coming up alongside Whidbey Island just above Bush Point when I spotted one of the Coast Guard's fast cutters heading down the sound from the north. His course was a little nearer the shore than the one I was on, so I decided just to hold steady and see what happened. When the cutter got within about a mile of the *Kitnayakwa*, they must have recognized us, because they suddenly turned to try and cut us off. As soon as that happened, of course, I changed course and opened up the throttles. I set out diagonally across the channel for Port Townsend. When I did that they let us have a blast from the one-pounder mounted on the foredeck. First we could see the puff of smoke from the gun as they fired; then we'd hear the shot. But they didn't come anywhere near hitting us. Maybe they were just firing warning shots; we didn't stay around to ask. They took four or five shots, but we were soon well out of range.

When we got to the other side of the channel near Port Townsend, another cutter was heading out to meet us. We were again able to swerve out and around it. Those big cutters were the fastest thing the Coast Guard had, but they could still only do about seventeen knots. Empty like she was that morning, the Kitnayakwa could do almost forty! It must have been frustrating for the crews on those boats. I knew that they wanted to get me in the worst way. I had heard from some of the Customs people on the Canadian side that there was a special reward out for me. I hated to disappoint them. There were plenty of other people in the rumrunning that they could pick on, though, so I didn't feel too badly.

When we got back to Victoria that morning, I bought Billy a ticket on the CPR boat and he headed straight down to Seattle. He showed the customer where the liquor was stashed under that wharf and picked up our money.

By this stage of Prohibition the Coast Guard and the federal agents were getting pretty serious about trying to stop the rumrunning. In looking back at those times, I'm always amazed that more people weren't killed. The cutters might give you one warning shot over the bows, but if you didn't stop then, they were shooting to disable the boat—or her crew! I'd heard that some of the fellows in the rumrunning down in the Seattle area were putting a bulletproof steel plate in the back of the pilothouse on their boats.

The steel was only one-sixteenth of an inch thick and was quite malleable. It didn't look very tough. One of the fellows who first installed some on his boat didn't think it looked like it would stop a bullet, so he took a shot at it with a 30-30 rifle. The bullet passed right through the metal like it was paper. Next they tried several thicknesses of the steel. But the bullet still passed right through. Finally they contacted the company that they had bought it from and discovered that the steel wasn't bulletproof until it was tempered. It was soft so you could mould it to the shape you needed, then you had to give it the heat treatment to toughen it. After they did that, the 30-30 only made a slight dent in the steel.

I thought about putting bulletproof steel in the *Kitnayakwa,* but I never quite got around to it. I used to stack a row of sacks of liquor up against the back of the pilothouse to deflect any stray bullets. But I was eventually to find out that liquor, glass and gunny sack did very little to slow them down.

I had made several deliveries to a fellow about halfway down Discovery Bay on the west side of Quimper Peninsula. Art was a nice enough guy, but he was really nervous. The whole time that we would be unloading, the guy would be worrying and fretting that we were going to be caught. The dropoff point that we were using was on a pretty deserted stretch of beach and seemed safe enough. The biggest threat, of course, was the fact that we were a couple of miles into a fairly enclosed bay and there was only one way out. When he handed me the payment for a load of liquor one night, Art told me his plan.

"Listen, I've got a connection in the Coast Guard," he said. "I can arrange it so they will not be anywhere around this area when you come in."

"Right." I answered. "You just go ahead and do that. And then you find someone else to deliver your liquor for you. You won't catch me making any deliveries anywhere when the Coast Guard knows that I'm coming. I don't care what kind of connections you've got! I'd rather take my chances on my own."

And that was the end of it as far as I was concerned. Art told me that he saw my point and wouldn't try to buy the Coast Guard off. But he lied.

The fool went ahead and paid someone to make sure that the cutters were not in the area of Discovery Bay when I came in with my next load. (At least that's what he tried to tell me later. It was either that or he was involved in a double-cross and was going to get cut in on the reward money they were offering for me. I never did find out which.)

In any event we came into Discovery Bay at about 11:30 p.m. on a very dark night in December. The cloud cover was thick and black and visibility was very limited. We were idling along at about four knots. I had my head and shoulders out the hatch in the top of the wheelhouse. I was keeping a very keen eye out just because the night was so black. We were fairly close to shore and I knew that, with the dark background of the forest that grew right down to the beach, something could get very close to us before I would see it. We were approaching our landing spot when, turning to look behind the boat, I was surprised to see what looked like a fire on the beach. I picked up the night glasses which were lying beside me on the roof of the pilothouse. I turned and had another look towards the fire.

What a shock I got when my eyes adjusted to the night glasses! I saw that what looked like a fire on the beach was in fact the phosphorescence of the bow swell of a Coast Guard cutter that was not much more than a hundred feet behind me! The night was so dark that without the glasses I couldn't see the boat at all. It was funny the way the phosphorescence in the water was the only thing that gave the boat away. And it was only churned up when the boat started to move at speed. It was amazing the way the phosphorescence looked from a distance. This was the second time I'd almost been fooled by it. Without the night glasses you could not tell what it was. With the naked eye it really did look just like a fire on the beach.

But I had no time to admire the wonders of Mother Nature! I hit the throttles and the *Kitnayakwa* flew ahead. The Coast Guard crew was ready for me, though. As soon as they saw the white water churned up by those Liberty engines, they opened fire on us with their machine gun. I quickly ducked down into the pilothouse and shouted to Tom to stay low. Then all hell broke loose!

Tom and I were crouched low—I had my head just high enough to see out the front window, though there wasn't much to see. Those machine guns were loaded with a tracer bullet every fifth or sixth shell so the marksman could tell where he was firing. Tom and I were facing each other, our heads not more than two feet apart, when one of those damn tracers went right between our noses! I'll tell you that for a second there neither one of us knew whether to faint or go blind! I can still close my eyes and see the orangey-red streak as that bullet passed inches from my face. I was looking right into Tom's eyes—and he into mine—and there was no confusion about what I saw there.

But that tracer missed us and buried itself in the bulkhead forward of the wheelhouse. And the sounds of other bullets flying all around us, and the rush of the *Kitnayakwa* through the water in the pitch black night didn't leave any time for reverie. We could see the glow where the tracer had lodged in the bulkhead, and Tom, fearing the boat would catch fire, jumped down and dug it out with his pocket knife. (As soon as he had it in his hand he realized that it was only phosphorescent and posed no danger.)

I knew that I would have no trouble outrunning the cutter; the problem was that I was pointed toward the head of the bay. If I kept on, they would very shortly have me trapped. I had to change course and do so fast. I climbed up on the box and stuck my head out of the hatch again. At that speed I needed to be able to see as much as possible. All of this took place in very rapid succession. Perhaps only thirty seconds had passed since I'd spotted the cutter. But they sure hadn't let up on the firing! Between bursts from the machine gun, I swung the wheel over as hard as I could and brought the boat around in a tight half circle. Before they knew what was going on, I was screaming down on the Coast Guard cutter at thirty knots. I flashed past them within a hundred feet. This time it was their turn to be surprised!

When the waves from the *Kitnayakwa* hit the cutter, I was treated to a marvellous sight. The marksman on the machine gun continued to fire at us, but he was being tossed around pretty good. Those tracer bullets were going everywhere but where they were aimed—some straight up into the dark sky, some down into the sea right near the cutter. It was such a funny sight that I called to Tom to come and have a look.

By the time they got their big boat turned around, we were well out of range of their guns. But it turned out that our troubles weren't over yet. The Coast Guard had reinforcements waiting for us further down the inlet. I counted five more cutters before we reached open waters. Each of them was hidden as long as they stayed close to shore and at slow speed. But as soon as they moved out of the blackness of the shoreline and picked up speed, I could see their bow swell and had little difficulty in avoiding the rest of them in the more open waters toward the mouth of the bay. It looked to me like they had planned a well-organized ambush. We were able to escape only because we had so much more speed than the cutters. Long live Liberty engines!

I knew there was also a good deal of luck involved in our escape that night. I'm sure the Coast Guard must have felt that they had us for sure. But I just had too much speed for them to ever catch me when the *Kitnayakwa* was fired up. I was just very lucky that I had spotted them when I did. If they had waited to come in on us until after we'd dropped the anchor, we would have been goners. And of course if they had ever scored a direct hit with the one-pound gun, I expect that the boat would have been disabled. But that never happened. And I guess you'd have to say that we were pretty lucky that night that neither Tom or I was hit by fire from the machine gun they were pounding us with. We kept that tracer bullet around for a long time! It became kind of like a good luck charm for the boat.

On the way back to Victoria we stopped and cached the load of liquor on D'Arcy Island. There were quite a number of broken bottles in that load. Whisky, glass and gunny sack are not too good at stopping bullets. Once back in the harbour I took the *Kitnayakwa* straight over to the float at Foster's. We put it up on the ways as soon as Bert arrived in the morning. I found eighteen bullet holes in the hull and cabin housing, and spent a busy morning drilling them all out with a one-inch auger and banging in wooden plugs. By eleven o'clock I had the holes patched and painted, and the boat back at Raymond's Wharf.

And lucky I did! About two that afternoon a Customs officer showed up. He had a good look at the hull. He didn't say exactly what he was looking for, and he didn't come on board, but he had a real close look at the stern and the side of the hull that was showing alongside the wharf. I knew very well what he was looking for, but I just played dumb and didn't say a word. Of course, there were no bullet holes to be found. (The Americans must have sent the word over, figuring that, even though they failed to get me in their well-planned trap, they could arrest me on the circumstantial evidence of the bullet holes in the hull of the *Kitnayakwa*. I hated to disappoint them again!)

And the funniest thing of all was that Art, the bootlegger who had likely set me up, had the nerve to come over from Washington a week or two later and ask me to make another run for him. He claimed that there had been some kind of a mistake and that it would never happen again! I told him that he was right about that. There had been a mistake all right! I had made a big mistake in agreeing to deliver the last load. But I sure as hell wasn't going to do it again! I told him to go to hell!

During the racing season I used to spend a good deal of time out at the Willows Fair Grounds and Race Track with some of my friends. I was never a heavy gambler—I would just place two-dollar bets—but it was a nice place to pass a sunny afternoon and a good spot to meet your friends. We'd either drive out or catch a 'jitney' out from town. (Some enterprising people offered rides out to the fair grounds for five cents. They were using mostly Ford cars; I don't think they were licensed or anything. They just picked up anyone who was willing to pay. We used to catch a ride right downtown on Government Street by the Post Office.)

I first met my first wife out at the race track. I ran into a friend of mine who happened to be with two girls. One was his girlfriend; the other was Pearl Bromley. I spent the afternoon with the three of them and we had a good time. After that I began to take Pearl out to dinner and dancing from time to time.

I found out that she was married and had a five-year-old daughter. She had been separated from her husband for about a year and was in the process of getting a divorce. She told me that she'd had a fair amount of trouble from her husband and that she'd really be glad when it was all over with. Pearl and I seemed to enjoy each other's company, and we started to see a lot of each other.

One evening Tom Colley and I were walking down the Causeway towards the Parliament Buildings, heading down to Raymond's Wharf, I think. Just as we turned the corner on Belleville Street, a man approached us and started calling me every name in the book. He was kind of a rough-looking fellow, quite a bit bigger than me. He told me that I had better stop going out with his wife, and began to talk about what was likely to happen to me if I didn't.

I didn't say anything at first. I just put my hands in my pockets and stood there as if I had all the time in the world, and was enjoying listening to his little speech. (When I did this Tom walked off a little ways down the street. He had seen me do it before.) When the guy seemed to be finished what he had planned to say, I started in on him. I took my turn at calling him all kinds of derogatory names, all the while just standing there with my hands in my pockets. I was hoping to provoke him into a fight. I was mad as hell, but I'd learned a long time ago never to show that. Instead I tried to show that I was as unconcerned as could be. I wanted the guy to take the first punch at me; then I'd let him have it. Trouble was, this fellow wouldn't fight. I guess he didn't expect me to go at him like I did, because after I was finished calling him every name that I knew, he just turned around and walked away.

When I caught up with Tom, he was laughing.

"I knew what was going to happen as soon as you put your hands in your pockets," he said.

Tom had seen me get into one or two fights before, and I had done the same thing. He'd been with me up in Ocean Falls when I had fought with the Japanese on the docks. Because I knew how to box from my youth and my army days, I always let the other fellow have the first punch. He seldom hit me with it, but I liked to let him try at least. I was very quick and I'd usually hit the guy five or six times before he knew he was actually in a fight and then he'd want to think about quitting. People always misjudged me because I was small.

Anyway, that was the last I saw or heard from Pearl's husband.

Eventually Pearl got her divorce, and we got married. We went down to Tacoma, where Pearl had a brother and some friends living.

We were married just before Christmas in 1927 in the Masonic Hall there. Mr. and Mrs. Bates, Pearl's friends, stood up for us.

For our honeymoon we drove down to Mexico. I had an Auborn car then. We took our time going down and looked at the sights in California. In all we were six days driving down and only three coming back. On the way back we stayed over in Tacoma with Pearl's brother for a couple of days.

Back in Victoria we stayed with Pearl's mother and father for a few weeks while we looked for a place of our own. We finally rented a house on St. Patrick Street in Oak Bay. We lived there for about two years.

Things were going pretty well for me in the rumrunning during this time. I was making good money, and didn't have too many close calls with the Coast Guard or the weather. I was always spending lots of money keeping the boat in top shape, but I was still able to put some away. After we had been living on St. Patrick Street for a year or so, we began to think about building a house of our own. We started looking around for a suitable lot. I naturally wanted to be close to the water.

One day we went driving out Cadboro Bay Road and ended up in the Ten Mile Point area. I noticed that there were lots for sale in what was known as the Queenswood subdivision. This was considered to be a long way out of town by most people. None of the lots seemed to have "Sold" signs on them yet. One end of the subdivision was very near Telegraph Cove, which offered a fairly protected anchorage except from the north winds that blew in the wintertime. I was immediately interested in this because I thought it would be nice to be able to moor my boat so close to home.

The next day we called the real estate agent. We went back out there with him and he showed us several lots. I picked the one that was closest to Telegraph Cove. The agent gave us $200 off the price of that lot because we were the first to buy in the subdivision. As soon as we had completed the deal, I began to clear some of the land and made arrangements to have a house built.

I designed the house myself with the idea that there would be lots of space where we could entertain our friends. The entry was on the eastern side, facing the ocean. There were several steps up to a porch and the front door. Off the entrance hall was a large

living room with a bay window and fireplace. Two crystal chande-
liers graced the ceiling. On the south side, folding glass doors led
to a sunroom. At the western end of the living room, two more
glass doors opened into the dining room, which also had a chan-
delier as a centrepiece. Double glass doors also led from the
dining room to the sunroom. My idea was that when all of the
doors were opened there was enough space to entertain a large
group of people. At the time it was fashionable to be able to dance
from one room to another. The way our house was laid out, we
could open the three rooms up for dancing.

The master bedroom, bathroom and kitchen were also on the
main floor of the house. The upstairs had a bedroom for Pearl's
daughter Doreen and a sewing room for Pearl. (The sewing room
became a nursery before very long.)

I hired W. M. Sutton, a local contractor, to build the house. It
cost me $10,200 and was finished in the fall of 1931.

We were not handy to any public school, so Pearl decided to
send Doreen to St. Ann's Academy in town. She boarded at the
school with the nuns during the week and came home on weekends. She went there for two years and then transferred back to
public school because Pearl decided that there was too much em-
phasis on religion at the Academy.

Telegraph Bay Road went right down to the water. I was able to
moor the *Kitnayakwa* right in the cove and be only five hundred feet
from my home. I really enjoyed that aspect of living out there.

Not long after we moved in, I was cruising out around the
Chatham Islands when I found a great big red cedar log that was
about six feet across at the top and seven feet at the butt. Actually
what I found was only half of the original tree; it was split right
down the centre. It was twenty-four feet long and flat as a table on
top. I could see that it would make a dandy float, so I towed it
home to Telegraph Cove.

On the beach there I poured a concrete block about four feet
wide and eighteen inches thick and put a big iron bar in it. I took
twenty-five feet of logging chain and attached one end to the log and
one end to the concrete anchor. Then I hooked onto the other end of
the log with a tow rope and dragged the whole thing out into the bay
with the *Kitnayakwa*. I now had a good float to tie my boat to during
the summer. I had a small rowboat that I just left hauled up on the
beach that we used to get back and forth from the float.

I wouldn't moor the *Kitnayakwa* in Telegraph Cove for any length of time during the winter because there was no protection from the vicious north winds that blew at that time of year. By this time I was keeping the boat out at Canoe Cove next to Swartz Bay most of the time. But I would still tie up down in the harbour sometimes, and once in awhile I would anchor in Cadboro Bay, which was also close to home. I liked to move the boat around because then no one could look in one place and know whether or not I was out on a run. I always felt I was much better off when no one knew for sure where I was.

I think that one of the reasons why I was able to be so successful in avoiding getting caught in the rumrunning was the fact that I never spent any time talking about it. Some of the fellows who were in the trade got carried away with the romance of it and like to talk about the thrills and the close calls that they had. But as long as I was still working at it, I never talked about it much at all. There were plenty of people who knew what I did for a living—certainly all of my friends knew and lots of others besides—but I never talked about it.

As far as anyone who didn't know better was concerned, I was an American who had made some money in a land deal down in the States and come up to Canada to retire. That was the story that I used when the income tax people came after me. They didn't believe it any more than I did, but they had no way of proving otherwise at the time. I paid some taxes and they left me alone.

Pearl got pregnant not too long after we moved out to Queens-wood. When her time came and she started to go into labour, I drove her into the hospital. After they got her all settled in, she told me to go home. I would have been happy to stay with her, but she said that she didn't want me waiting around the hospital all night. I went home because I didn't want to upset her at that time. I waited at home for her to call.

The baby was born that night. Pearl phoned her mother to tell her the good news, but she didn't call me. The next morning when I went into the hospital to see how she was doing, I was surprised to see that we had a son. Later on I asked her why she hadn't called me. She said that she was mad at me because I didn't stay with her at the hospital. She was the one who had insisted that I go home! But I was supposed to know that she had really wanted me to stay! Most of what they say about pregnant women doing strange things is true.

Anyway, in spite of the fact that my wife was mad at me, I was a proud father. I went out and bought a bottle of champagne. I took it back down to the hospital to have a celebratory drink with the doctors and nurses. The bottle must have been shaken up pretty good when I was driving down there, because when I took the wire off the top, the cork exploded out of the neck of the bottle and hit me square in the right eyeball. That was quite a shock! Within a few seconds the whole of my eye was blood red. One of the nurses shone a flashlight into it and I could just barely see the light. She said that if I could see any light at all, I wouldn't be blind in that eye. But it was quite a few days before I could see anything. (That eye is almost completely blind now.)

Fortunately we lost very little of the champagne out of the bottle and, after all the excitement over my eye died down, we were able to drink a toast to our new son.

Unfortunately, after the birth of Johnny our marriage was never as good as it had been early on. Pearl had one characteristic that I could never get used to living with. Anytime that we had a disagreement, or if she got upset over something, she would stop talking to me completely. Sometimes she would carry this on for days. And sometimes I would not even know what it was that had upset her. And with her not talking to me, it would be very difficult for me to find out.

I was the kind of person who would say what I had on my mind. If I disagreed with what another person said, I would say so. But I was always willing to talk about it. But not Pearl. If she didn't get her own way sometimes she would just clam right up. Later on in our marriage it could be a week or ten days before she would talk to me again. It was ridiculous. She would send messages to me through Doreen or anyone else who happened to be around and she would expect me to do the same thing. Once near the end of the marriage there was a whole month when she would not talk to me. This went on even while we were living in the same house, eating at the same table and sleeping in the same bed. If there was something that I had to know, she would tell little Johnny to tell me, even if I happened to be right in the same room. I never did get used to that treatment.

STORMY WEATHER

I HAVE SAID that I built all of my boats with a low profile to make them as inconspicuous as possible. This was especially important for all the night running that we did. On the *Kitnayakwa*, just as on the *Miss Victoria II,* there was a hatch just above the steering wheel. I could stand on a box with my head and shoulders above the deck and have an unrestricted view to all sides. This was most handy as we approached our rendezvous points. I always felt safer being out in the open where I could see and hear as much as possible.

In front of the hatch I put a windshield of about twenty-four by sixteen inches to provide some protection from the wind and weather. Even at twenty knots, raindrops hit like bullets. That windshield was made of quarter-inch plate glass, but even that wouldn't stand up to the weather sometimes. I had to replace it more than once.

On one occasion when we were heading back across the Juan de Fuca Strait after delivering a load on Whidbey Island, the weather turned really nasty. Before long it was blowing at gale force from the southeast. The wind was almost directly behind us. To compound the problem the tide was running against the wind, and the seas got very big and very steep in no time at all. Suddenly a huge wave all but buried the boat. It washed right over the pilothouse, smashing the glass in the windshield like it was fine china. Naturally that wave washed right over me as well, soaking me to the bone and leaving two or three inches of water in the cabin.

On another trip the same thing happened; once again we got hammered by a following sea. That was one of the worst nights that I can remember as far as the weather was concerned. Unfortunately, it was also an occasion when I had planned to make two deliveries in one night from two different pickup points. The plan was that we were to make the first trip from Discovery Island over to Port Townsend. Then we would run back to pick up a second load from a seine boat at East Point on Saturna Island, and haul it over to Anacortes. In good weather it would have been a busy night, but we could have managed it easily.

When we headed out of the harbour in the late afternoon, there was no wind to speak of, only a slight swell from the southeast. We loaded up at Discovery about a half hour before dark, and were soon on our way across the strait.

We were only about thirty minutes out from Discovery when the wind started to pick up. And boy did it come up in a hurry! In another fifteen minutes or so we were in the midst of a gale—it was blowing at least sixty knots. And we were heading right out to meet it!

That was one of the roughest trips that I can ever remember! The wind was so strong that it was all I could do to keep the *Kitnayakwa* pointed in the right direction. The wind was gusting fiercely. The seas soon built up to tremendous size. Sometimes a gust would hit the boat while we were on the crest of a wave and you could feel her shudder right down to the keel—the battle between the elements and those Liberty engines seemed to be dead even.

I fought that storm all the way across the Strait of Juan de Fuca. The *Kitnayakwa* was a good boat; she proved that she was up to the challenge. As we approached our rendezvous point near the garbage dump just west of Port Townsend, the eastern tip of the Olympic Peninsula gave us some shelter.

But when we finally reached our destination, there was no one there to meet us. I couldn't figure out why. Because of the weather we were a little late getting there, but I knew that our connection would have expected that and waited. I wondered what could have happened. An hour and a half later I found out. When the party arrived, they were very surprised to find us there. They were sure that we wouldn't have been able to make it across the strait in those conditions. While driving up along the Hood Canal from Seattle, they'd had to stop several times while trees that had been blown down were cleared from the road. Sixty-mile-an-hour winds were wreaking havoc all along the peninsula.

Once we had the load ashore, there was nothing to do but start back for the Canadian side. If we hadn't arranged for that second load to be delivered, I would have waited the storm out along the coast for a few hours at least. I knew the Coast Guard wouldn't be out in that weather, that was for sure! But I also knew that there was a load waiting to be picked up at East Point, and I'd said that I would be there.

I found it hard to believe, but once we were back out in the open, it seemed that the wind had actually increased in strength. My God, but there was a sea running out there!

On the way back we were running before the storm. It was all that I could do just to steer the boat. The seas had built to fifteen-to-twenty feet high. It was a wild ride! I had to constantly use the power of the engines just to keep the *Kitnayakwa* out of trouble. The boat would get to the top of a wave and start down the other side. Then I would back right off on the throttles as she would surf along on the crest as the wave broke—sometimes we would go for what seemed like a quarter of a mile on one wave. Finally the wave would break out from underneath us and I'd have to power up to ensure that the following wave did not crash right over the stern. Then the *Kitnayakwa* would climb the back of the next wave and the process would start all over again.

About three-quarters of the way across the strait we got into an area where the tide-rips were standing the waves right on end. When you get an area where a strong tide is running against the direction of the wind, things can get pretty hairy. That night it was as wild as anything I'd ever seen. The tide-rips cause the waves to get much steeper than normal. They seemed to be straight up and down. You had to be really careful—if the boat got crosswise at all, it could easily broach, almost like falling off the crest of the wave.

The tide-rips would also cause the pattern of the waves to be very unpredictable—you never knew what was coming next. I had the *Kitnayakwa* under control, coasting down the front of one of those huge waves when suddenly a second swell broke out of the first wave. The boat had no time to lift and that wave simply rolled over her. Tons of water smashed down on top of us. The windshield in front of me was broken, and I was knocked right off the box I stood on. All of the windows in the pilothouse were also smashed and the cabin was flooded. Water was everywhere. Fortunately most of it ran down into the bow and not back into the engine compartment. Billy managed to get the pump in the forward cabin going quickly and soon had most of the water out of there. I fought to regain control of the boat. We were lucky that the engines weren't flooded and that neither of us was hurt. I had cut my fingers where I had been trying to hold onto the two-by-two at the edge of the hatch, but didn't even notice it until things had settled down. We were soaked through and cold, but the *Kitnayakwa* had sustained no permanent damage.

We battled our way north and eventually got some protection from the weather in the lee of the San Juan Islands. It was still only eleven o'clock when we arrived at East Point to pick up our second load, which was being brought down from Vancouver on a seine boat. I wasn't all that surprised when the boat was not there to meet us. The Strait of Georgia would be a hell in this wind as well.

There was nothing to do but wait. And waiting proved to be no fun at all. We were wet and cold. Everything in the boat was soaked, and the little stove in the galley was totally inadequate for drying anything out. I kept hoping that the load would show up, so that we could get on our way. I would have delivered it that night if it had arrived. The crossing from East Point to Anacortes is mostly through waters sheltered by the San Juans.

Finally we tired of sitting shivering in the damp boat. There was a fellow who lived in the bay there and we tied the *Kitnayakwa* up to his float and went up to the house. He didn't seem to mind being imposed upon in the middle of the night—I guess he didn't get too many visitors. He gave us some clothes to put on while ours were drying in front of a roaring fire. We sat huddled around the fireplace until we were warmed, and had a cup of tea and a chat with our host. In a couple of hours our clothing was dry, and, turning down the fellow's offer to spend the night, we went back down to the *Kitnayakwa*. Once we were back on board, however, I immediately regretted my decision to leave the comfort of that house. The little stove could not compete with that big fireplace, and we were soon feeling the chill again. But I didn't want to miss our connection if they did show up.

As it turned out, we would have been better off to have looked after our own comfort. The seiner didn't arrive at East Point until four o'clock the next afternoon. By then at least we had the boat pretty well dried out.

The crew of the seiner had had a terrible crossing from Vancouver to Porlier Pass, bucking the southeaster all the way across the Strait of Georgia. They said they were taking water over the bow the whole trip. After a six-hour crossing they decided that they'd had enough for one night, and tied up at a fish camp in the pass. They were sure that we wouldn't have made it to East Point either. At first they didn't want to believe that we had been there waiting the night before. When they had a good look at the smashed windshield and windows in the pilothouse, though, they could see what we'd been through. What they didn't realize was the fact that I was used to running at night and in bad weather!

We transferred the load of liquor to the *Kitnayakwa,* and, as soon as it was dark, headed across to Anacortes. The previous night's storm was only a memory now, and the seas were calm. Even so, the crossing was colder than usual due to the fact that we had no windows in the pilothouse. Still it wasn't so bad; by midnight we were back at Canoe Cove, very much looking forward to the warmth and comfort of our own beds.

Winter was the busy time in the rumrunning. During the summer months I took it pretty easy. We used to spend at least part of the summer up at Sproat Lake. We eventually bought a lot on the lake, which was just north of Port Alberni and about one hundred and forty miles from Victoria.

Pearl and I first went up to Sproat Lake shortly after we were married. We stayed at Klitsa Lodge, which was owned and operated by Mrs. Wark, who was one of the daughters of Victoria pioneer John Wark and his Indian wife, Josette. The lodge was built about halfway out on a long point that jutted into the lake. From the lodge there was a magnificent view both up and down Sproat Lake.

Most of the guests at Klitsa Lodge were people with lots of money who were looking for a place to get away from everything. The lodge was only accessible by boat and there was no telephone, so no one could get in touch with anyone once they were there. Many Americans from all over the United States were regular guests. One of the Vanderbilts stayed at the lodge one summer before I started going up there. He liked the area so much that he bought a small island that sat about a quarter of a mile from the end of the point that Klitsa was on. He built a good-sized house right on the top of the island, and had an electric power plant installed and everything. He only came up once or twice a year, but kept a caretaker there the year round.

The second year that we went up to Sproat Lake we stayed in one of the cabins that Mrs. Wark had built at the north end of the lake. We rented a boat and did a lot of fishing. We could always catch eight or ten nice trout in two or three hours of trolling up there. It was a very peaceful spot.

One day that summer I was talking to the manager who worked for Mrs. Wark. I suggested to him that they should have a speedboat for transporting guests, and for getting supplies to the lodge. At the time they only had small boats that were very slow and really only good for fishing. The manager agreed with me, and told me that he'd been trying to convince Mrs. Wark to buy a faster boat, but had been unsuccessful so far.

During the next winter back in Victoria I built a twenty-foot runabout and put a forty-horsepower Ford engine in it. When we went back up to Sproat Lake the next summer, I shipped the boat to Port Alberni on the CPR boat *Maquinna*. I met the ship with a trailer and hauled the boat the rest of the way out to the lake.

That summer we again stayed in one of the cabins at the head of the lake. We went fishing and running about. When we visited the lodge, I didn't say a word about selling the boat to Mrs. Wark, but I did talk to her manager about it. He told me he'd been telling her how handy that boat would be for the lodge.

The night before we were to head home we were at the lodge for dinner. During the course of the meal Mrs. Wark asked me what I planned to do with my speedboat.

"Oh, I guess I'll just haul it back to Victoria," I said.

After dinner Mrs. Wark asked me if I would stop by her office before I left. I knew just what she wanted to see me about. As soon as we were alone, she mentioned that she would like to buy the boat. I told her the price that I wanted and she agreed to it right away. And that was that. Both Mrs. Wark and her manager were very happy with that little boat.

Mrs. Wark didn't mind paying for something that she really

wanted. Just after we were married, I had bought a fox fur for Pearl at Mrs. Foster's Furs on Yates Street in Victoria. It had cost me ninety dollars and was a real beauty. For some reason or other Pearl had worn the fur up at Sproat Lake—it must have been a really cold day. Anyway, Mrs. Wark fell in love with that fur. She wanted to buy it in the worst way. But neither Pearl nor I wanted to sell it.

About halfway up Sproat Lake on the north shore there was an area that had been surveyed for a town site. There were twelve lots altogether and Mrs. Wark had bought them all. The road wasn't in yet, but when it went in, it was to pass right behind those lots.

Mrs. Wark wanted that fox fur so badly that she finally got around to offering us our pick of the lots in exchange for the fur. Well, that was an offer that we just couldn't refuse! We looked the lots over and made the trade for the biggest and best lot. It had over two hundred feet of waterfront and a really nice beach. There were small cedar trees growing all over the lot, with a lot of large firs at the back. It was just like a park and very beautiful. I think we did all right on that trade.

The next summer I bought one of the bunkhouses from a logging camp that was closing down on the lake, and moved that onto the property. We hauled it up above the high-water mark, put some partitions in it, and soon had a nice little summer cabin. It had two bedrooms and a large kitchen/living room area. I ran a pipe to a creek that was nearby and we had running water as well. I built a little twelve-foot boat and put a sixteen-horsepower outboard engine on it and we used that to get to our cabin and for fishing and running around.

We had a lot of good times up at Sproat Lake. We asked various friends up to visit at different times. Joe Fleming, Charlie Bright, and Carl Melby and his wife from Seattle all came to stay with us at one time or another.

Melby and his wife came up with us for a couple of weeks in the fall one time. Carl and I wanted to do some deer hunting. At this time our cabin was not yet fixed up, so we stayed at the Klitsa Lodge. It was nice not to have to worry about preparing our own meals or anything.

One morning all four of us went across the lake to an area where we thought we would pick up a deer. After hunting all morning without seeing anything, we stopped for lunch beside the lake. After I'd eaten I took a shot at a knot of wood that was sticking out of a log that was just beneath the water about a hundred feet offshore. Just the knot stuck out of the water. I was firing a 32-20 rifle. I hit the knot on the first shot and just missed it with the second.

"Here, you have a shot," I said to Carl's wife, handing her the gun.

"I wouldn't even know how to shoot," she laughed. "I've never shot a gun in my life!"

But she seemed like she wanted to try it, so I showed her how to sight and fire the gun. Needless to say we were all surprised when she hit the target with her first shot. We were even more impressed when she shot twice more and never missed! That Mrs. Melby was quite a shot! She shot several more times and never did miss that knot of wood. She thought it was great fun!

When she went back to Seattle, Mrs. Melby started going to the shooting galleries that were quite popular then. She was soon winning all the darned prizes they had. In a couple of weeks they barred her and wouldn't let her shoot anymore.

Mrs. Melby was as nice a women as you'd ever want to meet. She was good looking and had a very outgoing personality and was friendly with just about everybody she met. On top of that she could outdrink anybody that I knew. And you could never tell when she had been drinking. Her speech never slurred and she never got loud and abusive the way some people do. The only way you could tell that she had been drinking was that her face became more flushed, the more she drank.

Carl's wife had a great sense of humour and did some pretty funny things at times. I remember the story about when she and her husband and Pete Peterson were up in Victoria staying at the Empress Hotel. It seems they had decided to eat in their room and had just sat down to dinner. Peterson was sitting at one end of the table and Mrs. Melby was at the other. Carl was sitting between the two.

"Pete, I don't care much for this dinner, do you?" Mrs. Melby said to her brother.

"No, I don't like it either," Pete replied.

Without another word they both stood up and each gathered the corners of the tablecloth, lifted the whole thing up off the table and took the bundle and tossed it out the door of their room into the hallway. Then they phoned room service to order a new dinner! Peterson and his sister made quite a pair! They always seemed to know exactly what the other one was going to do. And when they had been drinking, they were apt to do just about anything!

Another time they were all staying at the Hotel Georgia in Vancouver at the same time that the Prince of Wales was in town. The Prince and his entourage were staying at the Georgia as well. Carl and his wife had ten or twelve cases of liquor in their room and were having quite a little party. I think it was New Year's Eve. It wasn't long before everyone in the hotel knew where the party was and was heading for the Melbys' room. Even the Prince of Wales heard about it. Somehow or other he managed to slip away from his guards and make his way to the party. He was there for about four hours before they found him. He was having a wonderful time. But I'm sure that some of the people who were supposed to be watching out for him were in a bit of a panic for awhile.

Carl Melby and his wife were good people. I always enjoyed my association with them. Carl was a good guy to do business with and was a lot of fun to be around.

FIRE!

I KEPT THE *Kitnayakwa* anchored in Cadboro Bay from time to time during the winter months. The anchorage was much more protected than Telegraph Cove, and it was still quite close to home. It was also handy to Discovery Island where we normally took on our cargoes.

One miserable night after we had delivered a load in a gale, Billy and I stopped at Discovery to see Joe Fleming about some business or other. It had been a rough crossing and we were both looking forward to a hot cup of coffee at Joe's before finishing the run to Cadboro Bay. I was also hoping that the wind might drop off while we were ashore.

We spent about three-quarters of an hour with Joe, but the weather didn't improve any. When we left the island, it was still blowing pretty good and the seas were rough. Then about halfway across to the anchorage in Cadboro Bay, the engine died. I soon discovered that the gas line was plugged. The line was mounted right at the front of the engine room on the side of the bulkhead. I quickly uncoupled a section of the line and cleaned out the copper pipe that supplied gasoline to the engine. All the while we were being tossed about in the heavy seas, and I ended up with gas all over my right hand. At the time I thought nothing of it.

Then, as I was putting the section of gas line back together, disaster struck. I was just tightening the last coupling when the wrench slipped out of my hand. The darn thing flipped into the air and bounced off the bulkhead, where it hit two electrical contacts on the ammeter. A spark flashed! In an instant the spilled gasoline burst into flames. My whole right hand was ablaze!

I jumped out of the engine room and up into the pilothouse. Billy saw immediately what was going on, grabbed a coat from the wall, and wrapped it around my arm to smother the fire. Then unfortunately, in our haste to get at the fire in the engine room, we took the coat off my hand too soon. It burst into flames again. We quickly wrapped it up once more.

As soon as we had the fire out on my hand, we stamped out the flames that were burning on the floor of the engine room. The fire hadn't had a chance to get established—it was still just the spilled gasoline that was burning—so we were able to extinguish it easily enough.

At first I didn't even feel the burn on my hand. I guess I was in shock because it was pretty well fried—the skin was hanging loose all over it. I managed to get the engine started and we were on our way before I began to feel the effects of my injury. I suddenly felt dizzy and weak and thought I was going to pass out. I told Billy to take the wheel, and sat down in the corner of the pilothouse for awhile. After a few minutes my head cleared. I was able to take the boat in to where I anchored it in Cadboro Bay.

But by the time we were anchored and headed into shore in the skiff, my hand really began to throb. I soon knew that I was burned badly! Boy, did that ever hurt!

That was one of the most painful things I ever went through. Dr. Kinning, who was a distant relative of my wife, treated my hand with tannic acid. He wrapped the hand in bandages and I kept them soaked with the tannic-acid solution. That was the only way I could get any relief from the pain. At night I'd just get to sleep and then the solution would dry and the hand would start to feel just like it was on fire again. I'd have to get up and soak it again. This went on for two or three days before the pain began to ease up at all.

The hand was burned quite deeply in some places. I guess the fire burned right down into the skin because the gasoline had had time to soak in. It was several weeks before those spots began to heal. Pretty near all of the skin from the wrist down came off.

It was while I had the *Kitnayakwa* that I decided it would be a good idea to have a smaller boat for fishing and running about. The rumrunners simply burned too much gasoline with those big Liberty engines. I designed a speedboat that was twenty-two feet long with a V-bottomed hull. I put a Hall-Scott two hundred-horsepower airplane engine in it. I called the boat *Pearl* after my wife.

I was never really satisfied with the *Pearl*, though. It was the only boat that I ever built that I was disappointed with. That was the only time I ever made a mistake in choosing the correct propeller for a boat. Even though it had lots of power for its size, the *Pearl* just would not plane. I felt sure that the propeller was a little too big. The motor would not turn up to the speed that it should. The trouble was I never seemed to find the time to change the propeller. I kept the boat down in the harbour and never did take it out to Telegraph Cove. I wanted to get it running right before I took it around.

Anyway, as it turned out, I did not have the boat long enough to get it running the way I wanted it. One day an American fellow who was in town was hanging around Raymond's Wharf and saw the boat. He wanted to buy it right away. Partly because I wasn't happy with the way it ran, I didn't have much problem giving that boat up. I sold it to him just the way it was.

Maybe the *Pearl* was jinxed right from the start, because the fellow I sold her to didn't have her for too long either. Although, in his case I'd have to put the problem down to his own stupidity rather than anything that was wrong with the boat. Naturally, he wanted the boat for rumrunning—it was small, but there were a lot of fellows into the business in a small way. But this guy went and put a four hundred fifty-horsepower Liberty engine in that little boat! I guess it would do about forty knots, but there was no way that boat was built for that much power.

One day he was carrying a load of liquor from Discovery Island down to Everett. He went through Deception Pass and then down behind Whidbey Island to his delivery point. The wind started to pick up. Pretty soon there was a real gale blowing right into his face. And the darn fool didn't have the sense to slow down. He ran that boat full speed right into the teeth of that gale. The waves were coming straight at him and he was just jumping the boat from the top of one wave to the next. Without knowing it, he soon pounded all of the caulking out of the seams in the hull. And pretty soon the *Pearl* started to fill with water. As soon as he realized that the boat was sinking, the fellow headed straight for shore—he wasn't completely stupid—but he didn't quite make it. He had to swim the last hundred yards or so.

What a darn fool thing to do! I never could understand anybody who would not have the sense to slow a boat down when they got into a rough spot. That fellow really took the cake, though! Not only was he stupid enough to lose his boat and cargo that way, but then he came back to Victoria and told me about it! He told me that he'd figured it did not jar him as much when he was running the boat at full speed! I don't know whether he expected sympathy from me or what! He didn't get any, that's for sure.

Anyway, that was the end of the *Pearl*.

I didn't use the *Kitnayakwa* only for rumrunning. One fall I decided to go on a hunting trip up to the area around Bute Inlet where my brothers and I had trapped before the war. Billy Garrard and Joe Fleming went with me. We left Victoria at eight o'clock in the morning and were at Fawn Bluff, about seven miles up Bute Inlet, by four that afternoon. The bay behind Fawn Bluff provided one of the only safe anchorages in the inlet if the weather turned nasty.

I knew the area well from the years I had spent hunting and trapping there with my brothers. August still lived further up the inlet. I stopped at Fawn Bluff to visit with Henry Leask and his two brothers.

The Leasks had quite a little place there. There were carefully built rock walls for a walkway around the beach and out to the point. There was a net shed built on a rock foundation out in the middle of the bay, well above the level of the highest tides. The brothers had run about three-quarters of a mile of large, wooden pipe back to a lake that lay behind the bluff. They used the water pressure it created to operate a water wheel that they had designed and built. They were planning to use the power generated to run a small sawmill. They had also built a stone kiln, and had poured a large piece of glass that they were carefully grinding into a lens for a telescope that they were making. The Leasks were well-educated men and were very interesting to talk to. It was kind of unusual to find such development out in the middle of the wilderness like that.

Late that afternoon I went hunting on the hill behind the house, and in about an hour I had a nice two-point buck. I left a good portion of the meat from that animal with the Leasks.

The next morning we continued on our way to August's homestead, about fifteen miles from the head of the forty-mile-long inlet. The bay where my brother had his home was the only place in the upper part of the inlet that gave safe anchorage in a north wind. Bute Inlet has a well deserved reputation for being a dangerous place to be caught in a norther. In the winter the wind can blow at a savage rate, sometimes for three or four weeks at a time. The locals call a norther a "Bute," and with good reason.

In the bay August had cleared a nice little area. His house and garden sat in the middle surrounded by fruit trees. Beyond that there was a long building which housed about five hundred rabbits which he raised for hides and some meat. The skins sold for five cents each. August always had some wild animals around as well. He liked to trap and keep a number of wild animals. There were twelve marten, several mink, a weasel, and a squirrel that was running around loose. Later on, he even had a couple of cougar as pets.

When we arrived we did not find August at home. His wife told us that he was up around the Southgate River at the head of the inlet. We left the rest of the meat from the deer I had shot the day before with August's wife, and continued on to see if we could find my brother.

When we got to the mouth of the Southgate, I decided to head up the river aways. I figured I knew the channel well enough to stay out of any trouble. But I was wrong. The river had changed quite a bit. A logging company had been working upstream and there were a lot of deadheads in the channel. We didn't get very far before we hit a sunken log and bent one shaft and propeller.

We hung around the mouth of the Southgate for a few days, but we never did run into August. I showed Joe and Billy the countryside. But I knew my brother well enough to know that there was no way of predicting when he would show up, so eventually we headed back down the inlet. One of the reasons that August lived up in that part of the country was that he liked to go out and roam around on his own. He might be gone a day, but he might just as likely be gone a week.

I went back to Fawn Bluff running on one engine. The Leasks had a rack of a ways on the beach that was big enough for the *Kitnayakwa*. I put the boat on it at high tide and when the tide went out, I was able to get underneath to work on her. It turned out that there wasn't too much that I could do. The shaft was bent and there was no way I could straighten it. About all I could do was take a hacksaw and cut the shaft off close to where it came through the hull so that we didn't have the propeller dragging anymore.

From Fawn Bluff we ran over to Duncan Bay on the east side of Vancouver Island. We stopped to do some hunting on the flats there, but it turned out to be a terrible place to try to hunt. It was an area that had been logged off. It had become so overgrown with bracken that you wouldn't have been able to see a deer if it was twenty feet away. There were all kinds of trails through the brush, so we knew that there was game around, but the ferns had simply grown too high to see over. I never did like to hunt on the flat anyway, preferring to hike up and down the hills.

After that we went up to Menzies Bay to have a look around. The logging camp that had been there when I was in the area with my brothers had moved out. But the place was just alive with deer. We all went out separately in the afternoon. I saw twelve or fourteen, but they were all does or fawns. Billy and Joe each saw lots of deer too, but they didn't see any bucks either.

The second day we again set off separately, and again I had the same luck. I saw plenty of deer, but no bucks. Late in the afternoon I was working my way along a sidehill that eventually led into a canyon. There was a lot of second-growth fir, about a foot to a foot-and-a-half in diameter growing in the bottom of it. I stopped when the sidehill became too steep and was looking down into the canyon when I spotted what looked like a small fawn in the shadows at the bottom of the hill about one hundred and fifty yards away. I sat down on the ridge to watch the small deer, which looked like it might weigh about fifty pounds. The animal crossed the flat and started up the hillside on the far side of the canyon. All of a sudden I couldn't believe my eyes! I realized that the deer that I had been watching was a buck with the biggest rack of antlers that I had ever seen! I quickly raised my rifle and tried to get a shot at him, but I could only catch fleeting glimpses of him running through the trees. I never touched him.

I was so astonished by this that I climbed all the way down

into the bottom of the canyon to check the animal's tracks. He was definitely one of the biggest bucks I had ever seen! How in the world I had been fooled I could never figure out. Maybe it had something to do with the distance and angle that I was looking down on him from. Or maybe the shadows of the trees hid his rack. Or maybe it was just that I had become so used to seeing only does and fawns, that my eyes tricked me. I would never know.

So that was another day's hunting without success. My partners didn't fare any better than I did. But I was the one who had to tell the story of how I had missed the only buck that we had seen so far.

My luck finally changed on the third day of our stay at Menzies Bay. I went back to the same area I had hunted the day before. I saw about twenty-five deer and, in the space of about an hour, I shot a spike buck, a two-point and another spike. That made one for each of us. Billy and Joe did not see any bucks on that day either.

The next day we headed back to Victoria. Running on just one engine, the trip home took a lot longer than coming up, but it was easier on fuel.

The three of us went back up to Menzies Bay the following year. We were surprised to find the conditions vastly changed. There were almost no deer to be found in the area that had been alive with animals the year before. There was plenty of evidence that cougar had come in and killed a lot of deer. The rest must have moved off to safer grounds. On the one day that I hunted, I found remains of deer hair and bones in dozens of places. I was lucky enough to get a clean shot at the one spike buck that I saw all day, so we didn't go home empty-handed. But after seeing all the evidence that the deer had been driven out of the area, we only stayed the one day. There didn't seem to be any point in staying around to hunt for deer that weren't there, so we went right on back to Victoria.

I enjoyed deer hunting a great deal and always tried to get out in the fall. I enjoyed the peace and quiet of the woods. I guess it reminded me of those years up around Bute Inlet when I was so young. In all my years of hunting there were several times when very odd things happened to me.

One of the strangest incidents occurred on a trip to an area just south of Duncan on Vancouver Island. I was hunting alone in heavy timber. It was only mid-morning, but I'd been in the bush since dawn. So far I hadn't seen a thing. I was working my way slowly up a fairly gentle hillside when I spotted a two-point buck about fifty yards ahead of me. He was standing behind some low brush with his head and shoulders showing clearly through the trees. The buck dropped as soon as I shot it. Then, to my surprise, it was on its feet again, and looking down the hill at me. Before it could run off, I shot it again. Down it went. When I walked up to where the deer lay, I found two dead animals with their noses almost touching. I guess they had been resting there, and one had got to his feet just as I arrived. And, of course, when I shot that one, the other one stood up.

I had a heck of a time getting those two deer out of the bush. They were both a good size, and I was a fair distance from the road. I ended up working really hard for those two. Although I had only wanted one, I could not bring myself to leave one carcass to rot in the bush. I knew that somebody would be able to use the second one.

Another time, I went up on the Malahat just north of Victoria looking for a buck. I parked my car near the summit and hiked back into the hills. I walked and walked, but didn't see a thing. I must have covered ten miles at least. Finally, late in the afternoon I'd about decided that I wasn't going to get a deer that day, and was heading back to my car. Then, just as I came over the last rise that led down to the road, there was a nice two-point laying in a protected cove under a rock. He had his back to the rock and was looking down the hill. I fired; he just lay his head down, and never made another move. I waited, expecting the animal to jump up and run. But he didn't. When I went up to him, I found that I had shot him right between the eyes. After spending a whole day tramping through the bush, I got that deer within a hundred yards of where my car was parked.

But I didn't always have to work so hard to get results. I went out the road that goes up past Sooke Lake very early one morning. I knew of a meadow near a series of small lakes right at the top of the divide that I wanted to hunt right at daybreak, so I went up while it was still dark. I sat on the edge of a hill overlooking the meadow, which was about three hundred yards long and a hundred wide. As dawn approached I could see a dark object down below me. Pretty soon I could see that it was a deer. Not only that, but I could also make out that it had two companions in the meadow. But it still wasn't light enough to see if any of them had horns.

But I didn't have long to wait and the deer didn't seem to be interested in going anywhere. The dawn brightened and I could see that the largest of the deer was a buck. But it was still too dark to get a good sight on the animal. Pretty soon though, I had enough light to make a good shot. I could also see that one of the other deer was also a buck. The third was a small doe. I shot the largest of the bucks. The second one started to run, and I shot it too. The doe quickly ran off.

That meadow was about two hundred yards from where I had parked my car. I cleaned the two carcasses, got them into my car and was down at the Poodle Dog Café in Victoria having my breakfast just after six o'clock. That was one hunting trip when I got great results with very little time and effort.

A strange incident with a deer happened to my brother August one day when he was cutting wood on a gravel beach in Bute Inlet. August was working away when he happened to look out into the water and noticed a doe swimming towards the beach. The deer made it to the shore, but it could not get out of the water. The animal was exhausted, its legs stiff from swimming a long distance in the icy waters of the inlet. August figured that it must have been chased into the water by wolves and had swum the two-and-a-half miles across the inlet.

August went down and pulled the deer out of the water. He carried it up the beach to where it was dry, and lay it on some driftlogs. He tied a rope around its neck and covered the animal with a blanket. He tied the other end of the rope to a log. The doe just lay there limp while August went back to work.

After about twenty minutes August noticed that the deer was beginning to perk up. Its head and ears were up, but it still lay under the blanket. Ten minutes later the doe stood up, shaking off the blanket. It started to walk away. When it came to the end of its tether, that doe went straight up into the air, trying to kick the restraining rope off of its neck with its hind feet. It reacted with such fury that August was sure it would injure itself. The doe fell down once, but before August could get near it, it was on its feet again, kicking wildly. It kept right at it until it again fell down. This time it appeared to be winded. My brother was able to move in and remove the rope from the animal. He felt this display of energy proved that the animal had recovered from the effects of the long swim.

When the doe got its wind back, it stood up and immediately began to jump and kick at the rope that was now no longer holding it. It looked like it was trying to kick its ears off! After a bit of that, it stopped and appeared to assess the situation. It just stood there, looking around, twitching its tail nervously. After a moment or two it took one cautious step towards freedom. It stopped, looked, and twitched its tail. It took another step and then another. It moved off that way for quite a distance before it seemed to fully convince itself that there was no longer anything holding it back. Then it bounded off into the bush.

RUM ROW

CONSOLIDATED EXPORTERS LTD., the company that I was hauling for, had offices in both Vancouver and Victoria. As well as the liquor that we were running across the Strait of Juan de Fuca, they also sold whisky all up and down the West Coast of the United States from large ships that sat outside American territorial waters. There were a number of ships in the fleet on Rum Row: *Malahat*, *Coal Harbour*, *Stadacona* and others. The motherships acted as large sea-going warehouses, and supplied smaller vessels that ran the liquor to various points along the coast. The big ships never went into American ports at all. They would pick up their cargo either from a bonded warehouse in Vancouver or Victoria, or at the duty-free port down in Tahiti.

The mothership would anchor off the California coast about one hundred miles north of Los Angeles, and just sit there and wait for its customers to arrive. There was a three-mile territorial limit to begin with, but before long the United States government changed the law so that ships carrying liquor had to stay forty miles off the coast. Outside of that limit the American patrol boats could do nothing but watch.

From the mothership several large purse-seiners that were owned by Consolidated Exporters would pick up loads of two to three thousand cases, and transport those cargoes to different places up and down the coast where they would sit and wait for contact to be made by smaller speedboats that ran the goods into shore in lots of two to three hundred cases.

Both Consolidated Exporters and the Reifel Brothers, who had a distillery in New Westminster, were keeping motherships off the West Coast. The Reifels, in fact, were apparently even shipping some of the liquor they produced down to Tahiti and then back up the coast. That way they did not have to pay duty on it.

The Consolidated Exporters operation was controlled by the "shore captain," Charlie Hudson, whom I came to know well. Captain Hudson controlled the whole operation by wireless from Vancouver. No money changed hands on the high seas. Payment was made in Vancouver. Coded wireless messages revealed the location of the liquor ship and arranged a rendezvous time. American speedboats would arrive at the rendezvous site, and present the captain of the liquor ship with half of a dollar bill, the other half of which the captain already had. This was the proof that the buyers were legitimate and had paid for their liquor.

It was not too long after I built the *Kitnayakwa* that we began to hear rumours that there were going to be some changes in the rum trade in Pacific Northwest waters. The United States government was putting a lot of pressure on the Canadians to change their laws and crack down on all the liquor that was being shipped out of Canadian ports and consigned to places that everyone knew it would never reach. For the first few years the Canadian government did not want to lose the tax revenue that this trade provided. It was perfectly legal to consign a load of several hundred or a thousand cases of whisky to Bowen Island, even though there was no one there to drink it. Nevertheless, because the liquor was being bought and shipped legally, taxes were being paid on every bottle. The government was reluctant to give up that revenue. But the United States government kept the pressure on, and we knew that eventually there would be restrictions on running liquor right out of Canadian ports.

I knew that once the laws were changed I would have to go offshore to get my liquor. That would mean running out the west coast and into the open Pacific. The only trouble with that was the fact that I had specifically designed the *Kitnayakwa* for the protected inside waters of the Straits of Georgia and Juan de Fuca. It was certainly fast enough, but it was a little too blunt for the large ocean swells.

Once again I started to think about building a new boat. I knew pretty much what I wanted. I carved another wooden model on a scale of one inch to the foot. This boat would be fifty-six feet long with a beam of twelve feet. I designed the bow with a deeper V, more like a destroyer, so that it would cut through a wave rather than ride on top of it. I figured that with the extra length and beam this boat would be able to handle the ocean swell and still make good speed.

In the boating magazines I had been reading about yet another type of airplane engine that was being adapted for use in boats. This was an eight hundred sixty-horsepower Packard. I decided that two of those powerful engines would give the new boat the speed that I wanted. The only problem was that those Packards cost about $7,000 apiece. The whole package, boat and motors, would run me $23,000 or $24,000. I could have built the boat, but at the time I didn't have enough money to put the engines in it.

I went down to the Consolidated Exporters office in Victoria and asked them if they would consider giving me a loan to get the new boat built. They agreed right away. They knew that the law was going to change soon, and that I'd have to start running out the west coast, and they liked the idea of a bigger boat because I could haul larger cargoes.

The Victoria directors of Consolidated—Harry Barnes, Jimmy Hunter and George Gardiner—and I went over to a meeting with the rest of the directors in Vancouver. After the proposal was explained to them, all of the Vancouver directors of the company seemed to be in favour of the plan. Then the company's lawyer, who had been sitting quietly at the back of the room all the while, came up with some darn-fool, technical, legal question that seemed to catch everybody by surprise. I didn't even understand what it was he meant. It had nothing to do with the boat—he didn't know a damn thing about boats! But whatever his point was, he soon had them all shaking their heads. In five minutes he had killed the whole deal.

Naturally, I was discouraged by this turn of events. However, there was not a thing I could do about it, so I just kept on hauling with the *Kitnayakwa*. For awhile, at least, it was back to business as usual. As long as I could get my liquor in the strait, the *Kitnayakwa* was a great boat.

But the changes in the laws finally came. When they did, I was left to do the best that I could with a boat that was less than well suited to its purpose. I now had to run out the west coast and rendezvous with a ship that would come up from further south and wait for me about ten miles off of Pachena Point Lighthouse. The *Chief Skugaid* was a purse-seiner about ninety feet long. It would run up from its normal position down off the mouth of the Columbia River.

It was a trip of about one hundred miles from Victoria to the rendezvous point. I had to be much more careful about the weather when I started to go out into the open ocean. I did not want any accidents. I would start out at about ten o'clock in the morning, and run out at my normal cruising speed of about eighteen knots. About five hours later I would be at Cape Beale. Another hour's run would take me out to the *Chief Skugaid*. But if the weather was too rough, I would head into Barkley Sound and find a quiet anchorage among the Broken Islands. There was a nice protected bay on Village Island and another on Copper Island. The *Chief Skugaid* would sometimes have to lay out there for several days waiting for me if we got a spell of bad weather.

It would usually take us about an hour to transfer a load to the *Kitnayakwa*, depending on how large the swell was running. Moving the liquor from one boat to the other could be a fairly tricky job in rough seas. But we had lots of practice and got pretty good at it. As soon as the load was stowed on board the *Kitnayakwa*, I would head back in, trying to get in somewhere close to Sooke before it started to get dark. By the time we were heading down the strait off of Victoria, we would have been out for twelve hours or more.

The trip down Puget Sound and back, depending on where we were to make the delivery, might be almost the same distance that we had already travelled and could take another twelve hours. (This was why we did most of the rumrunning in the winter months when the nights were long and dark.) It ended up being a very long day. I would normally be up for at least thirty-six hours because I always found that there was something to be done with the boat when we arrived back in Victoria. Anyway, I was never able to sleep very well during the daytime.

At about the same time that they passed the laws that forced us to go offshore to pick up our cargoes, the Canadian government also built two fast cutters to patrol their portion of the Strait of Juan de Fuca. One of these was forty-five feet long and the other thirty-six. They were designed and built especially to go after the rumrunners.

I only ever came in contact with one of these ships; the other one I never even saw. But I did have several encounters with the *Imperator* which was the larger of the two cutters. It was powered by two, two hundred and fifty-horsepower Sterling engines. A fellow by the name of Biddencourt was the captain of the *Imperator* and he soon became more of a thorn in my side than all fifteen of the American cutters that patrolled U.S. waters.

The main trouble was that the *Imperator* was fast; it was getting too close to the speed that I was able to make. I had to keep a sharp eye out for it whenever I was in Canadian waters. If they got me in their sights, Biddencourt and his crew were very persistent in trying to tag along behind when I headed out the west coast to pick up a load.

I remember one time when I got the better of Biddencourt and the *Imperator*. I was out in the *Kitnayakwa* with a friend, Wilkes, who was a furrier in Victoria. We had fished out around East Point for three days. The fishing had been good. We had about a hundred salmon all nicely iced down in the skiff that was pulled up on the deck at the stern of the boat and covered with a heavy canvas.

On the way back to Victoria we were coming down the east side of a small island near Sidney Island when I saw the *Imperator* heading toward us.

"I think I'll have some fun with them," I said to Wilkes.

I turned the *Kitnayakwa* and went back around the end of the island and down the other side. Just as I had hoped, Biddencourt figured I was trying to avoid him, so he turned and went down and around his end of the island to head me off. We met about halfway on the west side of the island. As they approached, the *Imperator* signalled us to stop and came alongside.

"Can I come aboard?" Biddencourt asked.

"Sure, that would be fine," I replied. They brought the cutter in close, and lines were tossed to hold the two boats together. Biddencourt and one of his men came on board the *Kitnayakwa* and quickly had a look around. Funny enough, they looked every-where but under the canvas that covered the skiff.

"What have you been up to, Mr. Schnarr?" he asked.

"Oh, just a little fishing and cruising around," I told him. Knowing how disappointed he was at finding nothing on my boat, I had a hard time keeping a straight face.

"Fishing, eh," Biddencourt said, sounding very much like he didn't believe a word of it. "And how was your luck?"

"We did pretty good, I guess. Would you like a salmon or two?"

"Why, yes. That would be very nice," he replied. I think he still thought he was calling my bluff.

I loosened the cover on the skiff. Biddencourt looked pretty red-faced as I picked out a couple of nice fish for him. He thanked me and handed them quickly to his mate. At that point he sud-denly seemed to be in a big hurry to be on his way!

George Norris was Chief Customs Inspector in Victoria during the period of Prohibition. He certainly knew that I was in the rum trade; nevertheless, he was always friendly when we met. He did try to get me to give information on others, though. He would say, "I am not asking you anything for the record, but perhaps you can give me an idea about who is hauling from the American side." He wanted to know where they were coming from and where they were delivering to, but, of course, there was no way that I would give him any information at all. I always simply said that I didn't know anything about it. Sometimes that was the truth, sometimes it wasn't. Several times Norris hired a boat to take him out to Discovery Island, but I don't think he ever actually caught anyone there.

Norris tried to catch me with an airplane once, but that did not work either. When I arrived at Cape Beale on one trip, it was too rough to run out to the *Chief Skugaid,* so I went into Barkley Sound and anchored in a bay on Village Island.

I had not been there more than an hour when a plane came down the sound from the direction of Port Alberni. It cruised around overhead for a time and then left. It was pretty obvious that whoever was in that plane was looking for someone or some-thing. In those days it was not at all a common thing to see a small plane out in that area. I was pretty sure that they had spot-ted me. Later that afternoon, about four o'clock, the plane came down the inlet again. They had another good look around.

The next day the weather was still bad, and I was forced to spend another day just waiting. As soon as it was light, however, I moved about ten miles further into Barkley Sound and anchored near Copper Island. I wanted to see if that plane was really coming out to keep track of me. Sure enough, about nine in the morning it appeared. And once again they cruised around until they found me.

They made another pass at about four that afternoon. By this time the sea had calmed, and, as soon as the plane was out of sight, I raised anchor and headed out to pick up my cargo. I had delivered that load down to Seattle and was back in Victoria before daylight the next morning. I like to think that I was fast asleep in my bed at Telegraph Cove while Norris and his pilot were searching the waters of Barkley Sound for any sign of the *Kitnayakwa*! To my knowledge that was the only time that they ever tried to keep track of me with an airplane. It was not at all successful and far too expensive, I suspect.

Having to run all the way out the west coast to pick up my cargoes meant using a lot more gasoline in the *Kitnayakwa* than I had planned on when I built her. In fact, it meant using more than she could carry in her four hundred-gallon tanks. I solved this problem by loading four or five, forty-five-gallon drums of gas into the back hatch before we left Victoria on each trip. By the time we got out to Barkley Sound, the tanks would be down enough that I could pump the fuel from the drums into the tanks and toss the drums overboard to make room for the load of liquor.

By doing this I always knew that I had enough gas to make the trip down Puget Sound and back to Victoria. I would normally have about one hundred gallons left when I arrived home. But I looked upon that as insurance in case we had to run from the Coast Guard or hide out for a day if we couldn't deliver a load for whatever reason.

There was one particular trip that I remember when that extra gasoline came in very handy! I had both Tom Colley and Billy Garrard with me and we had picked up a load from the *Chief Skugaid* out off Pachena Light. It was late afternoon when we were on our way back down the strait. I was keeping fairly close to the Vancouver Island shore, trying to get as far back in as possible before dark. Then, just before we got to Sooke, who did we see but the *Imperator* heading out from Victoria to meet us!

I immediately swung the *Kitnayakwa* around and headed back in the direction we had come at full throttle. Unfortunately, the *Imperator* was capable of almost as much speed as I could make with a load on. She followed right along behind us.

By the time we were back out as far as Port Renfrew, I could see that I was slowly pulling away from them, but they showed no signs of giving up the chase. Perhaps they were hoping that they would run me out of fuel. At the time I had no idea what their plans were, but I did know that I wasn't going to let them chase me all the way up the west coast of Vancouver Island. I turned away from the shore and headed across the strait toward the American side.

And then the engines started missing! I had been pressing them for all the power I could get, and suddenly they both started missing in an irregular way. I had no idea what the problem might be. I gave Billy the wheel and went down into the engine room to have a look. The first thing I noticed was that there was water on the top of the engines. When I had a closer look, I could see that the water was coming through tiny holes in the engine casing around the spark plugs. Tiny jets of water were squirting out, causing the plugs to short out from time to time.

I quickly made some little wooden plugs with my pocket knife and managed to jam them in all of the holes I could find. That seemed to solve the problem for the time being. The engines quit misfiring and we were able to keep our lead on the *Imperator*.

Once we passed the midpoint in the strait, we were in U.S. waters, and the Canadian cutter gave up the chase. But our problems were far from over. For the rest of the trip I spent most of my time in the engine room carving plugs as more and more holes developed in those Liberty engines. Running through American waters with a full load of liquor on board was not the time that I wanted to be without all the power that those big engines could provide.

By the time we reached the American side of the strait, it was getting dark. We turned and headed east toward Port Angeles. But this was not to be one of our luckier days! It wasn't long before I spotted two American Coast Guard cutters up ahead of us. I saw them long before they saw me. One was running in close to shore, and the other was further out than we were. I was hoping to be able to just slip between them in the darkness, unnoticed. As long as the engines held up, I knew that I could easily outrun the American boats anyway.

But we weren't so lucky. Both cutters seemed to pick me up at the same time, and they turned on us. I gave the *Kitnayakwa* full throttle and was by them before they could get us within range of their guns. Thankfully the engines held out. We ran fast enough to keep increasing the distance between ourselves and the American boats all the way back down the strait. By the time we were due south of Victoria, we had left them far behind and out of sight.

By this time I had decided not to risk making a delivery with the engines performing the way they were and with the Coast Guard on our tail. I headed back over to Canadian waters. I passed by Discovery Island and headed up Haro Strait towards Sidney. I was keeping the boat out at Canoe Cove at this time. I stopped at a small island between Sidney Island and D'Arcy Island to cache the load of liquor. There was a bit of a depression in the middle of the island. We were able to pile all two hundred cases in there where it was well hidden by the brush that grew all around. No one was likely to be out on that little bit of rock at that time of year anyway.

I anchored the *Kitnayakwa* in my usual spot just off the end of the wharf at the Canoe Cove Marina. I was friendly with the Rodd brothers who ran the marina. They kept an eye on the *Kitnayakwa* for me, and always let me use their telephone to call my wife for a ride home. I bought an awful lot of gas from them. That night we stopped in to see Hugh and told him what had happened out on the water.

"They'll probably send a patrolman out this way to see if your boat is here," Hugh said.

"As far as I am concerned, it never left," I replied.

I had hardly said these words when we could hear the sound of a motorcycle approaching. We had no trouble deciding who it was.

"You fellows just pop into the bedroom and stay out of sight," Hugh said. "I'll take care of this."

From the back room we heard the knock at the door. Hugh invited the young officer in and asked him what he was doing way out there at that time of night.

"Is Johnny Schnarr's boat, the *Kitnayakwa*, out there?" the policeman asked.

"Yes, it is," Rudd replied.

"Has it been away?"

"Not that I know of," Hugh said. "As far as I know, it has been there for about two weeks. You can go out and have a look if you want. It's usually anchored about one hundred feet off the end of the wharf."

That seemed to satisfy the policeman.

"Well, I guess it's been there all along, so I won't bother," he said. I suppose he didn't want to go to the trouble of rowing out there in the dark. With that, he thanked Hugh for his help and went out and got on his motorcycle and left.

Tom, Billy and I came out of the bedroom. I also thanked Hugh for the way he had handled the cop. We talked about how lucky we were that we had made it back to Canoe Cove just when we did. Had we been twenty minutes later, we would have been dropping the anchor just as the policeman drove up, and would have had a bit more explaining to do.

But, as it turned out, that wasn't our only bit of luck! We were very fortunate that the young officer didn't have the enthusiasm for the short row out to the *Kitnayakwa* that night. When I went on board the next day, I found a half a case of liquor under one side of the coaming at the back of the boat. Somehow we had missed it when we were caching the load on the island! If the policeman had gone out to the boat, he would have found the engines warm and that half case of liquor, and would have had us! Luck was with me again!

After that I called Pearl to come out and get us. Then we sat around and visited with Hugh Rodd until she arrived. It had been an exciting evening, and not one that I would soon forget.

I never saw the *Imperator* around after that. I always wondered if the stories that I later heard were true. The way I heard it was that she had burned out the bearings in her engines trying to keep up with the *Kitnayakwa*. It sounded entirely possible to me. After all, they had chased me for a good forty or fifty miles, and they were losing ground the whole way, so you could bet that they were pushing those engines for all they were worth, trying to keep me in sight. And then there was the story of the reward money that the Americans had apparently put up to go to anyone who caught me. I guess they had motivation enough. But I always thought it funny that I never saw that cutter around again.

I now had engine problems of my own. The next day when I

had a look at the engines in the daylight, I discovered that the casings were being eaten through by the salt water. I learned that the Liberty engine was built so light around the water jacket that it did not last more than a year or so in salt water. The worst of it was that the casings seemed to be thinnest right around the spark plugs, so that was where the first holes appeared. And that's what led to the shorting problem.

For awhile I kept making little pegs to plug the holes, but I knew that was not going to work for any length of time, as the casings were steadily rusting away and getting thinner all the time. I knew that I had to have a new boat soon anyway, so I didn't think about replacing those engines. I didn't use the *Kitnayakwa* for too long after that. I sold her just the way she was.

But the surprises from that trip weren't over yet! The next day when I went out to pick up the liquor cached on the small island, it was gone. I had to call Consolidated Exporters and arrange for another load before I could complete the delivery. I found it very hard to believe that someone had simply stumbled onto the liquor by accident. But to be honest, I still didn't really suspect that I was being double-crossed by my friends. I guess I was pretty naive about things like that. It was still awhile before I came to realize that every time that I had cached a load of liquor, I'd lost it. But it wasn't too long before other events taught me that you couldn't always count on honesty from your friends.

DECEIT

SHORTLY BEFORE THE incident when we had been chased by the Imperator, I had delivered a load of liquor to a new customer down near Seattle. It was on a run when I made several deliveries to different spots in Puget Sound. The new customer had ordered fifty cases. Everything went fine except for the fact that the fellow didn't have the money to pay me when we dropped off the liquor. He promised that he would get it to me as soon as the booze was sold. Well, I didn't like that very much, but my only other option was to load the liquor back on the boat and haul it home, and I wasn't keen to do that either. I told the fellow that I didn't work on credit, but, seeing as it was his first time, I'd wait a couple of weeks for the money.

Well, I waited pretty near a month for my money, but didn't hear anything from this fellow. Finally I decided I had better do something about it. I told Billy I'd pay his way to Seattle and back on the CPR boat if he'd go down there and see if he could find out what was holding the money up. For all I knew the guy could have been in jail, but I wanted to know one way or the other. Billy agreed to go and find out what was going on.

When he got back a couple of days later, he reported that he'd had no luck collecting the debt.

"He says he's got no money and can't pay you," Billy told me.

Well, I figured that was probably one debt that I'd just have to forget about. I guess you get them in any business. And, in fact, the rum trade was probably at least as honest as most businesses. It was a fairly close-knit group, and anyone who started stiffing people soon found that they had no one to do business with.

Anyway, I'd all but forgotten about that unpaid delivery fee until I was in the Consolidated Exporters office a couple of months later when, who should I see, but the fellow who owed it to me. And there he was making arrangements to buy another load of liquor. I decided to find out what was going on by putting him on the spot right there.

"Hey, how come you didn't pay me for that load I delivered to you?" I asked bluntly.

The fellow looked surprised.

"Hell, I gave the money to Billy Garrard when he came over to Seattle two months ago! Didn't he give it to you?" he said.

My strategy had backfired. Now I was the one who was embarrassed. I had to admit that I had never received the money from my close friend. I must say I was shocked by the whole thing. I couldn't believe that Billy would have done that kind of thing to me.

Billy and I had worked together right from the beginning of my involvement in the rumrunning—from the time we were hauling with Fred Kohse's boats through the days with the *Moonbeam*, the *Miss Victoria I* and *II* and the *Kitnayakwa*. On top of that we were the best of friends; we practically lived together. Before I was married, we had shared a summer house out on the Gorge. We went to dances and parties and chummed around together. And we had been through some rough and very exciting times in the rumrunning. And, you know, we'd never even had an argument. Now all of a sudden I find out that Billy has stiffed me! It was a shock.

I went to see my old friend.

"What the hell is the idea of lying to me about that money I sent you to pick up in Seattle?" I asked him straight off.

I told him how I'd run into the fellow in the Consolidated office and that he had told me that he'd given him the money. Billy was caught off-guard; at first he obviously didn't know what to say.

"Well, I really needed the money, Johnny," he finally answered. "And I was afraid that if I told you about it, you wouldn't let me have it."

I found it very hard to believe that Billy could have done a thing like that to me when we had been such close friends. I was pretty angry about the whole thing.

"You're finished with me right now," I told him.

I fired Billy right then and would not have anything more to do with him. That whole episode was a real shock to me. I guess it taught me a lesson, though. I don't think I was ever so trusting of anyone else again. I really had trouble believing that Billy would have stolen that money from me. I had just given him $700 not two days before I sent him down to Seattle to try to collect the money.

It was awhile before I was able to come to terms with that experience. When the shock of it had worn off, I realized that Billy and his wife had been living pretty high. I think they got carried away with the lifestyle that they were caught up in. Billy knew a lot of big shots from his university days, and his wife really liked to go out a lot. Billy was a very pleasant and likeable guy. I think he just had a lot of trouble saying no to his wife.

Anyway, whatever the reason, he was finished with me.

After that I used different people as crew on my runs. I still used Tom Colley and Joe Fleming the most, but there were a few others that I used as well.

I even took my father-in-law along on one trip. He was about seventy-five years old at the time, but still in good shape. I told him that I'd give him $500 for the trip and he jumped at the opportunity. He was a little fellow, about my size, and he really liked adventure. He'd worked on the sealing boats up and down the coast for a number of years before they closed it down. He was a gunner and was used to an exciting life, I guess. Anyway, he turned out to be a bit more trouble than he was worth, so I only took him on the one trip.

When we ran out to the *Chief Skugaid* off the west coast, we often had to make the transfer of the liquor in pretty rough weather. The big boat had huge truck tires hanging all along one side. I would bring the *Kitnayakwa* up alongside and we'd tie the two boats together using the tires as bumpers. The engines on the purse-seiner would be kept running to keep us moving slowly ahead. That way the two boats would rise and fall at the same time, and we could make the exchange even if the seas were running ten or twelve feet. We would pass the liquor from one to the other, being careful not to fall between the two craft. It would usually take the better part of an hour to complete the transfer.

On the day I took my father-in-law along there was a good-sized swell running.

"Now you stay on the *Kitnayakwa* and wait until someone passes you a sack," I told him.

But the old fellow just wouldn't listen. He was reckless as hell. He would jump from one boat to the other to grab a sack and then jump back again. He was just too impatient to wait for some-one from the other crew to pass him a case. I figured the old fool was going to end up squashed down between the two boats, and I kept shouting at him to stay where he was on the *Kitnayakwa*, but it didn't do any good.

He made me really nervous. What he was doing was danger-ous and stupid. With the swell running at about ten feet, you just never knew when the deck was going to rise up or drop out from underneath you. You were safe only as long as you stayed put. When the force of the seas pushed the two boats together, those great big truck tires were flattened right out. It was pretty obvious what it would do to anyone who fell down into that gap. I sure did not want to see my father-in-law crushed between the two boats.

Anyway, one trip with the old guy was enough for me. He was just too much of a live wire. After that I always made sure that I had someone else to go along with me.

One of the hardest things about the rumrunning business was the long hours I had to put in without any sleep. If everything went according to plan on a trip, I would be up for about thirty-six hours. In the early years we wouldn't leave until evening, but, be-cause I was never comfortable sleeping during the daytime, I would have been up all day. Then I'd be up all that night. And quite often after a trip there would be something or other that had to be done on the boat, so I normally wouldn't get to bed again until that night.

Later, when I had to run out the west coast to pick up the liquor, it was even worse. I would start off earlier in the day, and, although I might not be up any longer, the hours at the wheel of the boat would take their toll. It was kind of hard, but you got used to it soon enough. I just accepted it as part of the job.

Of course, if for some reason a load couldn't be delivered the first night, then we'd either have to cache the liquor or hole up somewhere out of sight. And if we did that we'd have to keep a sharp lookout for patrols all day and try to make the delivery on the second night. Then we'd be looking at a sixty-hour work day!

It was while I still had the *Kitnayakwa* that I stayed over on the American side for the third time. Tom Colley and I had taken a load down to a spot between Everett and Edmonds in Puget Sound. For some reason or other our contact did not show up at the delivery point. We had run all the way in from out the west coast, and it was getting pretty near dawn by the time we decided that they were not going to show up. I didn't really want to run all the way back to Discovery Island in the daylight. By this stage the Canadian cutters posed more of a danger to us than the Americans. Instead of heading back across the border, I decided to take a chance on laying over in the Hood Canal.

Before it got light I ran the *Kitnayakwa* across the sound, past Point No Point and up around Foulweather Bluff into the canal. I went down and anchored in the small bay behind Hood Head. This seemed to be a perfect spot as I could see for quite a distance both up and down the canal. The bay was more of a lagoon with a low stretch of mud flats that connected the mainland to the head. From our position I could see over the flats out towards the mouth of the canal. And I also had a clear view a good long ways south into the canal. I would have been able to spot a cutter approaching from either direction in plenty of time to be able to outrun it. I'm not sure what I would have done if they'd come at me from both directions at once! But I really didn't think that there was much chance of a patrol boat being in the canal during the daytime, anyway.

Still I kept a very sharp eye out and didn't get any sleep that day. As it was, the time passed uneventfully, and we were able to deliver our cargo on the second night. We were happy to get back to Victoria the following morning for some much-needed rest.

REVUOCNAV

ABOUT A YEAR after the law was changed to force us to run out to the motherships to pick up our cargoes, I got a call from the fellows at the Consolidated Exporters office in Victoria. The head office over in Vancouver wanted to talk to me about the boat that I wanted to build.

I went right over. This time the lawyer, who had spoiled it for me earlier, kept his mouth shut, and all of the directors agreed to give me the loan that would allow me to build the boat. In fact, they were most anxious that I get started on it as soon as possible. It was agreed that I would put up $7,000 for the boat, and that they would back me for the engines with a loan of $15,000. We went straight to the bank, where Captain Charlie Hudson co-signed the loan for me. I walked out of that bank with a cheque for the full amount of the loan. I immediately started things in motion to get the boat built.

The deal that I made was that Consolidated Exporters would get forty percent of the fee for every delivery that I made with the new boat until the loan was repaid. (As it turned out, I had the debt cleared in the first year that I was hauling with the new boat.)

I had already carved a wooden model of the boat I wanted to build. In order to give the shipwrights the measurements that they needed to build the boat, I took the model, which was carved on a scale of one inch to the foot, to a draughtsman who transferred my design onto paper. It was kind of funny because that draughtsman told me that there was hardly any difference in the hull design between my model and Thornycraft designs which he had worked on in England. He said that there was only about two inches of variation in one part of the hull. Thornycraft was known as one of the best speedboat designs in Britain.

Once I had the blueprints, I took them to a Japanese shipyard on Coal Harbour in Vancouver. I chose another Japanese boatbuilder because I knew that they did excellent work, and they also always seemed to do it for a better price. Just as an example, there was another shipyard right next to the one doing my boat, where a sixty-five-foot boat was being built at a cost of $70,000. My boat was fifty-six feet long, and the cost was $22,000.

The other thing that I liked about the Japanese boatbuilders was that they didn't seem to mind working long hours to get a job done quickly. Three months after they laid the keel, my new boat was finished. They knew that I was in a hurry to have the boat, so they had a crew of eight or ten men working on it. They were also building another boat in the yard at the same time.

The hull of the new boat was double planked. The first planking was of half-inch red cedar laid diagonally; the outside was planked with five-eighths-inch yellow cedar, fore and aft. A heavy canvas was glued between the two layers of planking. I used yellow cedar on the outside because it is tough. Finally all of the outside seams were caulked.

The shipyard built the hull and cabin and installed the two, six hundred-gallon gas tanks under the floor of the cockpit at the stern. They also did the through-hull work for the drive shafts. I did the installation of the engines, the rudder, propellers, and all of the steering and controls. I also did all the finishing work inside and all the painting. I always painted my boats a dark grey so they would be as inconspicuous as possible.

During the time when the boat was being finished off, I was spending half my time in Vancouver working on it, and the other half still making liquor runs with the *Kitnayakwa*. I flew back and forth several times on a plane that was flying a regular route between Vancouver, Victoria and Seattle. It used to land in Victoria in a grass field out near the corner of Shelbourne Street and Hillside Avenue. That airline company was not in business for much more than a year, I don't think. I remember that I made my last trip on it, and then two days later read in the paper that it crashed off of Port Townsend. From what I remember they never even found the wreckage of that plane.

After the problems I'd had with the thin casings on the *Kitnayakwa* and the *Miss Victorias*, I had made up my mind not to use any more Liberty engines. With the new, bigger boat I knew I had to have all the power I could get. I soon settled on the Packard motor, which produced eight hundred and sixty horsepower. I would install two of them side by side.

The story on those Packard engines was typical. Apparently the United States Army was using them in a number of planes that they were flying all over the world. Then, when one of the engines began to have oil problems, they discarded them all. Some smart guy in California bought them all up really cheap, and started designing a clutch for them so they could be used in boats.

Getting a clutch system that would work turned out to be easier said than done. The fellow had to do a lot of experimenting before he came up with a clutch that was strong enough to hold an engine that powerful. He tried a two-and-a-half-inch Tungsten cold-rolled steel shaft, but even that twisted when he put full power on. When he complained to the manufacturer of the shaft, they told him that it would have to be heat treated for that much power. And that seemed to solve the problem. But all of the experimenting that went on really drove the price of those engines up. They cost me $7,500 each.

When I designed the new hull, I wanted the fastest boat I could get with a load on. With the faster Canadian cutters now also in the game, I wanted to maintain the edge in speed that I had so far enjoyed over my opponents in the rum game. As far as I was concerned that was one of the main reasons why I hadn't been caught.

The *Revuocnav* was all that I dreamed a boat should be. It performed just the way I had planned. (I used the same principle in naming the new boat that I had with the *Kitnayakwa*—I wanted something that people would have trouble remembering if they only saw it once. Revuocnav was Vancouver spelled backwards.)

With those two, eight hundred and sixty-horsepower Packard engines the boat would do better than forty knots with a full load on. The bottom of the boat was built like a hydroplane with a six-inch step in the hull thirty-four feet back from the bow. Twin

six-inch exhaust pipes came out under water right at that step.
Inside the hull there was also a ten-gallon oil drum on each exhaust to act as an expansion chamber to muffle the noise. There
was also an above-water exhaust outlet that I used for starting the
engines, but I had it fitted with a valve so I could shut it off once
they were running. Putting the exhaust underwater really helped
to deaden the sound of those big engines. Once we were underway, the Revuocnav ran very quietly—the main thing you could
hear was the sound of water running over the hull. You could
hardly hear the engines at all.

When the speed got up to about sixteen knots, I could feel
the boat ease up on its own and begin to plane. Then I could
bring the throttles back ten percent or more without losing any
speed. My cruising speed with the *Revuocnav* was about eighteen
knots. That was where I seemed to get the best fuel efficiency. And
I didn't have those two, six hundred-gallon gas tanks on her for
nothing! Those engines could really guzzle the gas! Even at cruising speed they were burning about forty gallons an hour. At full
speed she would suck back one hundred and twenty gallons an
hour! If I had to run at full speed for any length of time on a run
that took us down into Puget Sound, I might arrive back home
with less than a hundred gallons of fuel in my tanks. But I never
griped about what I had to spend on gasoline. I was always glad
to have that power and speed there when I needed it. With the
money I was making I figured it was better to spend a little more
if it kept me out of trouble!

When I first installed the Packards in the *Revuocnav*, I used a
half-inch gas line from the fuel tank to the motors. But when we
took the boat out for sea trials, we soon found out that that wasn't
big enough. When I got the engines up to full throttle, they would
only run a couple of hundred yards at full speed, then slow down.
I tried it several times, always with the same results. I quickly
realized that the engines just weren't getting enough fuel to keep
running at full speed. I had to change to a three-quarter-inch line.
And then they ran perfectly.

I bought most of my gasoline at bulk price from the Imperial
Oil station at the entrance to Victoria harbour. They sold it to me
for one cent a gallon cheaper than they sold it to gas stations
around town. The reasoning was that they didn't have to haul it
anywhere for me. At that price we both gained.

I would often go in there with the boat one morning, take on maybe a thousand gallons of gas, and then be back in the next morning for another thousand gallons! They knew what was going on, but never asked any questions. I was quite friendly with the fellow who ran the station. He was in the business of selling gasoline, and, as far as he was concerned, I was in the business of using it up! In those days no one made much of a fuss about the rumrunning anyhow. If you were smart, you kept it as quiet as you could, but you did not have to worry about most people.

I carried two hundred and fifty cases of liquor on every trip with the *Revuocnav*. With each case weighing about forty-five pounds that added up to over five and a half tons of liquor. Add another five tons or so of gas when the tanks were full and you had quite a load. But with the *Revuocnav* it was hard to tell the difference when she was loaded or empty. She would run at better than forty knots either way!

By the time Consolidated Exporters decided to help me get the *Revuocnav* built and in use, there was a great deal of competition in the business of hauling liquor. This was the early 1930s and times were tough. There were so many American boats going outside to bring loads of liquor in the Juan de Fuca Strait that they had driven the price we were getting for hauling down to five dollars a case. This made it tough for me. I had been getting eleven dollars a case up until that time. But in order to compete I had to drop my price too. The trouble was that the delivery cost me a lot more with the *Revuocnav* than it did someone who was willing to take a chance on running the Coast Guard blockade with a slower boat. But that was the way it was. There was no use crying about it. From then until the end of Prohibition, the price stayed at five dollars a case for delivery.

I still gave my crew the same one-third split as before, so they were making less money too. But it was still a lot better money than most people were making in those days. I was the one who took the worst of it from the drop. Now there were lots of trips when the one-third share for the boat did not even cover the cost of the gasoline and any minor repairs that I might have to make after a run.

At times my customers wanted me to carry three hundred cases, but I always refused. Two hundred and fifty was as far as I was prepared to go. I wanted to be sure that I could outrun those fast Canadian cutters if I had too.

Even with all the care in building that I took with the *Revuocnav*, disaster struck on our very first trip. I had both Tom Colley and Joe Fleming along with me at the time, and we were just on our way back down the strait after picking up a load from the seiner off the Pachena Light. It was evening and already dark. We were cruising along at eighteen knots just east of Port Renfrew when the thing we all feared most about night running happened. Suddenly there was a tremendous crash and the sound of wood being torn and wrenched. We were almost thrown off our feet by the jolt of the collision. We had hit a huge log in the water.

The night was pitch black and I did not get even a glimpse of that log before we hit it. It was a big fir, six feet through at the butt and eighty or ninety feet long. We hit it at an angle and the boat glanced off, but that log did not give an inch. The force of the blow sheared the lower part of the bow of the boat right off. Above the waterline the bow was still there, but down below there was nothing—planks, ribs, keel and bowstem were gone for six or seven feet back.

Tom Colley thought that we were sinking for sure when the bow dropped as water flooded into the forward section of the hull.

"Let's get the hell out of here before this thing sinks!" he shouted as he headed for the skiff.

"Just hang on a minute 'til we see what's going on," I argued.

Luckily there was no wind and no swell to speak of that night. I looked the situation over. The water was being kept in the bow of the boat by the bulkhead in front of the wheelhouse, but it was only a couple of inches below the top of the wall. I could soon see that we were in no immediate danger of sinking. As long as the forward bulkhead held and the water was kept out of the engine room, we would be OK.

The problem was what to do now. With the gaping hole in the bow there was no way to pump the water out. First I tried running dead slow. I used one engine on idle and just barely moved the boat ahead. That was OK, but when I tried speeding up a bit, the water immediately began to rise up the bulkhead, dangerously close to the top. I ran along very slowly for quite awhile. But I knew it was too slow, much too slow! We had a load of liquor on board, and we'd be sitting ducks for the Canadian cutters if we were still there when daylight came around. And there was no way I wanted to jettison that cargo. All the while I was trying to come up with a solution to the problem of the hole in the bow.

Finally an idea came to me. I wasn't sure it would work, but anything was worth a try. I remembered the heavy canvas that we used to cover the liquor in the open cockpit. It was twelve feet wide and twenty-four feet long. I told Tom and Joe to roll it, and take it up and drop it down over the bow. When they did this, the force of the water moving under the boat took the canvas down over the hull and covered the hole. Then they lashed it down as securely as they could.

Now I tried speeding up a little to see what would happen. Just as I had hoped, the water level began to recede as the bow of the *Revuocnav* was able to lift itself out of the water behind the canvas. I speeded up some more and more of the water was sucked out. It worked even better than I had hoped! In a matter of seconds there was virtually no water left in the bow.

Now I was able to run at about twelve knots. On the one hand, I didn't want to go too fast for fear of tearing the canvas loose and being right back where we started from. But, at the same time, I wanted to get the *Revuocnav* to Vancouver in order to have the repairs done in the shipyard that had built the boat. And I knew that I couldn't go into Coal Harbour with two hundred and fifty cases of liquor on board. Once again I had to find a place to cache the load. I came down past Victoria and around Ten Mile Point and headed up Haro Strait. We cruised in close to Sidney Island and ran down the east side. We were lucky enough to find a place where we could get right in next to the rock and offload the liquor directly from the boat without having to use the skiff. This saved some time.

The funny thing was that when we stopped to unload the liquor onto the island, the bow of the boat didn't fill up with water again like I expected it to. I guess the water pressure held the canvas against the hull. Anyway, very little seeped in.

Once we'd lightened the load, the *Revuocnav* rode even higher in the water, and we had no trouble at all on the run over to Vancouver. It was a very sad sight for me to see that gaping hole in the bow of my new boat when they pulled it up on the ways at the boatyard in Coal Harbour. I wasn't too happy either when I learned that that big fir tree floating in the ocean was going to cost me $2,400 in repairs. They had to replace the bowstem and keel and all of the double planking on the forward section of the hull.

The *Revuocnav* was a well-built boat to begin with, but after my little mishap with the fir tree, I decided that I wasn't about to risk the same thing happening again. I had an eighth-inch steel plate welded over both sides of the bow back about five feet and right down to the keel. This was fastened to the ribs with screws about two inches apart. If I hit any more logs, that coat of armour would provide some protection at least.

It was kind of a tough way to start out with a new boat, but I guess that's just the way it goes. I always knew how dangerous it was to run in the dark. Given the amount of driftwood and debris that was floating around in the Strait of Juan de Fuca, I just counted myself lucky that it hadn't happened sooner or more often. Or in a more serious situation, like when I was being chased by a Coast Guard cutter! Anyway, all my friends were amazed and amused when they heard the story of how we used the canvas tarp to cover the hole and were able to run all the way from Port Renfrew to Vancouver, a distance of about one hundred miles.

FOG AND OTHER HAZARDS

AS I'VE ALREADY said, I always did most of my hauling during the wintertime when the nights were long and dark. The darker the night, the better I liked it. Long, dark winter nights with a low cloud cover were my favourite, because I always wanted to attract as little attention as possible. I never had any trouble finding my own way around in the dark. But fog was something else.

A heavy fog lying right down on the water made it almost impossible to find your way around. If we got into a spell of really heavy fog or very bad storms, I would not do any hauling at all. I'd simply wait out the weather. But the trouble was that a lot of the time we didn't get any warning about the way the weather was going to be. The weather in the Juan de Fuca Strait could change in a hurry. To a certain extent the strait was protected by the Olympic Mountains in Washington State, and a lot of storms from out in the Pacific would pass to the north of us. But you never could count on it. If you just followed the forecasts from the weather office, you'd have to stay at home all winter! You had to use your own judgement. And there was no one who was right all the time. So I ended up getting caught out in bad weather plenty of times. On the one hand, winter nights were good for the rumrunning because they were long, but on the other, the weather was at its worst. We had to take the bad with the good. I always liked to remind myself that the weather was always just as bad for the guys in the Coast Guard, and that, on the really bad nights, they were much more likely to be in some protected bay than out in the open.

I remember one trip when we were going down Puget Sound to make a delivery halfway between Seattle and Tacoma. We were just off the lighthouse at West Seattle when the fog just settled down on the water and everything disappeared. Suddenly I couldn't see a thing! Luckily I had a good bearing on the lighthouse and knew the direction that we had to run. I figured the speed that we were travelling and ran straight down the sound until I estimated that we were opposite the landing point. Then I turned the boat ninety degrees and headed directly for the shore. I slowed the boat right down. And it was lucky I did because I didn't see the beach until we were within a hundred feet of it. I stopped and flashed the light in one direction. When I got no answering flash, I turned and flashed the other way. I immediately got a signal back. I couldn't believe my luck! I had run for several miles completely blind and landed right on the spot where I should be!

But I wasn't always so lucky. On another trip we were fogged in just after we passed Port Townsend on our way back from a run down Seattle way. We were about three-quarters of a mile off the lighthouse there and within a few minutes the curtain of mist rolled over us so thickly that you could barely see the bow of the boat.

I had Joe Fleming and Tom Colley with me on that trip. Tom had a Coastal Pilot ticket, so I asked him to chart a course to Discovery Island. He spent a few minutes at it, and then gave me the heading to follow. I followed the course he set exactly. I also kept a very close watch on the speed we were making. When I figured we should be getting close to Discovery, I sent Tom and Joe out onto the bow of the boat to see if they could hear the fog horn on the island. Tom popped back into the cabin a few moments later to report that they could hear nothing. I sent him back out with orders to keep a sharp eye and ear out.

I had been cruising at about eighteen knots in order to hold a steady course. When I sent Tom and Joe out onto the bow, I should have slowed right down or stopped the engines so that they could hear better, but I did not. In fact, I was just thinking about slowing down when suddenly, right in front of the boat, I could see what looked like a big kelp bed emerging from the fog. Then I saw that we were heading straight for two big, dark humps of rock that lay surrounded by the kelp. I could see that there was a small gap between the two rocks. All of this happened in the blink of an eye! I had no time to do anything except shut the motors down and head for that gap.

In the next instant there was a tremendous crashing and tearing sound as the *Revuocnav* hit the rocks, jumped up and scraped its whole length over that low spot. I do not think there was more than six or eight inches of water there. It was probably fortunate that we were still travelling at a good speed because our momentum carried us right over the rock and into the deeper water on the other side. We would have felt pretty foolish if the stern of the boat had hung up there.

Tom and Joe were both still on the bow. They saw disaster coming at the same time I did. They had been able to grab the handrailing along the side of the pilothouse and managed to hang on for the rough ride over the top.

Although I didn't know it at the time, the hull of the boat suffered little damage. We left some paint on the rocks, but not too much else. That steel plate that I had installed on the bow had kept the boat from suffering any major damage. But the propellers had still been turning as we went over, and the blades were pretty banged up. All three of the blades on one prop were wrapped tightly around the hub. On the other propeller two blades were ruined but one was still straight enough to provide a bit of thrust.

The rock that we had hit lay just off the west side of Discovery Island. It only shows at low tide. If the tide had been a bit higher we would have gone right over it. It didn't take me long to realize what had happened.

"Did you take that course from the lighthouse at Port Townsend to the lighthouse on Discovery?" I asked Tom, already knowing what the answer would be. He answered that he did.

"My God, didn't you allow for us being three-quarters of a mile offshore?" He admitted that he had forgotten about that. I never even bothered to say another word about it—I didn't swear or anything. It wouldn't have done any good at this point anyway. Tom had made one of the most basic errors you can make when plotting a course on the water. He'd simply forgotten to take into account our position relative to the position of the two points that he was plotting.

With the one blade that I had left I could make about three knots. We slowly made our way over to Golf Course Point, where we landed and dropped Joe off. From there he walked all the way over to the harbour and got his boat, the *Eljo*, and set out to tow us in. We continued on our way towards Victoria and were about halfway in when we met Joe coming out.

It wasn't until I got the boat up on the ways that I was able to finally survey the real damage done to the *Revuocnav*. All in all, I think I got off quite lucky. The steel on the bow had a few dents in it, but it certainly saved some structural damage to the boat. The struts that held the propellers were fastened to a twelve-by-twelve timber on the inside of the hull that was shaped to fit the bottom of the boat. That timber was split where the bolts went through it. Those rocks did not give one damn bit! That was a couple of propellers that I didn't even try to straighten. I just took them off and put new ones in their place. I had to replace the shafts as they were bent out of shape as well.

It wasn't too long after that when we almost got into trouble again running in the fog on the way home from making a drop down in Puget Sound. We were four or five miles off of Port Townsend heading back to Victoria when we ran into a heavy blanket of fog. I knew that we were out in the middle of the strait, so I wasn't too concerned about running through it. We went along for awhile without slowing down much. Then all at once I thought that the fog must be lifting because I could see a star in the sky. I had no sooner mentioned this to Tom Colley when I was shocked to see that the star appeared to be moving!

The next thing I saw was the dark bulk of a huge ship looming over us in the fog! I was heading straight for the side of a large ocean liner that was making its way down the strait. I had no time to think! I jerked the wheel hard over and spun a quick ninety degrees. The whole ghostly vision disappeared into the fog as rapidly as it had come. I'm sure that no one on board that ship was even aware of our near collision. (We had to keep an eye out for the big ships all the time, though, as we were crossing the shipping lanes down and back on every trip. But that was by far the closest I came to an actual collision.)

Sometimes we would follow the CPR boats that ran down to Seattle. I didn't do it very often, but, if the passenger ship happened to be going at the same time as we were, it was possible to follow it all the way down to Seattle. We would sometimes pick the ship up over near Port Townsend, and then tag along behind it. Some of the American rumrunners did this often. The big boat didn't break up the swells any because we always stayed too far behind it for that. The only reason that we would follow them when it was convenient was that the big ship made it hard for the U.S. cutters to come in on us. If the cutters tried to come down one side of the ship, we could always escape by running up the other side. By the time the patrol got around the end of the passenger ship, we could be well out of range of their guns.

We got a bit of a shock when we were going down to Seattle on one trip. The American navy was having manoeuvres out in the sound. There were bases both on Whidbey Island and at Port Townsend. As we were passing through the channel there, all at once they started playing a huge searchlight over the water from the Port Townsend side. The beam of this light was terrifically powerful.

"My God!" I said. "If they turn that thing on us, we've had it."

Sure enough, before we knew it night had turned into day. We were sitting ducks, caught in the intense beam of that searchlight. We figured we were goners! But then, to our surprise, the light was quickly switched off again. I think the navy was no more sympathetic to the Coast Guard than we were. Whoever was manning the searchlight on that night was not the least bit interested in what we were doing!

As I've said before, I came to realize that I had very good night vision. This was another factor that helped to keep me out of trouble. I was always the first to see anything dark at night. I could pick up a dark object on the water long before anyone else who ever worked for me could. Often I would run half a mile closer before they would be able to make out the object that I had already seen. There were many times when I spotted a patrol boat a long ways off and simply avoided it. I would always do the spotting by eyesight first and then put the night glasses on to confirm the identification of whatever it was. You couldn't use the those glasses too much; they put a real strain on your eyes. They were great things to use to identify something you were not sure of, though.

On the other hand, I was never the best at seeing a light that was a long way off at night. Tom Colley was always the champion of that particular skill. He could often see a light three or four miles before I would be able to pick it out. I could never figure that out. Tom thought that maybe he had developed the skill in the time he worked for the Pilot Association when he used to head out the strait looking for the light of a ship coming in. I don't know for sure where he got that ability, but I do know that he had it. It seemed to me that there were just a lot of differences in the degree to which people can see.

I always tried to avoid fog if I could, and I did the same with heavy weather. I would never set out to make a delivery if the weather was really bad. But, given the fact that we were doing so much of our hauling in the stormy winter months, we got caught out in rough weather much more often than we would have liked. There was simply no way to avoid it. Especially with the speed at which the weather can change on the West Coast. We might start out on a run in a light breeze under slightly overcast skies, and, by the time we were heading home, we might be fighting gale force winds and huge seas.

I have been in some of the worst storms that it is possible to imagine. The inside waters of the Juan de Fuca Strait are notorious for the rough water created when you get the combination of a strong tide running against a good wind. The area that we were running in all the time, between Victoria and Port Townsend, was one of the worst around for tide-rips. When a strong tide was running against the wind, the waves would get so steep that they would be really dangerous.

There was only one time that a boat sheered on me, and I lost complete control of her. That happened with the *Revuocnav* right off of Trial Island near Victoria. I was returning from the American side early one morning. This was another case when the weather simply deteriorated during the night. We'd set out in fairly light winds, but by the time we were out of Puget Sound on the return trip, a strong southeasterly was blowing. And the wind just continued to pick up as we got closer to home. By the time we were approaching Vancouver Island, the waves were huge, better than fifteen feet high. It must have been blowing sixty or seventy knots. And the worst of it was, we had a following sea.

Just off Trial Island we ran into a powerful tide-rip. A strong ebb tide was just standing those huge waves straight up on end! This is very dangerous because the waves get so steep and so close together. Then the worst happened. All of a sudden both ends of the *Revuocnav* were out of the water at the same time! The engines roared as the propellers clawed at thin air. The props and the rudder were hanging there out in the open air and I suddenly had no steerage. (A boat can only be steered when it has momentum—when the flow of water over the rudder can be used to change the direction of the craft.) With the rudder and propellers out of the water, the boat lost her momentum, and with it I lost any ability to steer her. The *Revuocnav*, all fifty-six feet of her, was suddenly whipped around on the crest of a wave like a chip of wood. All at once she was broadside to the seas. I helplessly hung onto the wheel as she tumbled down the face of the wave. The boat turned right over onto her side. Tom Colley and Joe Fleming had nothing to hang onto and were tossed down onto the side of the hull, which had suddenly become the floor.

I hung onto the steering wheel as hard as I could, but my grip was torn loose, and I landed on top of my crew. The boat lay completely over on its side in the trough until the wave went out from under us, and she was able to right herself. I jumped up and got hold of the steering wheel again and, with the propellers now back in the water where they belonged, managed to get the boat headed in the right direction before another wave could bury us for good.

This whole incident lasted for only a matter of seconds.

Then we were on our way again. But it sure puts a fellow in a sober mood! The ocean has a way of making a man feel small and weak in a hurry!

That was the closest I ever came to capsizing any boat. Had the *Revuocnav* had a round-bottomed hull, I'm convinced that she would have rolled right over and stayed that way. It was only the steep V of the hull that kept us from going right over. The bilge water had put its mark on the bulkhead right up to the level of the top deck. I cannot understand why they keep on building round-bottom boats for use in these inside waters. The V hull is a faster boat for the same power and twice as safe. I know as sure as I am sitting here that we wouldn't have come through some of the storms that we did in anything but a V-bottomed boat.

UP THE COLUMBIA RIVER

ONE DAY I got a call to go down to the Consolidated Exporters office on Wharf Street in Victoria. When I got there, they told me they had an unusual delivery proposal that they wanted me to consider. A customer in southern Washington wanted one thousand cases of liquor delivered to a spot about fifteen miles up the Columbia River. They asked me if I would be interested in hauling the liquor up the Columbia from a ship off the coast. When I had listened to all of the details of the proposal, I agreed to do it. We made all the arrangements right then.

The liquor would be hauled down to a point off the mouth of the river by a purse-seiner. The buyer would send a man up to Vancouver to ride down with the shipment and show us where to make the landing up the river. Somehow or other, the liquor for that deal was shipped right out of the harbour in Vancouver. How they did it, I don't know; I did not concern myself with that end of the business. All I planned for was my part in the operation, the delivery of the load.

We arranged that I would meet the purse-seiner thirty miles off Cape Flattery on a certain date. The seiner would then tow the *Revuocnav* down the coast to save my fuel. I filled the gas tanks on the boat and then also loaded her down with twenty-five, forty-five-gallon drums of extra gas. That would be my fuel supply for the four trips that I would make up the Columbia River.

Three days before we were to rendezvous with the seiner, Tom and Joe and I left Victoria and went out to Port Renfrew. I had decided to take both Tom Colley and Joe Fleming with me on this trip. I left early so that if I ran into any of the patrol boats, I'd have lots of time to put them off. As it was, we had clear sailing out the west coast and saw no sign of the Canadian cutters. I went into Port Renfrew and tied up to a boom at the logging camp there. I had worked at that camp quite a few years before, so I still knew some of the people there. We visited in the camp that evening.

The next day was sunny and warm. As there was no sign of the patrol boat, I decided to do a little hunting. Leaving Tom and Joe on the boat, I took my rifle and set off up the mountainside to see if I could find a buck. I climbed way up one of the hills behind the camp. The bush was thick and I saw very little sign of any deer.

About the middle of the afternoon, I decided that I'd had enough of tramping around in the bush and started to head back to camp. I was about halfway down the hill and moving through some very heavy brush when I jumped down onto a log about three feet in diameter. The log was up against a small fir tree about four feet from where I had landed. At just the moment I lighted on the log, a bear jumped up out of the bush right next to the fir and started to climb right in front of me.

I was so startled by all this that I had no time to think before I shot. I simply swung the gun up to my shoulder and pulled the trigger. The bear was no more than four feet away. It dropped out of the tree and down into the brush, dead.

Now I stood there on the log, my heart still racing from the shock the bear had given me, thinking, what the hell did I shoot the bear for? I certainly had no use for a dead bear! I didn't have too long to think about it though, because just then I looked over the edge of the log and could see something moving alongside the bear. I climbed down off the log for a closer look and discovered that it was a tiny cub.

Now I really felt lousy! The cub was very young; it looked like it weighed only three or four pounds. Now, what am I going to do with this? I thought. I picked up the small ball of fur. The little guy did not seem to mind being held at all; he only squirmed around a bit.

I decided I had better make sure that the mother was indeed dead. I guess I was hoping that she might come back to life and care for her cub. But the surprises were not over yet. When I rolled her over, I found a second cub underneath the carcass. Things were going from bad to worse! Now I was suddenly responsible for two tiny bears. I began to wonder how the hell I was going to get back to camp with two squirming, clawing cubs—the second was not nearly so docile as the first—and my rifle. I was wearing a heavy Indian sweater with short sleeves, so I took it off and put the cubs inside. I doubled the ends of the sleeves over so they couldn't get out and carried them that way.

When I got back to camp, I went straight out onto the boat. I walked into the cabin still carrying the bundle of bears in my sweater.

"What have you got there?" Tom asked.

"I've got a couple of little bear cubs," I announced. By this time I was feeling kind of pleased with myself.

"Get the damn things out of here!" Tom shouted. "I do not want any bears around me." He immediately got up as if to leave.

I didn't know what was at the root of Tom's fears of bears, but I could see that it was real enough, so I took the bears out on deck. I let them run around on the deck for awhile. One was a male and the other a female. The male was just like a kitten; he was as cuddly as could be. The female, though, was a different story altogether. She didn't want to be held at all. She would squirm and claw and constantly try to climb out of your arms. The male loved the attention he was getting and was really friendly. I eventually even got Tom to hold him for awhile. After that he didn't seem to mind them so much.

We stayed in Port Renfrew for one more day and kept the cubs on the boat with us. They seemed happy to eat just about anything that we gave them. But I knew that we could not take them on the trip down to the Columbia River. That was out of the question. It happened that the bullock in the logging camps was a lover of animals—he had several dogs and cats that he had picked up here and there—so I asked him if he would look after the cubs for me until I got back. He was more than happy to do it. In fact, everyone in the camp seemed to enjoy having the tiny cubs around. They were a novelty, I guess. Anyway, they got plenty of attention.

On the third day we left Port Renfrew. We ran over to the rendezvous point off Cape Flattery. When the seiner arrived, we loaded the twenty-five drums of gasoline onto it, and then took the

Revuocnav in tow. In preparation for that I had made up a guide for the tow rope that bolted right on the top of the steel bow post. It was made of two pieces of heavy steel hinged on one side. An inch-and-a-half hole was bored through the centre, half the hole on one piece of metal, half on the other. When it was opened I could lay the towrope through it. Then I put a piece of split rubber hose around the rope at that point and closed and bolted the guide. It held the rope solidly so that there was no way it could chafe. It worked perfectly.

The weather was fairly good all the way down the coast. It was generally overcast with only light breezes, so we encountered no big seas, only a large swell. The *Revuocnav* towed beautifully; there seemed to be enough drag created by the two propellers to keep her from sheering from side to side. We were attached to the seiner by one hundred fathoms of towline.

To my dismay, I discovered something on this trip that I had not experienced before. When I was out in the open ocean swell for more than half a day, I became seasick. Joe Fleming had the same problem, only he became sick even sooner than I did. We were both sick all the way down the coast. The only time that we felt better was when we were up the Columbia River. As soon as we were back outside for awhile, we were sick again. Given the fact that I had spent the better part of the last ten years on the water, this was kind of a shocking discovery for me. But that's the way it was. No matter how rough it got on the inside, my stomach was fine. But put me out in the swell of the open Pacific in a V-bottomed boat, and I was sick in no time. And that condition didn't ever go away. It was always worse for the first few days, and then it got so I could live with it, but I never did really get my sea legs when I was out in the ocean swells in a hard-chined hull. Later on I was to learn that I was all right if I was in a round-bottomed boat, but I didn't know that at this point. So I suffered.

We made our way down to a position about forty miles off the mouth of the Columbia River. When we got there, we didn't anchor. The captain of the seiner was a good navigator, and was able to hold his position without any trouble. The first two days we were there, there was a big swell running and I refused to take a load in. Out in the open ocean it was only a big swell and nothing to worry about, but I knew darned well that it would be an entirely different matter when that same swell hit the shallow water near shore. And when it hit the river mouth and bumped up against the outward flow of water, it would be too much. I'd already had some experience with the bar at the mouth of the Columbia, so I knew what to expect.

On the evening of the third day the seas had calmed, and I made the first trip in with a load of two hundred and fifty cases of liquor. We had no trouble getting over the bar at the mouth of the river and ran about fifteen miles upstream to make the delivery to a small bay on the north shore. Having the fellow along to show us where to make the delivery was a big help. We dropped him off along with the first load.

After each trip that I made up the river, I would pump the *Revuocnav*'s gas tanks full from the drums of gasoline on the deck of the seiner. I always wanted to have enough fuel aboard so that if I did get into any trouble, I could make it back to Victoria, or if a storm came up, I would have plenty to see me through.

I ran another two hundred and fifty cases up the river the next night with Joe and Tom along to help with the unloading. Then it was too rough for a couple of days. We just sat around offshore feeling lousy. After that the seas calmed again, and we made two more trips on consecutive nights to deliver the final five hundred cases. Other than the bit of rough weather that slowed us down, the whole operation came off without a hitch. We never saw anything of the Coast Guard or shore patrol at all.

Returning from a delivery, I would come pretty close to where I figured the seiner was and flash a light. Pretty near every time, we would get an answering flash right away. We were right on the dot. On the seiner they would be watching for us because they knew pretty well when to expect us after the first trip.

As soon as we returned from dropping the last load, we put the towrope on the *Revuocnav*, and started back up the coast again. This was in the middle of the night. When daylight arrived, I flagged the seiner and they slowed down. Joe Fleming and I rowed up to the tow boat and climbed on board. We left Tom on the *Revuocnav* to keep an eye on things, just in case of an emergency, but there was really no need.

Joe and I had been seasick every day that we'd been out on the open ocean. Within fifteen minutes of going on board the seiner, we were both feeling just as good as ever. All of our seasickness disappeared with the different motion of that round-

bottomed boat. At dusk that evening we rowed back to the
Revuocnav, and were sick again within twenty minutes.

The trip back up the coast was as uneventful as the one
down. When we passed Cape Flattery, we fired up the engines on
the *Revuocnav*, dropped the towrope and ran ahead over to Port
Renfrew to pick up my bear cubs. We spent three or four hours at
the camp visiting with my friends, and then we loaded the cubs
onto the boat and left. Everyone in camp was sad to see the cubs
leave. They'd become real pets.

We caught up to the seiner again about ten miles past Port
Renfrew towards Victoria. We came alongside them to chat and
show them the bear cubs which we had been telling them about
on our trip. One of the fellows on the seiner had a camera and
asked if he could take a picture of the *Revuocnav*. To oblige I ran
back aways, and then came past the other boat at full speed. The
fellow took a picture just as the boat hit a wave, causing a huge
sheet of water to shoot out from the hull, obscuring everything
except a bit of the bow, the top of the pilothouse and the stern. It
was a great picture because it really gave the impression of how
fast the *Revuocnav* went. (I really liked that picture. But somehow
or other, that and all the pictures of my boats were lost over the
years, and now I do not have a single one.)

I brought the bear cubs home with me to Telegraph Cove.
They turned out to be great friends with my son Johnny, who was
about three years old at the time. We would turn them all loose
out in the yard, and they would have the greatest time playing
together. The cubs were still tiny, of course. The male weighed
about four pounds and the female, three. They sure were cute,
with huge feet that seemed several sizes too large for their bodies.
We also had a pup for Johnny, and he would get right in there
and play with the cubs as well. They were all good chums. I never
had any trouble with them.

The only time things got exciting was if you tried to feed both
of the bear cubs from one dish. If you did that, there would be a
battle royal! That darned little female would jump on the male and
start to fight as soon as the dish was put down. We soon learned
that the only way to ensure peace was to give a dish of food to the
female first, and then put one down for the male.

When those two cubs were fighting, you'd think that they
were killing each other the way they'd go at it. They'd be clawing

and kicking and biting at each other with a vengeance one minute, and in the next they'd stop and each walk off in a different direction as if nothing had happened. And the way they'd be going at each other, you'd be sure that there was going to be some damage done. But they would never be bothered by it in the least. I would sometimes have to have a close look at one of them afterwards to assure myself that it wasn't injured, but I could never even find a hair that had been pulled out.

After I'd had the cubs out to Telegraph Cove for a time, someone in the government found out about it, and they sent a fellow out to tell me that, because I didn't have a license to keep them, I'd have to give them up. A friend of mine, a man named French, had an animal clinic downtown just across the street from the old Post Office. He wanted the bears to put in his window to attract attention to his business. The cubs were still very small, so I let him have them for awhile.

But it wasn't very long before the government was after him about a license, too. So French gave them to a drugstore where they were also put on display in the window during the day. Actually, they were moved around to several drugstores in town. They were quite an attraction and always drew a crowd. But, eventually, the government people caught up with them again. They finally took them away and gave them to the Game Department in Vancouver. This was probably just as well because, by this time, those cubs were no longer so small. They had grown to the point where they would be dangerous before too long.

The bear cubs hadn't been gone long when I ran into a friend who had one more story about them. This fellow owned a sporting goods store in Victoria, and he happened to visit a friend of his in Vancouver who was a game warden. When he went into his friend's office, he found him in kind of a sorry state — his face and hands were all covered with scratches. The game warden explained he was keeping the two bear cubs in the back room there, and that every time that the went to feed them, they would start to fight! And he made the mistake of trying to separate them! I guess he hadn't yet learned the secret of feeding them in separate bowls! The Game Department finally gave those two bears to the Stanley Park Zoo where they stayed.

ENSENADA, MEXICO

ABOUT A YEAR after I started operations with the *Revuocnav*, Consolidated Exporters began to build a high-speed rumrunner of their own. They had twenty thousand cases of liquor stored in a warehouse in Ensenada, Mexico, and they wanted a craft capable of hauling twenty-five hundred cases at a time up the coast of California.

Captain Charlie Hudson designed the *Kagome*; it was built in a yard near the Rogers Sugar Refinery in Vancouver. The boat was seventy-nine feet long and was powered by two, four hundred-horsepower Liberty engines. Between the two big engines she also had a seventy-five-horsepower diesel engine as an auxiliary which could be used for just idling along or for cruising. The diesel engine was much slower, but it also used a great deal less fuel.

When it came time to install the big Liberty engines in the new boat, the people at Consolidated Exporters hired an expert from California. I don't know exactly what happened, but the fellow got about halfway through and then decided that he was not able to complete the job. It looked to me like he could not figure out how to wire all of the engines up and get the controls to the pilothouse. Anyway, he quit and went home to California, leaving the job in a shambles.

Captain Hudson knew that I had installed several Liberty engines in my own boats, so he called and asked if I would like to come over and finish the job for them. I had had lots of dealings with Charlie by this time and I like him. Even though he now spent most of his time on land as the "shore captain" managing the Consolidated fleet on Rum Row, he knew a great deal about boats and the sea. Whenever I was in Vancouver, I always spent as much time as possible talking with Hudson.

It was summertime when the new boat was being fitted out, so I wasn't too busy otherwise. I was only making one or two trips a month. There wasn't enough darkness to run down into Puget Sound and back, so I would only deliver to spots on the American shore of the Strait of Juan de Fuca or to Whidbey Island. Things were quiet enough that I decided to take a month off. I told Charlie Hudson that I'd be glad to come over and finish the installation of the engines for him.

I didn't have any problem at all getting those engines all hooked up. It took some time though, as a lot of it was finicky work. I guess I spent most of the month of July in Vancouver.

The *Kagome* was designed to carry twenty-five hundred cases of liquor and at least two thousand gallons of fuel. When it came to ordering the propellers for it, the "experts" at Consolidated Exporters had simply sent the specifications for the boat to Coolidge Propellers in Seattle, and had them send up the propellers that they thought appropriate. When the props arrived, I took one look at them and said that they were wrong for this boat. They were too small and had too much pitch to take the kind of load that the *Kagome* was expected to carry. The propellers were twenty-four inches in diameter and had a twenty-seven-inch pitch. I argued that those figures should be reversed—that they should be about twenty-seven inches in diameter with about a twenty-four-inch pitch. But at the time my argument didn't carry enough weight, and we installed the props that were sent up from Seattle.

After the *Kagome* was launched, we took it on a trial run for about twenty miles up Burrard Inlet. It was a real excursion. All of the directors of Consolidated Exporters and their families were aboard. It was quite a triumph as the boat ran just fine. And she was fast. But I wasn't convinced at all. The boat was running light; it wasn't even carrying a full load of fuel. I would have been really shocked if it wasn't fast, running light like that. But all the top brass were very happy with the speed that the boat could make.

And no one was interested in listening to me when I argued that the only real test of those props would come under a full load. I'd had enough experience by this point to know what a difference it made when you put a load on.

In the past, several different people had come to me for help in improving the performance of their boats, and every time I had been able to make recommendations that gave them better speed and improved fuel efficiency. Most boats seemed to be designed to get their maximum speed when they are run empty or near empty. But a boat is hardly ever run empty! Especially when you are trying to make a living with it!

Anyway, as far as the head office people were concerned, the trial run was a great success, and the *Kagome* was now all set for her maiden voyage down to Mexico. Captain Hudson offered me the job as engineer on her. I told him that I had no intent in doing the job full-time, but that I wouldn't mind going for that first trip down the coast. It sounded like an interesting adventure. By the time that first run was over, it would be fall, and I would want to get back to start up operations with my own boat again. Hudson then asked me if I knew someone I could recommend for the job, someone who could go along on that first trip with me and learn how to operate those Liberty engines.

Right away, Tom Colley came to mind. He was excellent with engines, had spent most of his life working on the water, and was reliable. He'd made quite a few trips with me, so he knew what the rumrunning was all about. He had also been running a pilot boat out of Victoria and was used to West Coast weather. In fact, Tom had always amazed me with his ability to sleep on board a boat no matter what kind of weather you were in. I'd seen him bunk down in the worst storm imaginable. He'd wrap his arm around one of the chains that the bunk hung on and hook his foot around the other, and there he would sleep, bouncing up and down with the action of the boat.

The next time I was back in Victoria, I talked to Tom about a job with Consolidated Exporters. He was very interested in it. He went back over to Vancouver with me and was hired on.

Shortly after that trial run, we loaded the *Kagome* with fuel and provisions for the trip to Ensenada. The boat had a crew of eight men in all. We carried about fifty, forty-five-gallon drums of extra gasoline on the stern deck. The boat's tanks could carry enough fuel to get us down the coast; then we would use the extra gasoline to make the return trip back to our rendezvous off the coast of California north of Los Angeles.

We set out from Vancouver on a nice sunny day in late August. There was a bit of a breeze blowing out in the strait, so we just cruised along with the engines running at about one thousand RPM. We ran down the Georgia Strait, through Haro Strait and around the tip of Vancouver Island and into the Strait of Juan de Fuca. We were making about fifteen knots. At that speed, everything was running smoothly. I felt that the engines could use more breaking in, so I didn't even suggest giving them full power until we were out past Cape Flattery. Once we were out in the open, however, the seas were fairly calm and I suggested to Captain Hudson that it might be a good idea to see how the boat was going to perform at full speed with a load on. The captain agreed, so I gave the engines full throttle.

What a disappointment! It was no real surprise to me, though. Instead of the 2,400 RPM that those engines should have been capable of, they would only turn at about 1,800 RPM under that load. And the speed of the boat only increased to about seventeen knots. The *Kagome* was designed to do twenty-five knots with a load on. Those propellers were all wrong. All they did was pile up a mountain of white water behind the stern. There was a six-foot mast on the transom and, running at full throttle, you could see water above the top of it.

I turned to Charlie and said, "Do you think that we have enough gas to get down to Mexico at this rate?"

"I'm not sure yet," he replied tersely. It was clear that he was not happy with the performance of his boat.

"I don't think that those propellers can carry a load," I told him.

We cruised along like that for a quarter of an hour or so. Captain Hudson didn't say a word, but he was obviously considering his alternatives. The way we were plowing along, we could actually run out of fuel before we reached Mexico.

"Well, this is no damn good," Hudson said finally. "If you were in my position, what would you do?"

I didn't have any difficulty answering that question.

"I'd turn this ship around and head right back to Vancouver and get a new set of propellers on her," I said.

"That's just the decision that I've come to," he said. "We would really be in a fix if we had to run from anything at this rate."

With that he turned the *Kagome* around, and we were on our way home again. When Captain Hudson explained what had happened when we'd opened the engines up, he got no opposition to the proposal for a new set of propellers. We had to hang around in Vancouver for a couple of days waiting for them to be sent up from Seattle, but when the new props arrived we were ready for them. We had them on and the boat back in the water in no time. We topped up the fuel tanks and took the boat out for a second trial run on Burrard Inlet before setting off again. This time she had a load on. The *Kagome* made close to thirty knots with the new props! What a difference!

Once again we headed down the Georgia Strait, made our way around the tip of Vancouver Island, and headed for the open Pacific. And once again, less than half a day after we passed Cape Flattery, I was seasick. I could not eat anything. And I stayed sick for a whole three or four days that it took to run down the coast to Mexico.

Ensenada is only about seventy miles south of the California border on the Baja California. The town is located on a large, shallow bay. We anchored out in the middle of that bay for several days while Captain Hudson made the necessary arrangements to get our liquor out of the bonded warehouse. Nothing is done quickly in Mexico.

There was a wharf that ran about a mile out into the bay. But even at the end of the wharf there was not enough water to allow large ocean-going ships to tie up. The large ships anchored out in the bay and ferried their goods and passengers back and forth on a barge. There was lots of water at the wharf for the *Kagome*. But we anchored out anyway and saved the cost of paying wharfage.

While we were sitting out there with not much of anything to do, we got to know an old beachcomber who used to row out to our boat. We invited him aboard, and he had quite a few meals with us. We got to know him quite well. He had been living down there for about twenty years, and told us all kinds of interesting stories about the life around that part of Mexico.

The old fellow lived on a little wee boat about twelve feet

long. It was quite amazing. He had an area of sand and gravel at the stern where he could build a fire to do his cooking. And there was a small foredeck that he crawled under to sleep. He tied his boat to the pilings alongside the wharf. He fished for most of his food and raised a bit of money by beachcombing. He really seemed quite content with his way of life.

One evening, the old beachcomber came rowing out to the *Kagome* at about ten o'clock. He was very excited.

"The bay is full of sharks!" he shouted. "I have lived here for twenty years, and I have never seen anything like it. The sharks have never come in here before, but now there are thousands of them."

The old fellow wanted to know if we had a spear. When we said that we did not, he asked me if I could make one. I said that I could. I went down into the engine room where we had a regular little workshop. We were pretty well equipped and could make just about anything that we might need.

I took a piece of half-inch pipe and hammered three or four inches of the end flat and cut it to a point. Then with a hacksaw I cut two notches into the point and spread them out to make barbs to keep the spear from pulling out. I then flattened the other end of the pipe and bore a hole through it so that we could fasten a rope to the spear.

With the spear ready for action, I climbed into the beachcomber's boat and we set off to go shark hunting. He rowed towards the beach. As we got into the shallower water, I could see that the old fellow had not exaggerated at all when he said the bay was full of sharks. They were everywhere! There were literally thousands of them scattered along the shoreline of that huge bay. It was an eerie sight. Everywhere you looked, dark fins stuck out of the water. As the night got blacker we could see the sharks by the phosphorescence that showed as they swam. You could see the whole length of them outlined in the water. They came in all sizes and looked to be from four to twenty feet long.

When a shark of about eighteen feet swam under the boat, I leaned out and drove the spear into its back. Then the action began! The water boiled as the big shark thrashed about. It was all I could do to hang onto the end of the rope. That shark had no trouble towing the beachcomber's little boat around. It was a good thing that it chose to run away rather than towards our little craft! The shark writhed and twisted madly, throwing water in all directions.

Then suddenly, the line went slack. The fish had freed itself from the spear.

After that I speared a dozen or more sharks, but each time they were able to tear free. When I found that I could not hold the large fish, I started looking around for smaller ones. I don't know what we planned to do with an eighteen-foot shark anyway. But it was certainly exciting.

I kept trying to spear smaller and smaller sharks, but they all got loose. We must have rowed along the beach for a mile or more. There were sharks everywhere! Finally, I got the spear into one about seven feet long and it held. The tip of the spear must have hit the backbone, because that shark did not fight nearly so hard as the others. But we still had quite a struggle getting it into a small boat. It must have weighed about one hundred and fifty pounds. We hauled it out to the *Kagome* for everybody to have a look at. It had a wicked-looking set of teeth. One of the fellows on the boat pulled them all and saved them. The old beachcomber was very proud of our catch. He had great plans to sell the meat in the market the next day.

The funny thing was that, when we woke up the next morning, the surface of the bay was unbroken and there was no sign of the sharks anywhere. In fact, for the rest of our stay, we never even saw another shark.

When Captain Hudson finally got clearance to move the liquor out of the warehouse onshore, we moved the *Kagome* right in alongside the wharf. The liquor was brought down to the dock on trucks. The bottles were still packed in their wooden crates. As we didn't want or need the extra weight of the boxes, they had to be unpacked. Inside the boxes, the bottles were packed in straw in gunny sacks. We hired a crew of eight men, half of them Mexicans, to break open the boxes and load the sacks of liquor onto a hand hoist, which would then be swung out onto the boat. Our own crew took care of the stowing of the liquor in the hold of the *Kagome*.

The fellows on the shore crew broke open the wooden boxes with hatchets. There was one Mexican in the crew who was very careless. He seemed to smash at least one bottle every time he broke open a case. I'll bet that guy broke sixty or seventy bottles during the course of the loading. And no one stopped him! That was what amazed me. Nobody seemed to care. The captain was there in charge of the whole thing, and he didn't even say anything. I never understood why they didn't get rid of that guy.

Those broken bottles ended up causing problems for our crew loading the liquor into the hold. The liquor running out of the bottles would soak the gunny sacks. Fifteen or twenty minutes after the loading got underway, the men down in the hold started falling over. They were passing out from the alcohol fumes. They would have to be hauled out on deck for air. We soon found out that a man could only work in the hold about fifteen minutes.

But then, quite by accident, Tom Colley solved that problem. Tom couldn't stand the sight of all the liquor that was dripping out of the sacks going to waste, so he went to the galley and got a big pot. Every time we got a case with liquor running out of it, he would hold the pot under it to catch the drippings. It wasn't long before he had a full pot. Then he had a drink and passed it around. And the funny thing was that, after having a drink, no one was bothered by the fumes down in the hold again. The loading was finished with no more problems.

As soon as the twenty-five hundred cases of liquor were stowed aboard the *Kagome*, we headed north. We set out for a position two hundred miles north of Los Angeles. Once again, as soon as we were aways out of the harbour, I became seasick.

I had bought a gunny sack full of abalone shells from the old beachcomber for fifty cents. There must have been fifty or more shells in the bag. On the way back up the coast, I spent most of my time out on the stern deck working on those shells. It is possible to chip off the rough outside until all that is left of the shell is mother-of-pearl. I was still pretty seasick and the only thing that seemed to help was being out in the fresh air. So I spent hours sitting out on the deck chipping away at those shells. But every time it seemed I would run into a thin spot on the shell before I was finished, and the thing would break. I finally got so frustrated with it that I tossed the whole darned sack into the ocean.

We arrived at our position forty miles off the California coast in the evening. The *Kagome* had a wireless and an operator on board, and we'd sent word of our arrival, so we were expecting to be met by a speedboat that would begin hauling the load of liquor ashore.

Captain Hudson made all of the arrangements through the office of Consolidated Exporters way up in Vancouver. They talked in code; otherwise the Coast Guard would have been able to listen in and make their own plans to ambush the rumrunners. But no boat showed up that night. I was still sick at this time. I had not been able to eat anything since we had left Ensenada. The seas were fairly calm, though; there was just the normal swell.

We sat out there all the next day and through the night before the speedboat finally showed up at about four the following afternoon. As soon as they were alongside, we were all set to begin loading the liquor into the speedboat, but the guy in charge said to wait until he'd had a chance to talk with Captain Hudson. After a long conference he managed to convince Charlie to take the whole load in to shore in one trip with the *Kagome*. It would have taken quite a number of trips with the speedboat to get the load ashore. This had not been in our plans, and Captain Hudson was leery of it at first, but the fellow running the speedboat finally convinced him that it was perfectly safe. They promised that they would have dories and a crew waiting to unload the cargo as soon as we got in. The run would be made that night.

Once it got dark, we followed that speedboat in and anchored about three hundred yards off the beach. It felt wonderful to be in out of the swell. Within a few minutes I was not seasick anymore. There was hardly any swell washing up on the beach, so it made it easy for the dories to land. The unloading of our cargo went really smoothly. We would be loading one dory, while the other was unloaded ashore.

It got that I was feeling so good that I began to get a notion about making a second trip down to Ensenada.

"I'm feeling so good now, I feel like going out again," I said to Charlie Hudson.

"Like hell you will!" he replied. "I saw you out there. You're going ashore right here. We don't want to be shipping you home in a box. You're to go in with the speedboat. They'll take you to Sugarman's. It's all been arranged."

There wasn't much I could say. I had been terribly sick and unable to eat all the time we were out in the open. I guess the funny thing is how soon you forget just how badly you felt.

When the load of liquor was all safely on the beach, I said my goodbyes to the captain and crew of the *Kagome*, climbed into

Sugarman's speedboat, and we headed for Los Angeles. We first went north about ten miles to a little gas dock where we took on a load of fuel. Then we started the long run for Los Angeles. That speedboat made about twenty knots.

We arrived near Los Angeles about nine in the morning and headed into a slough. That piece of water was not more than wide enough for two boats to pass each other—twenty feet in some places, less in others. There were boats tied up all along it. We ran up the slough for several miles, finally stopping at a small wharf where Sugarman had a car waiting to take me to his home in the Hollywood district. There had been a big oil find in that area a few years before and there were derricks all over the place. It was a really strange sight.

Sugarman lived in a fine home in the posh area of Hollywood. He was one of the kingpins in the rum trade in southern California and had many other business interests as well. I stayed at his home for several days recovering from the effects of the seasickness. I was still quite woozy. Whenever I lay down, I could feel the motion of the sea, as if the bed was going up and down on the waves. I guess my sense of balance was still out of whack. About all I could manage to eat was fruit and juices; I couldn't hold down anything like a real meal yet.

Sugarman treated me really well while I stayed with him. He took me around to show me all the sights of Los Angeles. Of course, Hollywood then was nothing like it is today.

Finally, after four or five days, I felt well enough to eat some real food and we began to talk about how I was to get home. At first Sugarman was going to make arrangements for me to return to Victoria by bus, then he changed his mind.

"How would you like to go on a plane?" he asked.

"That would be fine," I replied. "It would be a lot faster."

The next day I boarded a plane in Los Angeles and flew to San Francisco. I stayed there overnight and then flew north again with a stop in Portland before landing in Seattle. From there, I caught the CPR steamship home to Victoria.

It was nice to get home again. I had been away for over a month. It had been an exciting trip in spite of my battle with seasickness. But it was good to get back to see my family and friends again.

Later Sugarman had a boat built in Vancouver. He wanted a big, fast boat for the rum trade. The boat he built was about sixty feet long, and he put the same engines in it that I had in *Revuocnav*, two, eight hundred and sixty-horsepower Packards. But he never could get those motors to run right. (Those Packards had a major problem with the valve springs.) From the stories that I heard, Sugarman was never able to use that new boat for more than one or two trips without having major engine problems. I heard that he eventually lost over $125,000 on that boat!

I believe that Charlie Hudson stayed on as captain of the *Kagome* until they had hauled all of the twenty thousand cases of liquor up from the warehouse in Ensenada. Then he returned to Vancouver to resume his duties as "shore captain" of the whole of Consolidated Exporters rum fleet.

Tom Colley took over my job as engineer on the *Kagome*. They stayed down south running liquor from the motherships that came up from Tahiti and sat forty or fifty miles off the coast. Unfortunately, Tom got his foot caught in a drive shaft while they were out there. The foot was badly mangled and the injury not properly treated. It eventually developed gangrene. Finally Tom had to be taken ashore in one of the speedboats.

He was rushed to a hospital in San Francisco. The Customs and Immigration people placed a guard on Tom's room at the hospital. He wasn't under arrest or anything, but they knew that he was involved in the rumrunning, and they just decided to keep a watch on him. The fellow who was watching him was from the Coast Guard. I guess maybe they thought that Tom would be making arrangements for liquor drops if they didn't keep an eye on him.

Anyway, the whole thing led to an amazing coincidence that turned out to be pretty funny. After Tom had been in hospital awhile, he and his guard got to talking and swapping stories about what they'd done. It turned out that the guard's best story was the one he told about the time he was stationed up in Washington State a couple of years earlier, and was involved in an ambush to catch a rumrunner. He got quite excited as he explained how they had made elaborate plans to bottle the rumrunner up in Discovery Bay at the northeast corner of the Olympic Peninsula. According to him, they had ten cutters spread out at intervals along the inlet to prevent any chance of escape. They were sure that this time they had the culprit trapped. Then he laughed.

"Christ! We couldn't have caught him with an airplane!" he said.

He went on to describe how he had been on the cutter that had got closest to the rumrunner. In fact, he was the gunner on the machine gun firing at it. He excitedly detailed the brief chase and the quick manoeuvre that allowed the rumrunner to escape. Little did he know that he was telling the story to one of the fellows that his bullet had come so close to killing! All the while the guard was telling his story, Tom lay there in the bed, trying his darnedest to keep a straight face.

The Coast Guardsman went on to explain how disappointed they were when the rumrunner escaped, because there was a big reward for the capture of that boat. He claimed that the captain of the cutter that brought it in would get $10,000 and each of the crew would receive $1,000. (That was the first time that I had confirmation of the rumours that I had heard about a $25,000 reward being posted for the capture of my boat.)

Tom never did let on that he had been aboard the boat his guard had been firing at. He mostly kept quiet and let the Coast Guardsman do the talking. He was also able to find out that the Americans only used their fast cutters in the daytime. They considered it too dangerous to use them at night because of the risk of hitting driftwood. They were right, of course, about the danger. But I guess we just weighed the dangers of hitting driftwood and bending a prop or whatever against the danger of getting caught and going to jail! It's all relative, isn't it?

I was certainly aware of the danger of hitting driftwood. As I've already said, I spent a good deal of time and money repairing the damage done when I'd run into one thing or another. I guess you have to put it down to blind luck when you consider the fact that I never did hit anything when I was being chased by the cutters.

After he got out of the hospital, Tom came back up to Victoria. He lost his battle with the gangrene and they had to take his foot off. For a period of about ten years the disease would show up again and again, and they would amputate another part of his leg. Finally he lost the whole thing. Then it got into the other leg, and eventually he lost that one as well. One day he was sitting at a table with four or five other fellows playing cards, and he just fell right off his chair. He had taken a massive heart attack and was dead. That would have been about 1940. Tom would have been about fifty years old when he died.

Captain Charlie Hudson stayed on as "shore captain" for Consolidated Exporters right up until the end of Prohibition in 1933. I lost track of him for awhile, but then decided to look him up when I was over in Vancouver several years later. I got in touch with one of the directors from Consolidated Exporters and he told me that Charlie was a salesman for one of the high-class yacht brokers down in the harbour. I went down to visit him there.

This was just after Canada had entered into World War II. Charlie Hudson had been captain of a destroyer in the First War and he was going to go back into it again. In fact, he was just spending the last few days at his job before he was to report for duty. He asked me if I would consider joining the Canadian Navy to take charge of instructing in the operation of speedboats. He told me that he had already spoken to his superior officers about me. He told them that I was one of the best speedboat men in Canada, and apparently they were eager to get me to join up. I thought it over, but in the end decided that I wouldn't go. I would have liked doing the job, but I knew that because of my lack of education, I would not be able to handle all of the paperwork involved in it. I knew from my own army experience what that was all about.

That was the last time that I saw Charlie Hudson. I did hear that he came back to Vancouver after the war, though.

THE END OF PROHIBITION

AFTER I CAME back from the trip to Mexico and California, it was back to business as usual hauling with the *Revuocnav*. The way things were going, we all knew that Prohibition was coming to an end. We didn't know exactly when it would be over at first, but we knew that it couldn't last much longer.

I continued to run out the west coast to pick up my liquor from the *Chief Skugaid*. With the larger boat I was now hauling for up to five different customers each trip. On the way down into Puget Sound I might make one stop on the south side of Edmonds, one just north of Seattle, and a third one about fifteen miles the other side of Seattle. Then on the way back out I might make two deliveries on the other side of the sound.

The fourth and last time that I had to stay over on the American side all day was with the *Revuocnav*. I was bringing a load in from the outside when it started blowing from the southeast. Joe Fleming was crewing for me on that trip. In no time flat we were facing right into a terrific wind. The wind hit gale force when we were still out around Port Renfrew. It didn't let up at all. We bucked into that blow all the way down the strait. For most of the trip you could hardly see the boat, there was so much water on the deck. The waves were steep and short and every one of them was coming aboard. We had to slow down to deal with it. In those conditions I knew that we didn't have time to go all the way down to Seattle and be clear before daylight, so I started thinking about some place to hide during the daylight hours of the next day.

Normally, I would have headed for a small channel between two islands on the east side of the Discovery group. It offered a perfect spot to tie up that was well protected from the wind and seas. There was a sheer rock wall on one of those islands that I could get right next to on any level of the tide. I could tie right up to the rocks, put an old tire between the boat and the cliff-face and ride the tide up and down in comfort with no worries at all.

The problem was that, at this time, the *Imperator* had been particularly active, patrolling the waters at the southern tip of Vancouver Island regularly. I decided that it would be safer to spend the day on the American side of the border.

We fought our way past Discovery and bucked across Haro Strait to San Juan Island. On the southeast tip of the island, just around the corner from Cattle Point, there was a tiny cove that offered good protection from the weather. The bay was only about a hundred feet wide and two hundred deep. There was a piling in the middle of the bay and we tied up to that and sat there for the rest of the night and all the next day. As it happened, the farm above the cove had been homesteaded by Joe Fleming's father, and his half-brother was still working the land. When it got light, Joe went up to the farm to visit his relatives and make new arrangements for the delivery of the load the following night. I stayed on the boat. I felt pretty safe being out in the San Juans the way we were—the chances of the Coast Guard patrol being out there were slim—but I didn't like to leave the boat when it had a load on. The day passed uneventfully. The storm blew itself out and we had no problem making the delivery the next night.

I kept on hauling liquor right up to the end of Prohibition. I made my last run on the night of April 2, 1933—I delivered two hundred and fifty cases down to Seattle. Prohibition ended on April 4, 1933.

It's so long ago now that it is difficult to recall the way I felt when the whole thing came to an end. I'm sure I looked on the repeal of the Volstead Act with a good deal of sadness. After all, it put me out of work. Prohibition had provided me with a very good income, an interesting lifestyle and a good deal of adventure and excitement. I can't say I was happy to see it end. But it didn't end overnight, and we all knew that it had to end sometime. When I look back on it, it is much easier to remember the good points than the bad, the thrills and satisfactions rather than the disappointments. All in all, the era of Prohibition in the United States was very good to me.

As I've said all along, I couldn't help but think of myself as a pretty lucky guy. I had twelve years of doing something that I really enjoyed. And I was always well paid for it. Sure, it was illegal as far as the Americans were concerned, but that never bothered me too much. I couldn't see where I was doing anything terribly wrong. When it came right down to it, I never actually bought or sold any liquor; all I did was haul it. I think that history has shown that the Prohibition laws were made to be broken. But I'm not making excuses. At the time, I knew exactly what I was doing. I knew I was breaking the law. I knew the risks I was taking. And I knew the penalties I would face if I got caught. I guess that was why the pay was so good.

During the time that I was rumrunning, I had four or five different people come to me—all from the American side—and ask me to run dope for them. They made offers as high as $25,000 to take a suitcase full of dope and land it on the other side. I turned them all down flat. I wanted nothing to do with that. I didn't see it as the same business at all.

But I think as much as anything else—the money and the excitement and all—I enjoyed the challenge of the whole game that was involved in the rumrunning: the challenge of not getting caught.

In looking back on it, I'd have to say that that challenge of staying out of reach of the authorities meant as much to me as anything else. I certainly wasn't in the business just for the money. I could have made a lot more money than I did, if that was my prime motivation. I could have paid my crews a lot less than I did, that's for sure. I never did change my practice of equal shares all around. It was always one-third for my crewman, one-third for me and one-third for the boat. If I took two crew with me, then the split was in quarters. And many times I took a second man along even though I did not really need him. And I always did more of the work than any of my crew. No, I sure wasn't in the rum trade just for the money.

I thoroughly enjoyed my life during the Prohibition years. I loved working on and around the water. I took a lot of pride in my work, even if it was against the law. During my years of rumrunning I made more than four hundred runs; I delivered to ten different buyers, and made landings in thirty-six different locations along the coastline of Washington State. I never missed a spot where I was told to make a delivery, yet I never had any instruction in navigation. Usually, I would be shown a new dropoff site simply by someone pointing it out on a map. They might say, "Right about here is the bay." And I would go in there in the dark, flash a light toward the shore and nearly always get an answering flash right away. Looking back on it now, it seems hard to believe that I never had more trouble than I did, making all of those deliveries at night, often in bad weather. Most of the places I delivered to I have never even seen in the daylight, even to this day!

I like to think I was lucky. I had to be to stay out of trouble the way I did. There weren't too many who did. But the thing was I also felt that I made my own luck. I was always careful. I never took any unnecessary risks. And I always made sure that I had the best equipment available. I spent an awful lot of money making sure that I always had a boat that could outrun the opposition easily. I was always confident that I could do what I set out to do. I never really felt that I was taking any unnecessary risks at all. It didn't always seem that way when the bullets were flying, of course, but you couldn't prepare for everything!

And looking back on it now, I realize that what I was doing was not at all bad for the Canadian economy at the time. If you consider an average of about one hundred and fifty cases per trip, I freighted at least sixty thousand cases of liquor across to the United States. That would have amounted to more than four million dollars of revenue that I brought into Canada. And that was no small sum in the thirties!

The worst of it all was that, when Prohibition ended, I found myself with a very specialized boat; one that was far too expensive to operate for ordinary travel. There weren't a lot of people around interested in buying the gas to fill those two, six hundred-gallon tanks and feed those eight hundred and sixty-horsepower engines! Nobody could afford it! It didn't take long for me to decide that I couldn't afford to keep the *Revuocnav*. There was just no way to use that boat to make it pay for itself.

In fact, there was really no market for the boat as it was. I finally decided to sell the engines separately. And even at that, I had to practically give them away. I sold one to a mining company up north somewhere for $900. They wanted it to operate an electric generator for their camp. That Packard would be able to light a lot of bulbs for them!

I sold the *Revuocnav* to a group of millionaires that had a lodge up in Princess Louisa Inlet at the head of Jervis Inlet. I think I got about $1,500 for the boat.

When I finished the rumrunning, I had maybe $10,000 in the bank. That was a fair amount in 1933, but it didn't make me rich. I could have made a lot more if I had been a better businessman, but that wasn't my way. I put a lot of money back into boats and engines. I spent something like $75,000 on my various boats. In those days that was a lot of money. But maybe that was what kept me out of jail!

And I did build what was considered a fairly nice house at the time. We lived well and travelled in good circumstances for quite a number of years. I really enjoyed many of the people who I met in the rum trade. Captain Charlie Hudson and Carl Melby were fine people and there were plenty of others as well.

After Prohibition, of course, I had to find another line of work entirely. I went logging for awhile, first north of Victoria near Ladysmith, and then out on the west coast of Vancouver Island up in Nitinat Lake. I never got too far away from the water.

Eventually, I ended up making my living as a commercial fisherman out of Bamfield on the west coast of the island. I bought my first boat, the *Eljo*, from Joe Fleming. Later I went over to Vancouver and bought a thirty-four-foot fish boat. I used that boat, the *Margaret N*, right up until the time I retired in 1969.

I enjoyed the twenty-five years of fishing out of Bamfield up in Barkley Sound. It wasn't as exciting as the rumrunning, but I was still my own boss, and it was good, healthy work. And the funny thing was, I never had a problem with seasickness when I was fishing. My fish boat was round-bottomed and, even though I went through plenty of terrible storms out on the open Pacific, I was never bothered by seasickness. But every time that I had gone out in the open in a V-bottomed boat, I had been sick.

I was almost seventy-five years old when I finally retired. I felt I could have fished for another eight or ten years, but my second wife was not in very good health at the time, and I thought it would be better for her to be in Victoria, closer to a good doctor and the hospital.

Looking back on my life, I realized that I was indeed a very lucky person to have lived during such an unrestricted period in our history. Although my childhood was hard, I was blessed with a strong body and a good mind, which made it possible for me to overcome most of the difficult situations that I encountered. For the most part I enjoyed my work, no matter what it was.

My life wasn't without its hardships. I was pretty hard hit when my little Johnny died very suddenly when I was working up in the Nitinat shortly after Prohibition ended. And my first marriage was not very successful, and it ended not too long after our son died.

But I was lucky enough to meet a terrific woman later in my life, and we had twenty-seven wonderful years of marriage. My second wife died of a blood disease at the age of seventy-seven.

And now, having been retired for more than seventeen years, I think it's safe to say that the twelve years of rumrunning were the most exciting years of my life. I was young and eager, and I really enjoyed the thrills and adventure of that period. And I've often thought back to the time I was in Seattle buying the engine for my first boat, when the fortune teller predicted that I would be very successful in the "adventure" I was going into. I guess I'd have to say he made a believer out of me!

BIBLIOGRAPHY

The vast majority of the information presented in this book comes from the taped recollections of Johnny Schnarr. Additional details were gathered from the sources listed below.

Clark, Norman H., "Roy Olmstead, A Rumrunning King on Puget Sound." *Pacific Northwest Quarterly*, July 1963.

Lonsdale, Captain L.A., "Rumrunners on Puget Sound." *American West*, November 1972.

The *Seattle Post-Intelligencer*, various editions.

The *Seattle Times*, various editions.

The *Vancouver Province*, various editions.

The *Vancouver Sun*, various editions.

The *Victoria Daily Colonist*, various editions.

The *Victoria Daily Times*, various editions.